R.T.C. LIBRARY
LETTERKENNY

THE FALL
OF THE
ROMANOFFS

D1341494

C0007084

THE FALL OF THE ROMANOFFS

by
A RUSSIAN

with an introduction by
ALAN WOOD
*Senior Lecturer in Russian History,
Lancaster University*

R.T.C. LIBRARY, LETTERKENNY

947
· 084

Ian Faulkner Publishing
Cambridge · England

Ian Faulkner Publishing Ltd
Lincoln House
347 Cherry Hinton Road
Cambridge CB1 4DJ

First published 1918
by Herbert Jenkins Ltd

This edition copyright © Ian Faulkner Publishing Ltd 1992
Introduction copyright © Alan Wood 1992

All rights reserved. No part of this publication may be
reproduced, stored in a retrieval system, or transmitted,
in any form or by any means, electronic, mechanical,
photocopying, recording, or otherwise, without the prior
permission of the copyright owner.

A CIP record for this book is available from the British
Library.

ISBN 1-85763-003-3

Printed in Great Britain by Billings and Sons Ltd

INTRODUCTION

by Alan Wood

ON 2 March 1917, faced with public demonstrations, industrial strikes and military mutiny in his capital, Petrograd, the autocratic ruler of the Russian Empire, Tsar Nicholas II, abdicated his throne in favour of his younger brother, Grand Duke Michael. After due consideration, the latter declined to take on the onus of regal responsibility and thereby brought to a rather ignominious conclusion the dynasty which had ruled Russia since the early seventeenth century. The abdication of Nicholas Romanov both marked the culmination of one revolutionary situation in Russia and also signalled the inauguration of another: the first brought tsarist autocracy to an end; the second brought the Bolshevik Party and the first Soviet government to power. Ever since the first Romanov tsar was elected to the throne of Muscovy in 1613, the much vaunted popular monarchism of the Russian masses and their faith in and loyalty to the *Tsar-Batyushka* ('Little Father') had been punctuated with periodic outbursts of revolutionary upheaval which were a violent expression of the people's inarticulate opposition to a regime which kept them in a state of semi-feudal thraldom into the second decade of the twentieth century. When the militant workers and politically radicalised soldiers took to the streets of Petrograd during the last days of February 1917, forcing Nicholas to doff his crown, they were taking part in the penultimate act of a drama which has justifiably been described as the most important political event of this century.

The two revolutions which shook Russia, and the world, during 1917 brought about a situation which has dominated the political, ideological, economic, diplomatic and military relations of the planet ever since. Now, as the Soviet Union which was created by those revolutions itself begins to collapse and fall apart, a re-examination of the events, processes and personalities that contributed to the 'fall of the Romanovs' and the formation of the world's first Communist government is continuing in academic, historical, journalistic and political circles throughout the world, not least in the former USSR itself. It is, therefore, on the seventy-fifth anniversary of the Revolution, an opportune occasion to republish this idiosyncratic account of the fall of the Russian Empire, written by a contemporary observer, who, as his previous volume, *Russian Court Memoirs*, reveals, was on seemingly intimate terms with court, government, military and official circles in Russia as they slowly gyrated towards their inevitable demise.

The Fall of the Romanoffs: How the ex-Empress & Rasputine Caused the Russian Revolution was published in 1918, though written (according to internal evidence) some time in mid 1917, probably around June or July, and certainly before the Bolshevik seizure of power in October. It was, therefore, already out of date and overtaken by more climactic events before it was published, but nevertheless provides a curious insight into the mind and mentality of a member of the *ancien régime* and self-confessed admirer of the dethroned Emperor, struggling to come to terms with the forces of revolution which had swept his old world away and which he was not really equipped to comprehend. It is, of course, too much to expect that a reactionary-minded, chauvinist patrician such as the author obviously was could have much understanding of the deeper underlying social, political and economic pressures which built up to the revolutionary explosions of 1917 – obvious factors such as poverty, illiteracy, land-hunger, economic exploitation, military disaster and so on. He therefore has to cast about for conspirators, malign influences, perfidious foreigners, politicians of dubious loyalty and other evil geniuses to explain away the destruction of his cosy universe.

Chief among those to whom the author apportions blame and opprobrium is none other than the ex-Empress Alexandra, wife of the quondam Tsar and mother to his heir, the Tsarevich Alexis. In his opening paragraphs he states quite unequivocally that: 'The responsibility for the wreck of the Russian monarchy lies entirely with the Empress Alexandra Feodorovna, the most fatal of all the consorts of Russian sovereigns' (page 5). In marked contrast to the tone of his earlier loyal defence of the misunderstood Empress who, he previously asserted, was the victim of 'misconception and prejudice' due to her German origins (see *Russian Court Memoirs*), the author now spares no venom nor invective in his desperate philippics launched against the unfortunate woman. Doom and tragedy had apparently attended her and all in contact with her since the day of her conception – from the death of her brother by defenestration at the time of her birth(!), through the Empire's humiliating military defeat by Japan in 1905, down to Russian reverses in the First World War and the Revolution of February/March 1917 itself. Commenting on what he alleges was Alexandra's destruction of her husband's draft plan for a full constitution to be granted the country in December 1916, the author declares: 'If the Emperor had not listened to her . . . the Revolution would have been averted by one stroke of a pen!' (page 102). Obviously such simplistic causative attributions can enjoy no credibility with the modern reader, but it is worth while considering the reasons why a man of some intelligence, refinement and education should compose this kind of populist drivel, more appropriate to the gutter press for which he himself professes such haughty contempt. In order to do this, it is necessary to place the contents of his narrative into historical context and to examine briefly the state of the Russian Empire and the house of Romanov in their rapidly declining years.

When Nicholas succeeded his father in 1894, the realm over which he now reluctantly ruled was the largest land empire in the world, covering one-sixth of the earth's land-surface, from the Baltic to the Pacific, from the Arctic to the deserts of Central Asia. It possessed a huge multi-ethnic, polyglot population, only two-fifths of which were Russian by nationality – an empire fraught with social and economic tensions and riven by internal contradictions. The country had an overwhelmingly agrarian, peasant society, but had recently undergone an industrial revolution, spawning a politically aware middle class of businessmen, capitalists and their attendant professional servitors, and an increasingly militant, class-conscious urban proletariat of factory workers and recently migrated peasants. It boasted the biggest army in the world, but had not won a significant military victory over a modern European power since 1812. In the artistic and intellectual sphere, a glittering constellation of Russian writers, poets, painters, composers, choreographers and scientists were in the avant-garde of contemporary European culture, while eighty per cent of the country's population could neither read nor write.

Politically, the Russian Empire was governed by an absolute autocrat with all power resting in the hands of the divinely appointed Tsar and his personally chosen ministers. Such enormous power did not, however, sit easily on the shoulders of Nicholas Romanov, a mild-mannered but emotional and not particularly intelligent man, distrustful of clever people (even his own government officials) – and more at ease with his large, doting family of four daughters and one son than with the public responsibilities of his exalted office. In 1905, against the background of a disastrously fought war with Japan, the Russian people erupted in a revolutionary turmoil which forced the Tsar to concede a number of political reforms, including the convocation of a quasi-parliamentary body called the State Duma. The result was an experiment in what can only be described as 'constitutional autocracy' – patently unworkable and a political absurdity doomed to failure. Even the conservative fourth Duma (1912–17), elected on a franchise deliberately designed to ensure majority representation of the wealthy classes, found it impossible to work harmoniously with the Tsar's government, composed of a rapidly changing assortment of ministers appointed on the advice of the royal family's notorious friend, confidant and improbable guru, Grigory Rasputin.

Rasputin, who shares with the Empress the author's accusations of responsibility for the fall of the Romanovs, is a bizarre, almost legendary figure whose role in the grotesque politics of late imperial Russia deserves some comment. He was not, as he is so often described, a 'mad monk'. That is, he was neither clinically insane, nor an ordained member of any monastic order. He was, in fact, a semi-literate, lecherous, uncouth Siberian peasant who had gained a reputation for his allegedly thaumaturgical powers and had joined a fanatical religious sect of self-flagellants called the *Khlysty*. When his pilgrimages around Russia finally brought him to St Petersburg, he swiftly ingratiated himself by various means with a coterie of scatty-brained high society ladies who soon brought him to the attention of the imperial family. It was then that an amalgam of personal, medical, mystical and political factors began to affect the government of the Russian Empire. The heir to the throne, Grand Duke Alexis, was a sickly child, afflicted with haemophilia, which the ministrations of a motley succession of regular doctors, faith-healers, quacks and medicine-men had failed to alleviate. According to sound evidence, Rasputin was apparently able to bring some comfort to the young lad through his powers of hypnosis which slowed down the body's metabolism, thereby suppressing any haemorrhage or bruising. The mystically inclined Empress thought this nothing short of a miracle and began to regard 'Grishka' as a man from the simple people sent by God to save her son, the dynasty and the Russian Empire. News of his disgusting personal habits, his wenching and carousing around the taverns of St Petersburg and in various aristocratic boudoirs failed to shake Nicholas and Alexandra's faith in their new-found 'friend'.

That would have been all very well had it been confined to a purely private family affair. However, from about 1912, Rasputin began to meddle in high politics and to recommend the appointment or dismissal of state ministers in return for personal favours, hospitality or sexual gratification. A crate of Madeira, a gypsy girl, a word from Rasputin in the imperial ear was often all it took to secure a high government portfolio. Particularly during the first two years of the First World War, a game of what came to be known as 'ministerial leap-frog' took place, with one incompetent, senile, mentally deranged or simply corrupt official replacing another in rapid, debilitating succession.

Understandably, this tragi-farcical situation totally altered society's view, not only of the government, but also of the royal family, the court and the sacred person of the Emperor himself. After Nicholas took personal command of the Russian army in 1915, spending most of his time at military headquarters in Mogilev, domestic politics were seen to be increasingly under the influence of the 'German woman' and her bewitching adviser, Rasputin, a kind of latter-day, malevolent Merlin-figure court-wizard controlling the destiny of Russia. Relations between government and society finally deteriorated to the point where a conspiracy of courtiers and royal relatives murdered Rasputin in order to rescue the prestige – as they saw it – of the imperial regime. Not that the assassination of the 'Holy Devil' affected the fortunes of Russia as it plunged towards revolution. As has often been said, Rasputin was not a cause, merely a symptom, of the malaise which held Russia in its fatal grip. To change the metaphor, he was simply a scapegoat on which many people, like the author of this book, laid the blame for all the evils of the tsarist social and political order. In a paraphrase of Voltaire's dictum concerning the deity, one highly placed contemporary wag remarked: 'If Rasputin had not existed, it would have been necessary to invent him.' Our author, however, has no need for such invention. He is unambiguous in his contention that:

'Russian historians of the future will blame Nicholas II . . . for being culpably weak and letting the reins of power . . . gradually slip through his hands, to be caught up by the iniquitous and despicable villain Rasputine' (page 41).

And further:

'. . . the shot that killed Rasputine on December 17th, 1916, was the first shot fired into the monarchy of Russia' (page 114).

Most modern Russian historians do not, however, ascribe the collapse of the Russian Empire simply to such subjective, personal factors as Nicholas, Alexandra or Rasputin. All three were in a sense, and despite their apparently central role, only peripheral actors on a stage which was being increasingly occupied and dominated by the Russian people – the millions of common soldiers, seamen, factory workers and peasants who took over the streets, barracks and fields of Russia between February and October 1917. The vacuum created by the Tsar's abdication was temporarily filled by the formation of two centres of political authority: these were the Provisional Government, made up of a self-appointed coalition of ex-Duma politicians and businessmen representing, by and large, the interests of what may loosely be described as the wealthy, property-owning classes; and the Petrograd Soviet (i.e. Council) of Workers' and Soldiers' Deputies, its democratically elected members forming a kind of crude workers' parliament which enjoyed the support and confidence of most of the capital's military and civilian population. This situation was described by the Bolshevik Party leader, Vladimir Ilyich Lenin, who returned from his Swiss exile to Petrograd on 3 April, as one of 'dual power' (*dvoevlastie*), the complexities and significance of which were either ignored or not understood by the writer of the present book.

The first and second Provisional Governments, led by the non-party aristocrat, Prince G. E. Lvov (Lwoff) – quaintly described by the author as an 'ardent Radical' (page 91) – enacted a wide-ranging programme of democratic and social reforms, which caused even Lenin to describe Russia as 'the freest of all the belligerent countries', but failed to address itself purposefully to the two most urgent problems at the centre of popular grievances and frustrations. Those were Russia's continuing involvement in the First World War – the new government's commitment to which was manifestly unsupported by a battered and war-weary population; and the administration's reluctance to redistribute land to the peasants and so legally settle the agrarian problems which the rural masses were now taking into their own uncontrollable hands. The inclusion of certain socialist leaders from the Petrograd Soviet in the third Provisional Government, now led by Alexander Kerensky, tainted the parties which they represented with complicity in the government's unpopular stance on the two central issues of peace and land, thereby paving the way for the Bolshevik Party's rocketing popularity and numerical support throughout the summer.

On his return from Switzerland to Petrograd in April, Lenin had surprised even his own close comrades in the party leadership by declaring that the time for a transition from the 'bourgeois-democratic' revolution, which had just taken place, to a full-fledged 'proletarian-socialist' revolution, which would transfer 'all power to the Soviets', was already at hand. The vital role of Lenin and the Bolsheviks and of the Bolshevik-dominated Petrograd Soviet and its Military-Revolutionary Committee (chaired by Leon Trotsky) during the autumn of 1917 were of course unknowable to the author at the time he wrote his account. However, what he does do is to use Lenin and the misleadingly called 'Lenintzys-anarchists' (*sic*, page 166) as a pretext for elaborating one of his central obsessions: that is, that the Russian revolutions – both the one that had already overthrown the monarchy, and the one that was still going on – were entirely the work of the hated Germans.

In fact his paranoid Germanophobia informs not only his views on the February revolution, but on the whole course of Russian history. The robust defence of Russia's autocratic tradition which he mounted in *Russian Court Memoirs* is now skewed into a xenophobic attack on the fallen dynasty in whose veins 'not a drop of the Romanoff blood flows' (page 115). On the contrary, bad German blood had poisoned the royal household from the early eighteenth century, culminating, of course, in the ill-fated mar-

riage of Nicholas and the German-born Alexandra and the conse-
quent tragedy of February 1917. The author also inveighs against
what he describes as the 'ultra-monarchists' and members of
Russia's political 'right' as being 'fanatical partisans' of the German Kaiser. Respected ministers and close officials of the royal
court with Germanic-sounding names are also collectively con-
demned in a torrent of racialist abuse. At the other end of the
political spectrum, all revolutionary activists in Russia are dismissed as the hirelings and agents of German imperialism. There
is, of course, documentary historical evidence to prove that the
German Foreign Ministry did provide financial support for revolutionary organisations inside Russia as part of its *Revolutionier-
ungspolitik*, i.e. the policy of supporting subversive movements
within one's enemy country. It is also common knowledge that
Lenin and other radical figures were ferried back to Russia in the
famous sealed train supplied and guaranteed safe passage
through northern Europe by Berlin. But it is of course ludicrous
to suggest that those genuine Russian revolutionaries unscrupulously utilising this foreign source of income were nothing but
German spies. (Even more ludicrous is the author's footnote on
page 114 to the effect that Lenin was himself a German whose
real name was 'von Lehmann'!)

The author's obvious anguish and mental confusion about what
was happening to his country is perhaps a reflection of the
anguish and confusion that the whole of Russia was experiencing
at the time. He bemoans the end of autocracy, but talks of the
'rotten system of the old regime' (page 48). He regards the Russian
people as honest, loyal Christian folk, but 'not fit for self-
government; they have no idea of the value of time, no consciousness of duty, no standard of moral integrity' (page 198). He is
bemused by a 'topsy-turvy' world in which common soldiers may
loll in first-class compartments; where 'Manual labour is valued
much higher than intellectual work' (page 199); where women
have formed regiments and a wife 'struts off to her business
duties' leaving her distracted husband 'pacifying squalling infants, rocking cradles, or looking after the pots and pans in the
kitchen' (page 201). Finally, as he declares in his rather desperate
peroration:

'Russia with her sparkling façade – somewhat oriental in its
splendour – is no more to be recognised. All that was beautiful,

imposing and brilliant has disappeared – and what has remained is vulgar, paltry and mean' (page 198).

His own inability, and that of the social milieu of which he was
part, to recognise or come to terms with the real forces which
shaped the revolution are a testimony as to why that revolution
occurred.

THE FALL OF THE ROMANOFFS

HOW THE EX-EMPRESS & RASPUTINE
CAUSED THE RUSSIAN REVOLUTION

by the author of
'RUSSIAN COURT MEMOIRS'

MCMXVIII

THE EX-EMPRESS ALEXANDRA IN THE UNIFORM OF
THE EMPRESS ALEXANDRA FEODOROVNA'S
REGIMENT OF LANCERS

CONTENTS

R.T.C. LIBRARY
LETTERKENNY

Chapter I

THE EMPRESS'S FOLLY

THE events of the first days of March, 1917, o/s, which brought about the fall of the Romanoff dynasty, were welcomed by the majority of my countrymen, not because of their revolutionary tendencies, but merely because they saw in the new order of things the final extinction of German influence in Russia.

The responsibility for the wreck of the Russian monarchy lies entirely with the Empress Alexandra Feodorovna, the most fatal of all the consorts of Russian Sovereigns.

At the time of the death of Alexander III, the feeling of the nation towards the Imperial Family was one of deep and sincere loyalty. The last days of Alexander III seemed firmly to have attached to the dying monarch and the members of his family the affections of the nation. A wave of patriotism enveloped the whole country, and the last sad journey of the remains of the deceased Sovereign from the shores of the Crimea to Petrograd was one long triumphal procession. The Imperial obsequies in the capital gave rise to endless loyal manifestation to the memory of the deceased Tzar and to his successor.

During the anxious days when the life of the once powerful monarch was slowly ebbing away in Livadia (the Imperial residence in the Crimea), a great despondency fell upon the majority of his loyal subjects. They looked with misgiving towards the future, when the reins of power would be held by the weak hands of the inexperienced Emperor, Nicholas II.

With all his wisdom, Alexander III had not possessed the knowledge of how to bring up his son to be worthy of the mighty

Empire for which he was ordained by fate. The Empress Marie has often been reproached with having spoiled the race of the Romanoffs, who up to then had been renowned for their magnificent physique. The new Tzar had not inherited his father's imposing deportment; he was small and slight, with his mother's features and her glorious eyes, like those of an antelope. Unaware that his days were numbered, Alexander III had always put off initiating his heir into affairs of State. He considered him too young to be burdened with such cares, and wished him to enjoy his youth a little longer.

The childhood of Nicholas II was mostly spent in Gatchino, in the restricted circle of courtiers, with hardly any friends of his own age. The Empress Marie was a devoted mother, but she was strict, especially during the years of his adolescence. The repression lasted until the lad fell ill and the doctor held a private conversation with the Tzar, after which the reins were slackened. His English tutor, Mr. Heath, was replaced by General Danilovitch, whose mission it was to form the mind of the future Sovereign, but the worthy General was a man of limited abilities, totally unfit to be the mentor of a future Emperor. He had been chosen for this onerous task because of his honesty, loyalty and morality – qualities that both the Emperor and Empress prized above everything else.

The education the Tzessarevitch received was that of an average officer of the Guards. His mind was not sufficiently cultivated, and nothing had been done to strengthen his will-power. He had no taste for reading, but he liked music and possessed a good tenor voice, which, however, has never been trained. He likes all kinds of outdoor games, and is an indefatigable walker.

At the age of eighteen Nicholas entered successively the Preobrajensky regiment, and that of the Imperial Hussars in Tzarskoe Selo. Coming into closer contact with officers of his age, he became intimate with some of them, but, shy and reserved by nature and accustomed to repress his feelings, he never possessed the gift of making friends. They were his companions with whom he laughed and was merry, but no real trusted friendship united him to any of them. His only real friend was his younger brother George, who shared his studies. For many years, however, the Grand Duke George was obliged to live in the south of Russia, and he died of consumption about four years after his brother ascended the throne. That is one of the reasons for the Tzar's

{6}

subsequent isolation; he was surrounded by courtiers, more or less devoted to him, but he has not one single friend.

Feeling his end approaching, Alexander III wished before his death to witness the betrothal of his heir. The question of the Tzessarevitch's marriage had often been mooted, though nothing was decided. The Princess Alix of Hesse had frequently visited her sister, the Grand Duchess Elisabeth Feodorovna. Both the Grand Duchess and her husband, the late Grand Duke Serge Alexandrovitch, were eager to bring about a matrimonial alliance between the Princess and the Emperor's eldest son, but the Empress Marie was opposed to this plan. Was it premonition, motherly instinct or personal dislike? The fact remains that Her Majesty was always against the marriage. Kaiser Wilhelm had wished his youngest sister, Margaret, to become the future Empress of Russia, but the Empress Marie detested the Hohenzollerns, and the Tzar was likewise not prepossessed in favour of so close an alliance with the Court of Berlin.

It was rumoured that the handsome Princess Helen of Orleans had struck the fancy of the Tzessarevitch. This alliance would have been a very popular one in Russia, and would have delighted the Tzar and his Consort, but the Princess, belonging to the Roman Catholic Church, could not change her creed, and that would have been a serious impediment.

When the dying Tzar wished to see his son affianced, matters were hurried, and the choice fell upon Princess Alix of Hesse. The Princess, who since her first visits to this country had attained maturity, felt some misgivings as to her suitability for the part allotted to her. Unfortunately she did not listen to the inner voice that whispered that she was unfit to be the Empress of Russia. Her grandmother, Queen Victoria, strongly advised her to accept such a brilliant offer, and, as, since her father's death, the Princess Alix was dissatisfied with her position at the Court of Darmstadt, she finally decided to acquiesce.

In Russia it was known that the future Tzessarevna had been brought up in England under the care of her Royal Grandmother, and people fondly hoped that she loved England and was more English than German. A few days before the Tzar drew his last breath, Princess Alix was hastily summoned to receive the blessing of her future husband's father. She travelled to the Crimea with her eldest sister, Princess Victoria of Battenberg. Kaiser Wilhelm, with his usual somewhat obtrusive gallantry, hastened to greet his cousin at some German town, and gave her his escort for an hour or two. People have now remembered this against the dethroned Empress Alexandra, and say that during these hours a plan of conduct was sketched out for her by her cousin William, which she has faithfully endeavoured to carry out during the twenty-two years of her husband's reign.

By the advice of the Prince of Wales (afterwards King Edward VII), who was in Livadia at the time of his brother-in-law's death, the wedding was hurried on and, three weeks after the funeral of Alexander III, the new Tzar was quietly married to Princess Alix of Hesse in the Private Chapel of the Winter Palace. The bridal pair received an enthusiastic welcome from the crowds of people assembled in the streets. When they alighted at the Kazan Cathedral to worship at the shrine of the Holy Virgin and, Russian fashion, bowed low to the people, inclining themselves three times, they were greeted with tremendous bursts of cheering. Everything seemed promising.

The first discordant note was struck when the young Tzar received the deputations of the Zemstvo[1] in the ancestral halls of the Winter Palace. The address of the Zemstvo from Twer contained some allusion to the hopes of liberal reforms being granted. In his speech to the assembled deputations, the young Emperor expressed his firm resolve to follow in the footsteps of his beloved parent, and nipped all liberal hopes in the bud by calling them 'senseless dreams'. These two unlucky words gave rise to no end of discussion, and laid the foundation stone to the Tzar's unpopularity in liberal circles.

The Tzar Nicholas II is one of the most unlucky of men and ill-fated of monarchs. Fortune frowned upon him from the first day of his ascending the throne of his forefathers. Everything seems to combine against him, every event seemed to bring misfortune, and every blessing turned into a curse; but the most calamitous day of his existence was his marriage day. The Empress Alexandra brought only trouble and dissension into his life, and has been the evil spirit who has led the unfortunate Tzar to his doom.

The first year of his reign passed quietly enough, the Court was still in mourning. The young sovereigns led a retired life and the general public saw but little of them. The rumour began to spread,

1 The representatives of Country Courts.

however, that the young Empress repelled everyone by the stony haughtiness of her bearing during the receptions she was bound to attend. Deputations from all parts of Russia flocked to Petrograd to greet the young sovereigns on the occasion of their ascending the throne, as well as on their nuptials. Costly gifts were proffered, but neither gifts nor devotion moved the Empress out of her chilling impassivity. Nothing seemed to touch her or elicit a smile of gratification. Her Majesty entered the room, where the people stood assembled, bowing stiffly and looking rigid and stern. Without casting a glance at the exhibited presents, selected with such care and devotion, she muttered a few monosyllables of thanks and retired without entering into conversation with anyone.

The Tzar, on the contrary, was charming and endeavoured by the suavity of his manner to atone for his Consort's ungraciousness. Numbers of people, offended by their reception, returned to the provinces spreading the most appalling tales of the Empress Alexandra's supercilious haughtiness, of the disdain she openly showed for her husband's most loyal subjects. Her friends put forth her extreme shyness as an extenuating circumstance, but a quite different construction was put on Her Majesty's distant manner by the nation. It was attributed to the arrogancy of the German Princess, who looked down upon Russia and scorned its people.

It soon became noised abroad that the relations between the two Russian Empresses had become strained. The Empress Alexandra had not the gift of ingratiating herself, or even of inspiring sympathy. She never tried to conciliate those who could have been her true friends and advisers; nor did she attempt to disguise the fact that there were in Russia many things of which she did not approve, and which she intended to reform. With the members of the Imperial Family she was strictly polite without admitting any intimacy likely to lead to friendship. It soon became common knowledge that the young Empress was very difficult to get on with; her temper was harsh and violent, and she treated her immediate entourage with such disdain that it became difficult to get any young lady to accept the hitherto coveted position of lady-in-waiting.

One of the maids-of-honour attached to the young Empress soon after her marriage received a very severe rebuke. Perceiving the handsome gifts that some deputation had just presented to the Sovereign, the maid-of-honour delightedly expressed her admiration of them, adding ingenuously: 'I hope they saw how pleased Your Majesty was!' The Empress measured the unfortunate girl with a withering glance, remarking: 'I believe you wish to teach me a lesson.'

On another occasion a private concert was held in the Palace. The Marshal of the Imperial Court approached Her Majesty with the words:

'It has always been the custom on such festive evenings to invite the ladies-in-waiting to be present.'

'Quite unnecessary,' was the ungracious answer. 'They can open their doors and listen to the music from their rooms.'

Being a greater stickler for etiquette, the Empress insisted on the old-fashioned rigid customs of the German Courts being adapted to the Imperial household. These innovations caused much displeasure, and during the first years the ladies-in-waiting were continually leaving. The only maid-of-honour who found favour in the Empress Alexandra's eyes was Mlle. Anna Taneief, better known by her married name of Madame Vyrouboff. She became the evil genius of Her Majesty.

Faithfulness is one of the chief characteristics of the ex-Emperor Nicholas II. He does not share the predilection of most of the male members of the Imperial Family for gallant adventures. As a young man he only had one liaison with a celebrated ballet-dancer, a liaison which was broken off at the time of his betrothal. When he married his heart belonged entirely to his wife. The ex-Tzar is an ideal family man, and his devotion to his wife and children is exemplary. Loving his Empress as he did, trusting her blindly and having a high opinion of her superior judgement, he gradually became entirely subject to her influence. If anything he was rather in awe, not so much of her as of the hysterical fits she developed. These attacks were formidable weapons in Her Majesty's hands, and she used them unscrupulously to enforce her will.

The general opinion in Western countries that Nicholas II is not a clever man is a mistaken one. His greatest defect is a want of will-power and self-reliance, which renders him vacillating and has prevented him from enforcing his own wishes. His first opinion is always correct and his first decision right. If he had acted independently, and had been more spontaneous in his resolves, all would have been well, but the Empress interfered in everything. Her opinion rarely coincided with the Emperor's decisions, and his weak will could not withstand his consort's strong personality. He listened to her, began to waver, doubted his own judgement and finally let himself be overruled by her wishes. He committed the fatal mistake of allowing his wife to interfere in State affairs. Her influence continued to increase until it became unlimited. During recent years the Empress has been the all-powerful ruler of Russia's destinies. Believing as he did in her superior wisdom and in her integrity, it never struck Nicholas II that the country he was ordained by fate to govern did not trust her, and strongly objected to her rule.

Alexander III had been a wiser man in this respect, for, although he adored his wife and was a model husband, he never admitted the Empress Marie's interference in questions of government. She was at the head of all the educational and charitable institutions, she directed her children's education and took the lead at the Court. That was her proper sphere, but she had no control over State affairs, and she was too womanly and right-minded ever to attempt such an intrusion.

The first bitter disappointment of the young Empress occurred a year after her marriage. Instead of the ardently expected son and heir, she gave birth to a daughter. Six months later the Coronation took place in Moscow. The young Empress, whose unpopularity was already an acknowledged fact, received a cool welcome from the population, whereas the Dowager Empress was greeted with acclamation. The difference between these two receptions naturally produced an unfavourable impression on the Empress Alexandra, increasing the harshness of her demeanour.

One of the first mistakes of the young Tzar was the nomination of his uncle and brother-in-law, the Grand Duke Serge Alexandrovitch, to the post of Governor-General in Moscow. For many years old Prince Dolgorouky had filled that post, and it would be difficult to find a more popular Governor-General. Moscow loved and honoured him, and his sudden removal to make way for the Emperor's uncle broke the old man's heart, and was deeply resented by the people. On the other hand, the Grand Duke Serge was not the right man in the right place. He was harsh, tactless, arrogant, treated the people haughtily, and managed to offend those it would have been wiser to conciliate. His wife on the contrary, the Grand Duchess Elisabeth, charmed the Muscovites and gained their affections. She was called the Queen of Moscow, and her popularity lasted until the present war, when the former devotion changed suddenly to detestation. Her German origin was remembered against her, and sundry stories were spread regarding her predilection for German prisoners, and the preference she showed them in comparison to the wounded Russian soldiers.

A grudge had been nursed for some time against the Grand Duchess for becoming a deaconess. In Russia there are nuns, who live in convents, but up to this there had been no deaconesses. Several members of the Holy Synod protested against the innovation from Germany, where there are no nuns, but where 'diaconessen' and 'diaconessen-Stifte' (homes for deaconesses) exist. At the present moment the Grand Duchess Elisabeth is one of the most unpopular members of the Imperial Family.

But to return to the first period of the reign of Nicholas II. Time passed, and each year brought fresh hopes to the Empress of giving an heir to the throne of Russia; but these hopes were dashed to the ground. Four daughters were successively born to the Imperial couple. The Empress was desperate, and her excitement on each occasion was such as to cause serious anxiety, and those about her feared to let her know the disappointing sex of the new-born infant. This intense desire to give birth to a son became the Sovereign's fixed idea, and she had recourse to all kinds of expedients to enable her to give an heir to Russia. Prayers, vows, pilgrimages, sortilegy, hypnotism, etc., everything was tried.

Occult science had always attracted the Tzar and his Consort, and spiritualistic sittings were continually arranged either in Tzarskoe Selo, or in the old Palace of the Grand Duke Nicholas on the Italian Street, which has since been sold. The best mediums were commanded, and, although these sittings were kept a profound secret, still everyone knew of them, and the most amazing tales were spread. The spirit of Alexander III was invoked, and his son found great satisfaction in consulting him on State matters. Every impending reform was submitted for approval to the spirit of the departed monarch. The burning question of the next heir to the throne was naturally also a topic on which the spiritual oracle was consulted.

Hypnotism played a prominent part in the life of the Empress Alexandra. A renowned French hypnotist was sent for, and during a seance, whilst the Empress was under his hypnotic influence, he insinuated to her to conceive an infant of the male sex. After a very short time the Empress felt herself to be *enceinte* – an announcement that caused jubilation to reign at Court. The usual proceeding of consulting a specialist was this time omitted by the advice of the hypnotist, who insisted that, as the child was conceived under hypnotical influence, the intervention of a medical man could only do harm to the natural development of nature. The heir was expected in June, 1902. Everything was in readiness, and Her Majesty waited impatiently, but there was only disappointment. At last the Emperor was obliged to call in a specialist, who pronounced the Empress to be suffering from an illusion! The case was given a Latin appellation, scientifically explained, and the incident considered closed. But no pen could adequately describe the poignant grief and bitter disappointment suffered by the unfortunate Empress. The hypnotist, having proved such a dismal failure, was sent back to France in disgrace, where he died shortly after his return.

In the summer of 1903, the ceremony of Saint Seraphim's canonisation took place in the monastery of Saroff, where he had spent the greater part of his holy life, and where he was buried. The Tzar and his Consort were present at the religious rites, and took part in all the processions. A passionate appeal was addressed to God by the Imperial couple to send them the blessing of a son and heir. The ill-famed Rasputine, who later attracted so much public notice, but who at that time was an obscure person unknown to the Sovereigns, was present at the canonisation ceremonies, in the guise of a tramping pilgrim, or, as such men are called in Russia, 'Staretz'. He prayed for a long time before the silver shrine containing the relics, his devotional prostration resembling a trance. Subsequently he was heard to prophesy to the assembled crowd that a new miracle was about to take place, and that a year would not elapse before the birth of the long-expected heir to the Russian throne would gladden the country.

After ten years of anxious suspense, the Tzessarevitch Alexis was born on July 30th, o/s, 1904. The war with Japan was at its height, and our reverses dimmed the joy that in other circumstances the nation would undoubtedly have felt. For the same reason no public rejoicings commemorated the happy event, but the Tzar was lavish in the many bounties and privileges he granted. All petitions were conceded, and their numbers increased to such an enormous extent that a separate Chancery had to be established to investigate them. The christening was performed in Peterhof with great solemnity, and all the ladies present wore their Court apparel.

During these halcyon days the Empress was so engrossed with her nursery that she did not pay much attention to State affairs, and limited her interference to occasional remarks.

At about this time Mlle. Anna Taneief became an intimate of the Imperial household. Mlle. Anna Taneief's father held the position of Chief of His Majesty's Chancery. He had occupied this post since Alexander III's reign, but his influence at that time was quite unimportant. Taneief *père* is the son of the late composer Taneief, and he started in life as a professor of the Petrograd Conservatoire. Alexander III was passionately fond of music and had his own amateur orchestra, in which he played the violoncello. Music brought Taneief into touch with the Court, and eventually he exchanged his musical career for that of a courtier.

M. Taneief is clever and intriguing; he had the good fortune to impress the young Empress favourably and it soon became rumoured that he was becoming all-powerful. It was he who instructed his daughter so cleverly that she accomplished the difficult feat of finding favour in the Sovereign's eyes. Later on, he continued to pull the strings to such purpose that Mlle. Taneief was the first lady-in-waiting whom the Empress treated kindly and really liked. She adroitly insinuated herself into Her Majesty's confidence, and finally became quite indispensable to her Imperial Mistress. When Mlle. Taneief married Lieutenant Vyrouboff, the marriage took place in the Chapel of the Palace at Tzarskoe Selo, and the invitations were issued from the Court as for a Royal marriage. After the wedding of Her Majesty's favourite, the intimacy continued, and developed into a devoted friendship.

Madame Vyrouboff's conjugal life turned out a failure, and was speedily dissolved after a terrible scandal. No one knows with certainty what exactly happened, but the facts that have reached the public are as follows. Lieutenant Vyrouboff was appointed to a ship which was going round the world. Wicked tongues stated that the appointment had been caused by the wish to get rid of him. The young husband having taken an affectionate leave of his bride, who was spending the summer months in Peterhof, started for Cronstadt to join his ship. Arrived there he was informed that,

in consequence of an unforeseen mishap to her machinery, the
ship could only be ready to sail on the next day.

Glad of the opportunity to spend another day with his wife,
Lieutenant Vyrouboff took the next boat to Peterhof, and unexpectedly turned up at his wife's 'datcha' (villa). To his astonishment he found the house surrounded by police agents, who
prevented his entrance on the plea of the Empress's presence.
After a long walk in the park the young officer returned to his
house, where he found the police still in full force and his entrance
barred, although he was told that the Empress had left. The
impetuous sailor became furious at the idea of not being let into
his own house. He used violence and forced a way into the datcha.

What happened after his sudden appearance remained a mystery to the uninitiated, but a quarter of an hour later, Madame
Vyrouboff, dishevelled and shrieking, ran out of the villa and,
going straight to the Summer Palace of the Imperial Family, took
refuge with the Empress. Divorce proceedings were immediately
instituted, and Madame Vyrouboff unofficially resumed her
duties in attendance on the Empress. It was said at the time that
it was proposed to declare Lieutenant Vyrouboff insane and put
him under restraint, but the Minister of the Court, Baron Fredericks (he had not then been created Count) told the Emperor
frankly that such a measure would provoke great displeasure and
set public opinion against the Court.

The Dowager Empress was a pained witness of what went on
at the Imperial Court. She was naturally cognisant of all the
circumstances of her son's life, and her disapproval of many things
was manifest. The continual spiritualistic sittings inspired her
with displeasure and anxiety, her very soul revolting at the idea
of her dead husband's spirit being called forth. Her Majesty was
seriously annoyed with the Grand Duke Nicholas and his wife for
aiding and abetting the young Empress, encouraging her mystical
proclivities and looking out for new and powerful mediums and
celebrated occultists.

There was a time when the relations between the Dowager
Empress and the Grand Duchess Anastasia Nicolaïevna (the wife
of the Grand Duke Nicholas) became very strained. Her Majesty
accused the Grand Duchess of deliberately intriguing from personal motives against her maternal authority and influence, and
she flatly refused to meet Anastasia Nicolaïevna. But Her Majesty
could do nothing to check these ominous proceedings; her in-

THE FALL OF THE ROMANOFFS

fluence over her son, which had once been so strong, was now completely gone. The Tzar listened only to his wife, and the estrangement between mother and daughter-in-law continued to increase.

Until the birth of her son, the Empress held herself under some restraint; she considered that in not giving an heir to the Crown, she had failed in her duty towards the country and the dynasty, and the morbidness of her character only helped to emphasise this feeling. But with the birth of the Tzessarevitch she changed completely, and asserted herself in a way she had not hitherto attempted. One of the first consequences of this newly acquired self-reliance was the determined stand she took against her mother-in-law, and the breach between the two Imperial Ladies widened immeasurably. The Dowager Empress withdrew completely from public and social life and seldom appeared at her son's Court, where in the eyes of the young Empress, she was an unwelcome guest.

Nothing, however, not even his devotion to his wife, could make the Tzar waver in his affectionate allegiance to his mother, but though he loved her, he was often guilty of offending her, owing to his wife's influence. The close intimacy that had formerly existed between the Emperor and his sisters ceased by degrees, and the ties of friendship with some of his cousins were severed. The Empress brought dissension into the very bosom of his family, she came between him and all his affections, and she alienated him completely from his kinsfolk.

Chapter II

THE CLOUDS GATHER

NAPOLEON would willingly have crushed the Kingdom of Prussia completely after the Battle of Jena, dethroning the King, Frederick William III, and turning the country into a large province. The French Emperor was only hindered from this extreme measure by the interference of the Russian Emperor Alexander I, who, moved by the beauty and sorrow of the unfortunate Queen Louise of Prussia, chivalrously resolved in this instance to act as her champion. Russian historians and politicians have often reproached Alexander I for advocating the cause of Prussia, and not considering the interests of his own country, for the abolition of the kingdom of Prussia would have been a political advantage to Russia. The Hohenzollerns have never got over the humiliating role they were obliged to play, and Prussia never forgave Russia for the fact that she owes her very existence to the generosity of the Russian Tzar.

The German Kaisers have always played a double part towards Russia. Notwithstanding the close tie of kinship that bound him to the House of Romanoff, and his professed friendship for his brother-in-law, Nicholas I, his nephew, Alexander II, and his great-nephew, Alexander III, the Kaiser was always wary in his politics. Whereas the Russian Tzars, Nicholas I and Alexander II, were sincere in their loyalty to Prussia and their devotion to the German Sovereign, Alexander III disliked the Germans and mistrusted them; but he held his old great-uncle in high esteem, although he thoroughly detested the latter's grandson, the present Kaiser Wilhelm.

Instigated by Prince Bismarck, William I saw an everlasting danger-signal in the developing power of the mighty Empire so close to Germany's frontier. He strained every nerve by intrigue to stem the tide of Russia's power and progress. His grandson, William II, zealously followed this system, even more eagerly, for in his case the traditional friendship with the Russian monarchs, Alexander III and Nicholas II, was only a pretence.

The present war has revealed many things, and numerous damning circumstances have been brought to light. A widespread German spying net has been for years ingeniously woven and stretched all over Russia. German agents filled the country. Some of them lived in Russia for years, having established themselves as wholesale merchants, shopkeepers, brokers, land-agents, etc. Others came over as bank-clerks or business men. Most of these Germans seemed to be quite accustomed to their new country and boasted of their devotion. At heart they were traitors to the nation that had given them such generous hospitality. Their mission consisted of spying and carrying out German orders to Russia's detriment. Nothing evil happened in Russia without Germany's connivance. The wires were pulled in Berlin. It has been irrefutably proved that many revolutionary movements and acts of terrorism in this country were inspired from the banks of the Spree.

Germany did everything to weaken the Russian Government and further its unpopularity among the population. By sundry well-planned intrigues, Germany kept Great Britain and Russia from fraternising. She created obstacles to Russian politics in Persia, China and Turkey, and she played a perfidious part in the Balkans. Her aim was to isolate Russia completely from all political alliances and friendships. Being at the bottom of every political calamity that befell Russia, it is not to be wondered at that the Russo-Japanese war was to a great extent provoked by the clever machinations of Kaiser Wilhelm's agents. Berlin was far better informed of the state of our army, navy, and munitions than Petrograd. It was the object of the crafty Wilhelm and his satellites to implicate Russia in an unsuccessful war.

It must, however, be acknowledged that a great part of our failures was due to a fatal ill-luck, which pursued the Russians from the first day of the war. The reverses sustained caused great discouragement among the Russians and distrust of the way things were managed. Count Witte was sent to Portsmouth, U.S.A., to discuss the conditions of peace, but the Count inspired but little confidence. He was known to be a man of undoubted

CLOOO7084

intellect and mental strength, but he had the reputation of being utterly unscrupulous in his methods, and untrustworthy. People were therefore inclined to be sceptical when they knew that such an important mission was entrusted to him.

Many people in Russia, especially in military circles, considered the moment unfavourable for peace pourparlers. It was known that General Kuropatkine's successor, General Linevitch, had sent an urgent wire insisting on the continuation of the war. The Japanese were completely exhausted, and he had formed a powerful army ready for the attack. For these reasons the news that peace had been concluded was greeted with great reserve. The young Empress was especially insistent on peace being ratified, but her pacific endeavours were not appreciated by the nation. 'A German Princess cannot be expected to care for Russia's dignity' was said of her at the time.

The year 1905 was an exceptionally ill-fated one for Russia. The workmen's demonstration, which ended so tragically, took place on January 9th, o/s. Thousands of workmen, headed by the priest Gapon, advanced towards the Winter Palace, intent on exacting a Constitutional Government from the Tzar. The majority came from the neighbourhood of Petrograd. In great numbers they streamed in from Kolpino, Schlusselburg, the Putiloff foundry, etc., and were joined by the workmen of the capital. On reaching the square facing the Winter Palace, they formed a threatening crowd.

The authorities were well aware of the forthcoming manifestation, and made the great mistake of not stopping each separate procession, obliging all to go back. Instead they allowed their numbers to accumulate, and, instead of dispersing them gradually and preventing them from reaching the town, they were left unmolested until they had reached their destination and asked to be led before the Tzar. The Imperial Family resided as usual in Tzarskoe Selo. The crowd was ordered to disperse, they were told that the Sovereign was not in the Palace, but the assembled masses did not budge. They were warned that, if they did not move on, the order to shoot would be given. After the third warning, the first discharge was made and the square before the Winter Palace became the scene of bloodshed and confusion.

The late General Dmitry Trepoff was at that time the Governor-General of Petrograd. He was a man of energy and resolution, devoted to the Tzar and to the autocratic power of the

R.T.C. LIBRARY, LETTERKENNY
9607
086

monarch. At that stage only severe measures could stem the current. The General gave the order to shoot, adding the words that have since become famous, and which have often been used as a reproach against the Government: 'Do not spare cartridges'! And cartridges were not spared! Volleys of rifle fire succeeded each other, the place was strewn with bodies of the killed and wounded. The priest Gapon divested himself of his cassock, which concealed the uniform of a university student, and in this guise fled from the scene of slaughter. As to the rest of his flock . . . it was a general *sauve qui peut*.

This disastrous event, the cause of so much useless bloodshed and misery, produced the most painful impression on people of all parties. The victims were numerous. The workmen had chosen a Sunday for their demonstration and the traffic in the streets was greater than usual, and the casualties were very numerous. Among the killed and wounded were many quite unconnected with the demonstration, who happened to be passing near to the scene of disaster. The Tzar, on being informed of the tragic event, endeavoured to smooth matters over. He gave the order for all manufactories and foundries to select two deputies each, and send the assembled deputation to the halls of the Winter Palace. On the day fixed for the reception, the Sovereign came over from Tzarskoe Selo to the hall where the workmen were gathered. He took their collective petition, questioned them on the reason for their complaints, and promised that their claims should have consideration. After that interview the rights and privileges of the workmen were somewhat increased. The men's complaints ceased for a time, but they nursed their resentment. Mutiny was in the air.

As to the priest Gapon, who had inspired the manifestation and was the recognised leader of the workmen, he disappeared completely. At first no one knew what had happened to him after his flight, but the fact was soon revealed that the enterprising priest had been spirited away and had safely reached the Riviera. Here he was frequently seen at the gaming-tables of Monte Carlo. In fact his escape in the crowd and subsequently from the country, leaving no trace, was successful to the extent of causing sceptics to suspect the intervention of the police. This gave rise to the story that Gapon was an 'agent provocateur', but the men's trust in him remained unshaken.

After October 17th o/s, and the amnesty to all political emigrants, the priest returned to Russia, and played the part of mediator between the Government and workmen. A few months later he vanished, and for a long time his fate remained an unfathomable mystery, until his body was unexpectedly discovered hanging in one of the rooms of an uninhabited datcha (villa) at Ozerky, a summer resort at about half an hour's distance by rail from Petrograd. He had obviously fallen a victim to his enemies lying in ambush for him. No one knows with certainty what occurred on the fatal day of his disappearance. Was Gapon murdered by order of the secret police, who feared he knew too much? or had his partisans discovered the double game he was playing and taken their revenge? The circumstances of his murder were shrouded in mystery and gave rise to numerous stories. The real facts are known only to those who planned the ghastly drama – and they have kept their own council.

A story was current at the time that an engineer, Ruthenberg, in the guise of a police-agent, had entered into negotiations with Gapon and, on the day he was made away with, had enticed him to Ozerky to receive a large sum of money in return for services he was to render to the secret police. Several of his partisans were secreted in the isolated house. When they heard the evidence of his treachery, they came forward, overpowered the defenceless man, sat in judgement upon him, sentenced him to death, and he was forthwith executed. The engineer Ruthenberg – some people state the name was only an assumed one – was lost sight of at the same time, but the rumour was circulated that he had been heard of in Switzerland.

A few months prior to those Gapon demonstrations, the Minister of the Interior, M. Plehve, had been killed by a bomb hurled into his carriage by a student named Sazonoff, a member of a secret revolutionary society. When death overtook him, the Minister was on his way to the Baltic Station to take the train to Peterhof, where the Tzar resided. This assassination was a misfortune to the monarchy, for the Tzar lost in him one of the strongest pillars of autocratic rule. Plehve was a powerful man, full of mental vigour, ability and energy, who never wavered in his resolutions. All his numerous successors, not excepting even Stolypine, seem pigmies in comparison to him. Plehve struggled with the revolutionists according to his lights and kept them at bay. Had he been alive, the political movement of the workmen would have been nipped in the bud. He would likewise have found means to suppress Rasputine at the beginning of his career, before his demoralising influence had become so great.

This all-powerful hand safely removed, the revolutionists and socialists breathed, and hastened to proceed with their agitation. The next terrorist act was the assassination of the Grand Duke Serge Alexandrovitch, which occurred on February 4th o/s, 1905, in Moscow. The Grand Duke was disliked in Moscow. The arbitrary methods of his administration gave rise to serious displeasure, and, above all, he was feared for the influence he wielded over the Tzar. An attempt on the Grand Duke's life had been for some time expected. The Grand Duchess Elisabeth even received anonymous warnings not to accompany her husband if she did not wish to share the fate that was in store for him. Knowing that her presence protected him, the Grand Duchess kept continually at his side in public.

On this ill-fated day the Grand Duke was going to visit one of his favourite friends, and his wife did not accompany him. He was hardly out of the portals of the Kremlin Palace when a terrible explosion was heard. The Grand Duchess rushed out hatless, with a wrap carelessly thrown over her shoulders, and was in time to see the police collect the remains of what had, only a short time before, been her husband. The head of the murdered Grand Duke was not disfigured, but all the rest of his remains that could be gathered together filled only a small square box. The arrested murderer, a student, Kolaeff by name, was only slightly wounded.

The bereaved widow visited the murderer in his prison-cell, and asked him the reason for his act. Kolaeff was greatly taken aback when he saw the Grand Duchess in her weeds standing before him. He was visibly perturbed; still he answered her question and told her that men like the late Grand Duke were the enemies of mankind, being the repressors of liberty and progress, and they had to be removed. He wept when she asked him if, when he planned the murder, he had thought of her grief.

He refused the small medal-ikon she wished to give him as a token of her forgiveness.

This visit to the prison-cell of her husband's murderer was interpreted in various ways. Everyone judged the step from a different standpoint, but the majority were critically inclined, and considered the visit a serious breach of good taste. At the trial it was revealed that Kolaeff had for some time watched for an opportunity to throw the bomb he kept in his pocket for that purpose. He had for several days hovered near the Kremlin Palace, but each time he saw the Grand Duke his wife had been with him, and, callous though the assassin was, the fear lest she should share the doom of her husband stayed his hand.

It has since transpired that the assassination of M. Plehve and the Grand Duke Serge would never have succeeded but for the machinations of one of the most despicable individuals who combined the part of revolutionist and police agent, being traitor to both causes. Owing to the revelations of M. Burtzeff, one of the most notable of Russian political emigrants, who spent many years in Paris, the treacherous share of Azeff, one of the most valued secret agents of the police, in the organization of these murders, does not leave room for the slightest doubt. Seven years later the Prime Minister, Stolypine, fell, shot by a similar agent-provocateur.

The Tzar was deeply grieved at the terrible fate of his uncle and brother-in-law, with whom he had always been on the most affectionate terms. The shock sustained by the Empress has never been entirely effaced. Her health gave way and her nerves became utterly unstrung. Both the Sovereigns wanted to start for Moscow, but the state of mind of the people there made this undesirable, and, much against their will, they were persuaded to relinquish this purpose. The Tzar's youngest uncle, the Grand Duke Paul, who was exiled from Russia in consequence of his having contracted a morganatic marriage with Madame Pistohlcorse against the Tzar's wishes, was immediately sent for. The Grand Dukes Serge and Paul had been brought up together and had been devoted to each other. A reconciliation between uncle and nephew took place. The Grand Duke Paul and his cousin, the late Grand Duke Constantine, were the only representatives of the Imperial Family present at the obsequies in Moscow.

The next blow was the disaster of Tsussima, which by the irony of fate occurred on May 14th, the Coronation day. This was a blow not only to the Imperial Family, but to the whole nation. The destruction of Admiral Rogestvensky's fleet, the loss of so many lives, the dramatic circumstances attending the battle, all were a great trial to the nation. Some people had, from the first, been against the useless sacrifice of sending Admiral Rogestvensky at the head of a fleet composed of antiquated warships, but the disapprobation increased to a clamour after the overthrow of Russia's hopes. As a matter of fact the fleet had been equipped partly to assuage public opinion; the Chiefs of the Admiralty had but little hope of the success of the enterprise. Even Admiral Rogestvensky felt that he was going to his doom.

For months before the fleet sailed, the newspapers published articles full of upbraiding and indignation at the indifference of the Admiralty in not sending a fleet to relieve Port Arthur. They pointed out the available ships, indicating the repairs necessary, and blamed the Naval Authorities. It was Captain Klado who wrote the most uncompromising articles about the hesitation manifested in sending the fleet. He did not mince matters and boldly accused the Admiralty of committing a crime by their slackness.

These articles, which daily appeared in the *Novoe Vremia*, fired public opinion, for Captain Klado was a sailor and had an eloquent pen. His opinion was considered authoritative, and he became the hero of the moment, especially after his arrest in consequence of having written articles on naval matters without the authorisation of his chief. During the days of his punishment his room was turned into a bower of roses, and all his readers vied with each other in showing him all kinds of attentions. But alas! Captain Klado had been wrong in his optimistic views, woefully wrong!

The ex-Tzar has often been accused of not having felt deeply the reverses of the Russo-Japanese war, and being indifferent to the disaster of Tsussima, but in this case the reproach is unmerited. The Sovereign was very much depressed, and did all in his power to assist the widows and orphans. Many pensions were paid out of his own private purse. Orphan boys were taken gratuitously into cadet corps and other educational establishments. The administration of Palaces all over the country was entrusted to officers who had been through the Manchurian Campaign. But Nicholas II is by nature extremely reserved; he exercises a wonderful self-control, his pallor being the one visible sign of agitation he manifests. It is only those who know him intimately who can detect when he is under the stress of some painful emotion.

When the Members of the Duma came to Pskov to persuade him to resign in favour of his son, the Tzar was the calmest of the three. When later on, in Mohilev, he was told that several members of the Duma were on their way to arrest and escort him in his train to Tzarskoe Selo, he showed an imperturbability that was astonishing, and even had the presence of mind to suggest that the deputies should be invited to dinner.

But to resume the thread of this narrative I must return to the events of 1905. The summer months passed quietly enough, but the storm was brewing, displeasure reigned amongst the people, centring mostly among the working classes. In the first days of October the strikes in Petrograd commenced on a gigantic scale. There was no electric light, no water, no daily papers, the trains were forcibly stopped and no post delivery admitted. At this period of the year the days are very short, darkness sets in early and numbers of hooligans invaded the dimly lighted streets, stopping carriages, molesting inoffensive pedestrians, smashing shop-windows, sacking, pillaging and destroying what they could lay hands on. Everything was in a state of confusion. This lasted for several days.

It was at this juncture that Count Witte (he had just returned from America, and the title of Count had been conferred on him), with the aid of the Grand Duke Nicholas, persuaded the Tzar to make concessions and grant a Constitutional Government. The Manifesto embodying these things was hurriedly composed without due deliberation, by Count Witte. It contained many weak points, but its principal feature was the approaching convocation of the Duma. This would give the power to the representatives of all classes of the population to deliberate on the measures and reforms required for the weal of the nation.

The well-known journalist, M. Menshikoff, relates in his diary that a few days before October 17th o/s, he was invited to call on Count Witte, who requested him to draw up the Manifesto under consideration. For several days the eminent writer remained closeted in his study, weighing every word to be included in a document that would have become historical. The draft was duly delivered to the Count; but it never saw the light of day. Quite a different Manifesto appeared on October 17th, and M. Menshikoff has never heard why the one drawn up by him was discarded. The assembling of the Duma was fixed for the following month of May. The Government was to be somewhat modified, but the Ministry was not to be a responsible one, as is the case in England and France. It was said at the time that the German Emperor, from motives of personal interest, had strongly dissuaded the Tzar from granting a responsible Ministry. It was to be a 'United Ministry' instead.

The strikes ceased as if by magic, but the riots continued, and it was only thanks to the energy of the Minister of the Interior, the late M. Peter Nicolaïevitch Dournovo, that order was again restored. Count Witte was appointed Prime Minister, but he occupied this post only for a short time. His attitude was strange: it seemed as if he did not wish to appease people's minds, and his transactions with the representatives of the Labour Party were extremely doubtful.

Count Witte was succeeded by M. Stolypine, who filled the post until the day of his death, about six years later. M. Stolypine took the portfolio of the Interior likewise, for his predecessor M. Dournovo, though a very able man, was considered retrogressive, and was unpopular in Liberal circles. It was therefore thought injudicious to keep him at the head of such an important administration at such a critical moment. Notwithstanding the Manifesto and the concessions granted, the disturbances continued. Moscow became the scene of an insurrection, which after much bloodshed was finally repressed by the Governor-General Dubassoff. Agrarian disorders occurred in most parts of the country, and numerous estates were totally destroyed. A year later the Letts and the Estonians revolted in the Baltic provinces, and had to be repressed by armed force.

It was known throughout the country that, at the first signal of danger to the throne, German troops were in readiness to crush the insurgents. Everyone knew that the order given out by General Trepoff, 'Don't spare cartridges', was inspired from Berlin.

Both the first Dumas were failures. The elections took place at a time when people's minds were still in a state of ferment. Numerous members were elected who had neither the required education nor the necessary enlightenment to fulfil the requirements of a deputy. The majority of the elected members had not the most elementary notions of Parliamentary proceedings, and they formed a heterogeneous assembly. The sessions developed into a series of storms and cyclones. Both the first and second Dumas were short-lived.

The third and fourth Dumas were more judiciously composed, although the partisans of the Right were all the time in a large minority. It was a perpetual struggle between the Government and the Duma, and the polemics bore the character of a wrangling feud, with occasional brilliant speeches and smart utterances. No

THE CLOUDS GATHER

serious work could be done under such conditions. The Government accused the Duma of hindering all its efforts, and the Duma upbraided the Government for having no efforts to hinder. Those were the relations between the old Government and the Duma during the first ten years of the latter's existence.

About this time (1905–1906) the strange conduct of the Empress Alexandra became noticeable. Her Majesty never appeared in public, private audiences were unwillingly granted and only in the most urgent cases, Court receptions were abolished. On those occasions, when a Court pageant or banquet could not be avoided, it was the Dowager Empress Marie who, at her son's side, came forward to greet the assembled guests. No one, except the restricted Court circle, saw the Empress, and all kinds of rumours spread about regarding her peculiarities. Some said that, fearing to grow stout, she had followed the system of a German 'Entfettungscur' (a cure to dissolve the increasing fat) against the advice of her doctor, and the result was a complete breakdown of the nervous system. Others stated that she suffered from nervous eczema, which at times covered her face and hands and prevented her showing herself in public. Some affirmed she was the victim of an acute form of neurotic heart disease, and at times could not bear the presence of more than one person in her vicinity. Others believed she was simply mad.

Her Majesty began taking a vivid interest in Church matters and clerical affairs; her devotion taking a fanatical turn. She showed a marked predilection for pilgrims and monks. At this inauspicious moment the name of Rasputine was first mentioned in connection with the Court. In a fatal moment Rasputine was taken up by the Bishop Theophanus, the confessor of the Imperial Family. The Bishop introduced him to the Dowager Countess Ignatieff, whose renowned clerical Monday receptions were the rendezvous of distinguished prelates, theologians and people interested in Church questions. Rasputine achieved a decided success in the salon of the Countess, especially amongst the ladies, some of whom became his ardent followers, one of his principal 'disciples' being Madame Golovine, the elder sister of the Grand Duke Paul's morganatic wife, Princess Paley (better known abroad by her former title of Countess Hohenfelsen) and her two daughters. Rasputine began to be talked about!

When it was discovered that Rasputine was gifted with a marvellous hypnotic power, Bishop Theophanus, knowing the

THE FALL OF THE ROMANOFFS

vogue of hypnotists at the Imperial Court, spoke of him to the Empress and brought him into her presence. The Empress's friend, Madame Vyrouboff, had previously met Rasputine at one of the smart houses of Petrograd, and had fallen under his spell. It was at her instigation that Bishop Theophanus introduced the 'staretz' at Court. Her Majesty found the priest's presence had a soothing effect upon her shattered nerves. Thus commenced the favour of Rasputine that was to lead to such fatal developments.

Later on, when the Bishop discovered the true character of the scoundrel who posed as a saint, when he had proofs of his profligacy, he deeply reproached himself for having lent himself to the introduction of this obnoxious creature into high spheres. The Bishop tried to undo the harm he had caused. He openly disowned him, and endeavoured to prevail on the Emperor to have him sent back to his native village in Siberia. He disclosed the true nature of Rasputine, but it was too late. The influence this pseudo saint was gaining over the Empress's mind was daily increasing, and the sole result of the Bishop's warning was that he made an implacable enemy of the new favourite, and fell into complete disgrace with the Empress, with the result that he was removed to another diocese far away from the capital.

Rasputine came to Petrograd in 1906 and ever since has been the Court's evil spirit, who has steadily led the Empress, and through her the Emperor, to their downfall.

Quos Deus vult perdere dementat!

Chapter III

THE COMING OF RASPUTINE

THE question naturally arises, who was this mysterious Rasputine, who for so many years swayed the destinies of this mighty Empire, and what was the secret of the unbounded influence he wielded over the Empress Alexandra?

Gregory Rasputine was a simple mujik (peasant), hailing from the village of Pokrovskoe near Tobolsk, in Siberia. His real patronymic was 'Novykh', but he and his kinsfolk had earned the surname of Rasputine, which in Russian means dissolute. The name stuck to them and, owing to the Siberian custom, was inscribed on Gregory's passport. The record of his past was one of the worst imaginable. More than once he had been in prison for theft of horses, and he had been flogged for all kinds of dishonesty. He was a drunkard, and his licentious habits had made him the black sheep of the village. His profession was that of a driver, and this brought him into contact with all kinds of people.

One day he had been driving a high church dignitary, who turned out to be the Bishop of Kazan, Alexis. The prelate entered into conversation with him, and was struck with the depth of his religious faith. This colloquy had a lasting influence on the mind of Rasputine. He returned to his village a changed man, abandoned his profligate ways and after a time decided to give up his work, consecrate himself to God and become a 'staretz'.

A Russian staretz is a pilgrim who wanders from one monastery to another, going to different churches all over the country to worship at the saints' shrines, or before the sacred reliquaries. The ambition of every staretz is to visit Mount Athos, and above all to have worshipped in Jerusalem at all the places where Jesus

Christ lived and suffered. A staff and a knapsack are his sole
possessions; he accepts alms to help him on his way, and, if he
cannot get a gratuitous night's lodging, he spends the night under
some tree. The inferior classes of the Russians have a great
veneration for such 'startzys', and consider they lead a saint-like,
ascetic life, following God as the New Testament commands. On
the whole, therefore, these men and women, for among the pilgrims there are women likewise, fare pretty well on their journey;
for most people, especially among the small tradespeople and
peasants, consider it a religious duty to offer them hospitality. In
convents there are special barns allotted to the pilgrims, where
they are fed at the convent's expense.

At the age of thirty-six, Gregory Rasputine decided to become
a staretz. He parted his hair that grew long on both sides of his
face, developed a flowing beard and endeavoured to give himself
the outward appearance of saintliness and godliness. During
these wanderings his mystically inclined mind hit upon a doctrine, which to him appeared novel, but was in reality similar to
the one spread in the second century by the heretic Marcion. It
consisted of the axiom that to elevate the spirit it is necessary by
all available means to destroy the flesh. In passing through
Kazan, Rasputine was warmly welcomed by his old friend, the
Bishop Alexis, who was himself of a mystical turn of mind.
Convinced of Gregory's sincerity, the Bishop directed his steps to
Petrograd, giving him a letter of recommendation to his father,
the Rector of the Religious Academy; the latter introduced him to
the Bishop Theophanus.

In Petrograd Rasputine began by establishing a circle of ascetic
students. At that time there was a decided vogue for asceticism,
and this tendency was considered beneficial. The three of this
ascetic movement were the Bishop Theophanus, Rasputine and
another staretz, Mitia (derived from Dmitry) the Blessed. Rasputine was looked up to as the leader, for he had invented a special
expedient to deaden the flesh, which brought him numerous
followers belonging to the weaker sex. Women incessantly flocked
round him, and amidst them, strange as it seems, there were
many ladies belonging to the aristocracy. The rumour of Rasputine's fame began to spread and became tinged with scandal.
Amazing stories were repeated of the extremities these delicately
nurtured ladies were led to by the strength of their infatuation
for an uncouth mujik and his questionable doctrines.

THE COMING OF RASPUTINE

The triumvirate, however, soon dissolved; the first to sever partnership was Mitia the Blessed, who became an inveterate drunkard. Subsequently a serious breach occurred between the Bishop Theophanus and Rasputine. The Bishop, bitterly disappointed in his former protégé's ascetic life, revealed to the Tzar all that he had discovered, convicting Rasputine of the most revolting licentiousness. The reprobate was sent back to Siberia, where he had left a wife and four children. There he lived very comfortably, supplied with everything by his lady followers, until they succeeded in having him recalled to Petrograd. This occurred in the year 1911.

From the first moment of his introduction to the Imperial Court, Rasputine produced a wonderful impression on the Empress Alexandra from a mystical point of view. Her Majesty implicitly believed in his saintliness, and her faith in the power of his prayers was boundless. She had heard the story of his prophecy at the shrine of the newly canonised St. Seraphim, relating to the forthcoming heir to the throne of Russia, and the idea got hold of her mind that Rasputine's life was mixed up with that of the Tzessarevitch. The Lord had granted his prayer, because of his purity and superior worthiness; the Lord sent him to the Court to protect the boy's existence and ensure his parents' felicity.

Rasputine was a mighty tool in the hands of those who, wishing to gain their own ends, desired to obtain a hold over the Empress. Among Rasputine's admirers Madame Vyrouboff was the most ardent. She became his devoted friend, and General Woyeikoff aided and abetted her in her efforts to strengthen the Empress in her belief that all her hopes lay in Rasputine, and that his proximity prevented harm from attacking any member of her family, especially in regard to the little Tzessarevitch.

The continual presence of this mujik amidst the intimates of the Court circle shocked many of the courtiers, accustomed as they were to the old traditions of courtly elegance and refinement. Rasputine's evident uncouthness, coarse manners, greasy hair and above all his hands, with blackedged nails, were a nightmare to most of them. The Minister, Count Fredericks, in particular, regarded this unwarrantable intrusion with much disfavour.

'But who is this Rasputine of whom there is so much talk nowadays?' the Count one day asked the Emperor.

The reply was: 'Oh! quite a simple mujik, whose prayers are

{31}

carried straight to Heaven because of the sublime faith he is endowed with.'

Admiral Niloff once warned the monarch of the increasing displeasure Rasputine's presence caused.

'Better one Rasputine than ten hysterics!' was the Tzar's response.

This shows clearly that, whatever his crimes, Rasputine saved the Emperor from the hysterical outbreaks of the Empress.

The governess of the Grand Duchesses, the maid-of-honour, Mlle. Tutcheff, flatly refused to have anything to do with Rasputine, and objected to his visiting the schoolroom, especially to his being admitted into the Grand Duchesses' bed-chamber, to give them his nightly blessing after they had retired to bed. The result of this protest, which much incensed the Empress, was that when the Imperial Family went to Livadia, Mlle. Tutcheff was not included among the suite and, seeing the impossibility of enforcing her desires, which she deemed indispensable if she continued to undertake the responsibility of bringing up the Tzar's daughters, she sent in her resignation. No other governess has since taken her place.

Prince Orloff, when he was a member of the Court, never attempted to conceal his feelings of repugnance for the Empress's favourite, and even among the members of the family the sentiments towards Rasputine differed. It is well known that the Grand Duchess Olga loathed the man, and that the Tzessarevitch could not bear him. At the time of the latter's accident in Livadia in the year 1912, which for many months endangered the boy's life, Rasputine was absent. Finally he was sent for and the child's recovery was attributed to the power of his prayers.

The strange part of this 'Rasputine-madness' was that each time the Tzar was prevailed to send Rasputine into exile, something happened to the Tzessarevitch. It has since been proved that the staretz was hand in glove with an oriental quack doctor of some renown, who treated his patients with infusions of herbs brought from Tibet. It was insistently rumoured, especially during the last two years, that Gregory frequently brought the Empress philtres to give to the Tzar, to make him more amenable to her wishes. It may likewise have happened that a few drops of some cordial might have been added by a 'devoted hand' to the food of the Tzessarevitch, making him temporarily ill, confirming thus the Empress in her superstitious dread of the 'saint's' removal from her vicinity. As to the Tzar, some of the Ministers have noticed that he was lately subject to strange fits of depression, bordering on complete apathy. During these phases His Majesty was quite unlike his usual self.

Rasputine's influence continued steadily on the increase and began to insinuate itself into official spheres. It was universally known that no better intercessor in any business matter could be found than Rasputine, no more dexterous defender of the most hopeless cause. His small flat, consisting of three rooms, on the English Prospect, and subsequently on the Gorokhovaia, was filled every morning with men and women soliciting favours. More people were to be met in his rooms than in the halls of the most influential statesman. It was a heterogeneous assemblage: there were ladies in rich furs and diamond earrings, generals in full uniform, courtiers, merchants, actresses, adventuresses, all kinds of business men and officials. A pretty woman was always sure of a warm welcome.

In one of the rooms a table was laid for tea, with the inevitable samovar invitingly hissing. The intimate ladies of the flat clustered round this table, the newcomers waited in the first room, whilst the unkempt master of the flat, in a bright-hued silken shirt, attached round the waist by a leather strap, hovered fussily between the two rooms, occasionally taking someone for a private interview into the adjacent study. If an unknown woman entered, especially if she were a fine-looking one, the obnoxious staretz's eyes would begin to shine and he would assume his most benign air, tinged with vulgar familiarity.

Strange scenes occurred at these receptions. The following stories were related by an eye-witness: One day a good-looking young woman stood bashfully on the threshold of the room. Rasputine eagerly advanced to meet her, greeting her with incessant pats on the back, shoulder and hips. Returning with her to the principal room, where a titled lady sat ensconced in the corner of a sofa, he rudely pushed her aside with the words: 'Get out of the way fat cow.' The lady, obviously used to his boorishness, meekly submitted, rising without a word or sign of protest.

Another time a young man of good family appeared accompanied by his very pretty wife. Without any ado, Rasputine kissed her, under the eyes of her husband, who looked on beaming with gratification. It sometimes happened that his effrontery met with unexpected resistance. 'The spirit of the Lord has not entered thee,' was his only remark, anxiously adding, however, 'Look here, don't attempt to blab, for there,' with a characteristic jerk of the thumb to what he believed indicated Tzarskoe Selo, 'they think I am a saint.'

The staretz treated his women friends with scant ceremony, calling them by their Christian names and hustling them about in the most impertinent manner, making use of their services in preference to those of servants. Princess S. generally carried in the huge samovar, which she could hardly lift; another lady brought in a tray with wine or refreshments. Rasputine called such treatment of fine ladies, 'Purifying their spirit through humbling their pride.'

There was nothing prepossessing in the man's appearance. His hair was dark, long and untidy, his nose aquiline, but his eyes were the principal feature. They were light grey, set in a dark face, which made them look lighter. They had something hard, metallic, even compelling in their glance. The weird depth of his gaze and the deep furrowings on his rugged, long-shaped face, gave it in moments of repose a stern expression, although at times of relaxation he could be the merriest of the merry, but his mouth, at all times, retained a cynical expression.

Rasputine never refused a supplicant anything, for he liked to prove his boast that to him even the impossible was possible. Having heard the request, he would give the applicant a square slip of paper on which in his illiterate hand he traced the following words: 'Please listen to N.N. and do what he asks, I beg you.' Oh! these characteristic slips of paper, covered with his large rudely formed letters and badly spelt words! Ministers and statesmen were overflowed with them and, in most cases, they proved the 'open sesame' to all kinds of privileges, for the majority of re-cipients thought it their duty to comply with his requests.

There were some men of independent spirit, as for instance the former Minister of Foreign Affairs, M. Sazonoff, who took no notice of his intercessions, contemptuously throwing his papers in to the wastepaper basket. A lady once came to Count Ignatieff, at the time when he occupied the post of Minister of Public Instruction, provided with a note from Rasputine. The Count flung the paper away in disgust, and reproached the lady for having recourse to such a method of obtaining what she desired.

'If your cause is a righteous one,' he said, 'I will with much pleasure accede to your wishes. If not no man on earth could compel me to do what I should not consider just.'

Unfortunately most of the Ministers and Government officials thought differently. A lady once came to a general, who shall be nameless, with an urgent petition to recall her son for a day or two from the front to receive the blessing of his dying father. She was told that the reception was over earlier than usual because the general was busy. The lady insisted, pleading the urgency of her case. All was in vain. She was curtly informed that the general was engrossed with such serious matters that he could not be disturbed. The lady then took out of her handbag the precious paper square with which she had judiciously provided herself. Instantly the scene changed, the officer on duty hastened to carry the magic paper slip to his chief, the lady was received in the most courteous manner, all her wishes were attended to and the general, with much obsequiousness, personally saw the lady out of the vestibule.

There was hardly an institution or organisation where Rasputine had not placed some of his boon companions. Several years ago he insisted on an old friend of his, a monk named Barnaby, being made a bishop and given the diocese of Tobolsk. Barnaby, a former kitchen-gardener, was as uncouth and illiterate as Rasputine himself. There naturally arose many protests amongst the members of the Holy Synod at giving such a high clerical post to a man utterly unfit to discharge the duties incumbent upon him. Nevertheless Rasputine prevailed: Barnaby was made a bishop. One of the members of the Holy Synod[1] remarked, on that occasion: 'We are ready to appoint a black boar-pig as bishop, rather than offend the Tzaritza.'

Rasputine has been accused of taking large fees for these intercessions of his, but it hardly seems likely; for, after his death, the whole fortune he left his family amounted to 3,000 roubles (£300). It is far more likely that he revelled in the influence he wielded, and became intoxicated with his power. He was, however, surrounded by harpies; one of them, a certain prince, had a branch establishment where all kinds of affairs, depending on Rasputine's intercession, were arranged on a business basis, from the nomination of a Minister to the furthering of some commercial transaction. There were likewise his three secretaries, who prob-

1 The Bishop Anthony of Kharkhoff.

ably made profits out of the business. Personally the staretz preferred rich presents to money gifts.

Notwithstanding his position at Court, the adulation of his many admirers and the reverence he inspired with the Emperor and Empress, Rasputine continued to lead a dissipated life and spent his nights, far into the small hours, carousing in some favourite haunt, where he could listen to the orchestra and drink his fill. Vodka had given way to champagne and cognac. But his revelries mostly degenerated into riotous brawls. The annals of the former police could have divulged many a tale of these junketings, for in those days Rasputine was surrounded by police agents, his every step was dogged and his safety one of the most onerous responsibilities of the police.

In Petrograd the venerated staretz observed certain caution, for fear of some extravagance of his reaching the ears of the Empress, 'who thought him a saint'. He was less on his guard in Moscow, however, where some of his adventurous proceedings outdid the limits of scandal. When he was drunk, which was very often, he bragged in the most brazen manner, no matter of whom his audience was composed, of the Tzar's and Tzaritza's devotion to him and of his unbounded power.

'One word of mine,' he would hiccough, 'can make or unmake a Minister, my slightest desire is implicitly obeyed. I hold the whole Government in the hollow of my hand', and he would stretch out a heavy fist. To prove his familiarity, he would call the Sovereigns by their names: 'Nichlas' and 'Sascha' (the Russian diminutive for Alexandra). He would show the embroidery on his shirt, boasting that a high-born lady had worked it for him.

He took a keen delight in titles, and frankly avowed his predilection for princesses and countesses.

Dancing was one of this strange man's amusements: he could dance for hours. Eye-witnesses assure me that at such times he would undergo a regular transformation. His uncouthness vanished as if by magic, his movements became flowing and full of a weird grace, and his dancing produced an enthralling impression. The following story gives a characteristic illustration of Gregory Rasputine's rakish behaviour and of the Sovereigns' blind infatuation. It really looked as if a spell had been cast on them.

It was Christmas time, and the Imperial Family were busily preparing to light the luxuriously decorated tree. A discussion arose about a suitable present for the staretz: an embroidered shirt, a new coat, or something for his household. Rasputine was expected, and the Empress would not have the tree lit until he appeared. The Commandant of the Palace had received no telephone message that the staretz had taken the train for Tzarskoe Selo. After a long wait the telephone was set ringing in all directions: the Police Prefect, the Minister of the Interior, the Director of the 'Okhrana' (safety guard) were called up and apprised of Gregory's disappearance. At last a police agent discovered Rasputine in a private room of a well-known restaurant in a state of utter intoxication and in the company of chorus-girls. The police agents pounced upon him, took him forcibly to the station, and did everything they could to make him sober, for he had to be brought to the Palace or the Christmas festival would be spoiled. Arrived in Tzarskoe Selo, Rasputine made a tremendous effort and entered the Imperial presence, but the evening was nevertheless a failure, for never had the indecorum of the 'saint' been more apparent!

His misconduct was always explained as an attempt of the Devil to cast a spell over him.

The Emperor was warned several times by different people of the evil reputation Rasputine had acquired, and of the distressing impression his obvious influence at Court produced on people's minds. Rasputine would be temporarily sent home to his wife, but each time the intriguing coterie of courtiers, to whom his presence was indispensable, succeeded in having him recalled. During one of these absences, an attempt was made on his life by a peasant woman, but the wound she inflicted was not a mortal one.

When the news reached Petrograd that he was dangerously wounded, the perturbation amongst his admirers and followers was boundless. A surgeon and skilled hospital-nurse were sent out to his native village, but this was not sufficient. Madame Vyrouboff set out on the long journey to Siberia and remained some time in Pokrovskoe, until Rasputine was pronounced out of danger. Madame Vyrouboff's journey was kept a secret, but everyone knew that she had gone to nurse her friend, and it gave rise to no end of gossip. The most absurd stories were spread, and, what was much worse, they were thoroughly believed!

About a couple of years ago, after some outrageous scandal about Rasputine in Moscow, General Djunkovsky, who at that time occupied the post of Chief of the Gendarmes, requested an audience with His Majesty, and, without mincing matters, disclosed to the Tzar all that was known of the real character of Rasputine, not omitting the cynicism of his doctrine, the indecorum of his conduct and his boasts of the subjection in which he held the Tzar and the Tzaritza.

'Are you positively sure of this?' enquired the Sovereign.

'Absolutely, Sire,' replied the General.

'I believe you, but I have to convince the Empress; I must therefore ask you to institute an official enquiry on the subject. When that has been done, bring me the written statement duly signed.'

General Djunkovsky left the Tzar's presence with a gleam of hope in his eyes. He felt gratified at the way the Sovereign had listened to his accusations of the Empress's acknowledged favourite, and, certain of the facts, he was sure of being able to prove them. That night he started for Moscow. His first move was to give General Andrianoff, the Police Prefect of Moscow, the necessary instructions to have a minute dossier prepared of Rasputine's conduct during his last stay in Moscow. The proofs were irrefutable, and the story about as ugly as it could be.

The report was placed before the Tzar. He gasped, as he made himself acquainted with the record of the 'saint's' scandalous behaviour.

The Tzar went to the Empress and showed her the document. A violent attack of hysterics was the result. The Empress had to be attended to, Madame Vyrouboff was called to soothe the frenzied distress of her Royal mistress. When she was told the cause of the attack, Madame Vyrouboff was indignant at General Djunkovsky's officiousness. She persuaded the willing Empress that Rasputine continued to be the immaculate saint she fondly believed him, and that the accusations were a tissue of lies and barefaced calumnies. They were invented by the enemies of the dynasty that the saint, who was sent by God to protect them, might be removed from their presence. General Woyeikoff came to the rescue; he persuaded the Tzar that the report presented by General Djunkovsky was deliberately exaggerated and he offered to go to Moscow and investigate the matter himself and bring the Tzar a true statement. The Tzar agreed and subsequently sent for General Djunkovsky.

'Did you make the enquiry yourself?' he asked.

The General owned that he had entrusted the matter to General Andrianoff, as better able to give an accurate account.

'I asked you to make a *personal* enquiry,' coldly remarked the monarch.

As a matter of fact General Woyeikoff likewise turned to General Andrianoff, but the astute Police Prefect fully understood the aim of General Woyeikoff's mission. He had seen that General Djunkovsky was in earnest, and really wanted to tear off the mask of saintliness from the iniquitous Rasputine, and he had given him undoubted proofs of the latter's scandalous behaviour! General Woyeikoff, on the contrary, wanted to mend matters and condone facts. This was clear to the Police Prefect, and he resolved to be diplomatic. The second dossier was prepared in quite a different strain; it was benign and conciliatory. Armed with this document, refuting the former accusations, General Woyeikoff returned to Tzarskoe Selo. The Emperor felt relieved that he need not grieve his Consort and that, with a clear conscience, he could leave Rasputine unmolested. The Empress was overjoyed at the exculpation of her favourite, whilst Madame Vyrouboff and the staretz, who was, of course, apprised of the danger he had escaped by a hair's breadth, were in a state of exultation.

Soon after this incident, which excited great interest and heart-burning in Court circles, and in those coteries closely connected with high spheres, General Djunkovsky received his dismissal from the post he occupied and joined the active army. With his departure another honest, upright friend of the Tzar, a true prop of the monarchy, was removed. But General Woyeikoff remained, and both the Emperor and Empress felt more than ever convinced of his sincerity and devotion to them.

The Empress had received many hints of her growing unpopularity owing to Rasputine's presence and influence at Court, but she paid no attention to such warnings. She had always made a difference between Petrograd and the rest of Russia. From the first she had disliked 'St. Petersburg' and its society, and she had never sought to be in touch with them.

'Let Petrograd and the aristocracy be displeased' was her argument. 'Petrograd is by no means Russia. In the provinces, the Emperor and his family are very popular. The nation is mostly composed of peasants, and they are flattered that one of their class lives in our proximity. I know the Russians, and I have received many touching letters expressing this sentiment.'

In this the Empress made a grave mistake, and proved that she had never understood the Russian character, either that of the peasant or of those belonging to the higher classes. With all their former reverence for the Tzar and the Tzaritza, with all their past devotion, the feelings of the peasants were full of subtlety. They had a strong sense of the great difference between them and the Tzar and his family. To hear of one of their own class living on intimate terms with the Sovereigns and treating them with familiarity outraged their idea of the fitness of things. The knowledge that the Emperor and Empress permitted themselves to be imposed upon by an upstart from their own ranks, a simple mujik of questionable antecedents, lowered the standard of Sovereignty in their eyes, and injured their feelings of loyalty and respect.

The Russian peasants' conception of the Tzar is that of a powerful and imposing ruler. They love his kindness and simplicity, but they must feel it is the outcome of condescension. In the Tzaritza they do not see the woman; they only wish to reverence the Sovereign. They crave to admire the Tzaritza, to catch her eye benignly fixed on them, to sun themselves in the radiance of her smiles. For this reason the Empress Alexandra was never appreciated. Even as a sister of mercy she failed to comprehend the soldier's sense of what was to be expected from an Empress of Russia. To see her kneeling in front of him, bathing his feet, or dressing his wounds shocked him. Many officers objected to being sent to the Court hospital of Tzarskoe Selo, because it embarrassed them to accept such services from the Empress. If Her Majesty had confined herself to visiting the wounded as their Empress, of talking to them kindly, of showing a personal interest in them and their affairs, if she had questioned them about the war and listened patiently to their description of battle-incidents, she would have been adored. But the Empress never could understand that, in the eyes of her subjects, she must shine and be ornamental, but not useful in the trivial acceptation of the word.

The Empress was quite wrong in the belief that the nation was pleased at the exclusive position Rasputine enjoyed at Court. Her Majesty may have received letters confirming this belief, but were these letters genuine? Were they not written by someone who had an interest in strengthening the Sovereign's conviction that she was pleasing the people?

Each day that passed seemed only to strengthen the position of the staretz Rasputine. He brought over two of his daughters from Siberia, and later sent for his son, a youth of twenty, who was attached to Madame Vyrouboff's hospital-train. The daughters were educated at a gymnasium. It was suggested that they should be educated at the Smolny Institute, one of the most select boarding-colleges for girls, but the directress of this institute, the late Princess Lieven, protested against this unwarrantable intrusion, and as the Dowager Empress Marie was at the head of such educational establishments, the Empress Alexandra was unable to enforce her will.

Simultaneously with Rasputine's increased influence, the Empress's friend, Madame Vyrouboff, grew in favour. It was only since the outbreak of war that the fatal consequences of their power showed up in their true light foreboding danger to the country, putting every right-minded person against the reigning monarch and his Government. The most ardent advocate of monarchism had to own that things were getting desperate, and that such a state of affairs could not last. Every true friend of the Tzar, every honest servitor of the dynasty, had been removed by the Empress Alexandra; the Tzar was completely isolated, the easy prey of the Court camarilla. About nine months prior to the wreck of the Empire, the Dowager Empress Marie went to Kiev and did not return to the capital. She preferred not to witness the doings at Court, which she viewed with sorrow and dismay, but alas! could do nothing to stop.

The clouds were gathering. For some time the coming of a change was felt, anxiously expected by some, regretfully by others, but considered inevitable by all.

Russian historians of the future will blame Nicholas II, the last of the Romanoffs, for being culpably weak and letting the reins of power, which for over three hundred years had been in the hands of the Romanoff dynasty, gradually slip through his hands, to be caught up by the iniquitous and despicable villain Rasputine. Is it to be wondered at that the indignant nation brought about the Revolution and caused the downfall of the Tzardom?

Chapter IV

THE GREAT BETRAYAL

URING the first days of the war with Germany, there was
an auspicious moment when Nicholas II could have attached to himself the love and respect of the nation. Even
the Empress, if she had acted in the spirit of a Russian Tzar's true
Consort, could have regained the affections of her husband's
subjects. Never had the Emperor been so popular as at that
exciting time. The day of the publication of his Manifesto was the
most triumphant of his reign. When His Majesty, after the religious ceremony in the halls of the Winter Palace, stepped out on
the balcony to greet the people assembled in the Square in front
of the Palace, the people dropped on their knees, baring their
heads before the monarch, singing the National Hymn, 'Boje
Tzaria khrani' (God save the Tzar) and acclaiming him with a
thunder of cheering. Patriotism filled all hearts, real patriotism,
that made the people forget all past grievances and rally round
the throne, eager to defend beloved and Holy Russia from the
invasion of the hated Germans. In the moment of National danger
all parties joined. Political contests were forgotten in the unanimous wish to give the monarch adequate support to crush the
enemy.

But a few days sufficed to bring home to all the conviction that
these feelings of patriotism were far from being shared by everyone in the land. Strange reports were circulated about the Empress Alexandra and some of the Grand Duchesses, who were
German Princesses by birth. It transpired that Her Majesty was
not at all enthusiastic about the war. The idea of an armed strife
between her former Fatherland and her present country filled her
with pain and distress. Her attitude damped the Tzar's animation

in favour of fighting to the end until a definite victory made peace overtures acceptable to all the Allies.

The following anecdote, widely spread at the time, though a fictitious one, is illustrative of this general impression.

'I really don't know,' said the little Tzessarevitch to a friend, 'on whose side I am to be. When the Russians are beaten, Papa looks glum and when the Germans are beaten, Mamma cries.'

After two months of war it was whispered that the Empress was endeavouring with all her might to bring about a reconciliation between the Kaiser and the Tzar, and thus ensure a separate peace.

Meanwhile the fond delusion of the Russian people, that the Tzaritza had more of the Englishwoman in her than of the German, was being rapidly dispelled. The fact was suddenly revealed that at heart she belonged to Germany, and that she bore a serious grudge against England.

Rasputine was absent from Petrograd when Germany declared war on Russia, but his return to the capital was not delayed. He made no secret of his pacificatory inclinations, and openly assured everyone that a prolonged war would be Russia's undoing. He would, he assured everyone, never have let things come to such a pass had he been at Court. War would have been avoided. From the first, Rasputine manifested aversion to the bloodshed that was going on, and insisted on the necessity of peace. He even told the Empress that her son's safety depended on its being speedily concluded. This peculiar attitude of his towards the war at a time when the whole country had risen as one man, palpitating with indignation at the insults the German Kaiser had hurled against the Russian Tzar, eager to go to battle in defence of the country and the throne, made people suspicious of his motives, and the popular belief was that Rasputine must be a German agent, or the tool of some skilful German spy.

The Empress's friend, Madame Vyrouboff, followed the priest's cue, and thus the intimate Court camarilla, which surrounded the Sovereigns in a tight and exclusive circle, became impregnated with Germanophile sentiments, which they well knew afforded gratification to the Empress. All those who surrounded the Tzar, but whose opinions differed in this respect, were gradually but relentlessly removed from the monarch's vicinity.

About this time, Count Witte returned home from Biarritz. He had always been considered a friend of the Kaiser, and each time he passed through Berlin he was the object of marked attention from William II. Count Witte was never squeamish in his methods, he did not disdain having Rasputine for an ally, and there had been several interviews between the two men, which only added fuel to the flame. The Count's unexpected death a few months subsequently, shortly after the sensational revelations brought to light Colonel Miassoyedoff's arrest, was surrounded with legends, and the fact that no wreath had been sent from the Emperor to be deposited on the Count's coffin seemed to indicate that all was not as it should be.

Cases of treason towards Russia on the part of the Baltic nobility were pointed out by the newspapers, names were given of those barons who had gone over to the German side and were fighting in their ranks. This brought on an increase of bitterness against the Germans who for years had lived in Russia, enjoying many privileges, but at heart had remained obdurate Germans, ready to attempt anything which might endanger the safety of their adopted country.

The entourage of the Tzar became the subject of severe criticism: Count Fredericks, Count Benckendorff, Baron Meyendorff, General von Grunwald, Baron Hoyningen Huehne, Baron Korff, Count Nieroth, were all Germans. The Minister of the Imperial Court, Count Fredericks, in particular, attracted general mistrust. He was known to be the leader of the German party at the Court, and was suspected right up to the time of the Revolution of furthering German interests. This distrust and dislike on the part of the people went to the extent of accusing the old Count of being a spy, of using his position at the Court and the knowledge of military secrets he gained to give useful information to the Germans. The general indignation was such as to cause the Tzar to be coldly received in Moscow, because of Count Fredericks' presence, and the German names of his other courtiers.

It was the same thing in the army. When Count Fredericks shadowed the Sovereign, the soldiers gave the Emperor a cool welcome. Murmurs were heard on all sides, reaching the ears of the supreme Commander-in-Chief, the Grand Duke Nicholas. The Grand Duke mentioned the fact to the Emperor, advising him when he visited the front not to be accompanied by Count Fredericks. It was noticed that once or twice after this the Tzar travelled with only Russian courtiers bearing Russian names in his suite. It was likewise noised abroad that Count Fredericks would soon be relieved of his duties at Court. But when the Empress discovered the motives of her husband's resolve, she tartly admonished him on such disloyalty to an old and valued friend, a devoted servitor to his father and himself. She proved to her husband the folly of giving way to groundless prejudice, and assured him that his enforced resignation would break the old man's heart. The Emperor desisted.

News was filtering through from the front that the munitions of the army were far from adequate, as the War Minister, General Soukhomlinoff, had led the country to believe. There was a scarcity of rifles[1] that looked ominous, and wonder was felt at the War Minister declining the offer of Japan to supply the Russian army with munitions and rifles. The real blow, however, fell when the treachery of Colonel Miassoyedoff was established. The story of how his treason was discovered is most interesting and proves that it was by a mere fluke that Russia was relieved of a dangerous spy, owing to whose despicable machinations with the enemy so many of our efforts had failed to bring success.

It was about the end of the year 1914 that a Russian officer K. was taken prisoner in Prussia. He succeeded in deceiving the German military authorities by professing a great hatred of Russia, and stated his eagerness to serve the Germans. He spoke the language fluently, and proved so convincing that, for once, German astuteness was at fault. The man was implicitly believed, and his offer to do spy work for them accepted with alacrity. K. was taken to Berlin, where he was put in communication with a certain M. Brauermeister, who for many years had lived in Russia at the head of some kind of business. This occupation was only a blind to conceal his real profession of one of the mainsprings of the German spying organisation in Russia. M. Brauermeister, who disappeared from this country a couple of months before war commenced, and an Austrian spy, Altschiller, are alleged to have been intimate friends of General Soukhomlinoff's wife, and constantly received at the War Minister's house.

The reason that Brauermeister had not been discovered, and had never even excited the least suspicion, is to be found in the extreme caution he observed. He never wrote, and when valuable

---

1 In the indictment under the Revolutionary Government it was stated that towards the middle of October, 1914, 870,000 men at the front were without rifles.

documents had to be delivered in Berlin, his wife went abroad and smuggled them through in her handbag. This M. Brauermeister gave K. all the necessary instructions and told him to find out Colonel Miassoyedoff, who was one of their most valued agents, and to consult with him as to the best way of operating. Provided with necessary passports, and a thorough knowledge of the 'dessous des cartes', K. departed. Arrived at the first Russian garrison town, he gave information disclosing all that he had heard of M. Brauermeister's past and Colonel Miassoyedoff's present treachery.

A watch was set on Miassoyedoff's movements, with the result it was proved only too clearly that K.'s statements were correct. Miassoyedoff was arrested, tried by court-martial and hanged. Miassoyedoff's trial had, however, lifted only a small corner of the spying-web so dexterously spread over the country. One painful discovery led to another. The War Minister, General Soukhomlinoff, in whose house Colonel Miassoyedoff had been on the most intimate footing, was seriously compromised. Public opinion required his immediate removal, but protected by Rasputine, who was besieged by constant visits from Madame Soukhomlinoff and occasional ones from the General himself, and backed by the Empress, the Tzar left General Soukhomlinoff unmolested for several months. At last circumstances grew too strong to be ignored with impunity. The army was in a state of boiling indignation to have to fight without guns and munitions. Something had to be done, and General Soukhomlinoff received his dismissal, conveyed to him in the following letter of the Emperor:

Much esteemed
Vladimir Alexandrovitch,

I am much distressed in being obliged to inform you that I have come to the conclusion that, in the interests of Russia and with a view to giving satisfaction to the army's wishes, it is indispensable for you to give up the administration of the War Office. A conversation held with the Supreme Commander-in-Chief strengthens me in this resolution.

It gives me great pain to write this to you after our conversation on the day preceding my departure, and I remember with satisfaction that no misunderstandings have ever arisen during the prolonged time of our work together. History will appraise your activity: maybe its judgement will be less severe than that of your contemporaries.

With sincere respect,
NICHOLAS.

This letter was brandished about by General Soukhomlinoff, and shown with pride to his colleagues of the Upper Chamber, as well as to his friends.

When the Emperor returned from the 'Stavka' (Headquarters), both he and the Empress received the desolated Minister in the most amiable manner, and kept him to lunch with them. The Sovereign's gracious reception of the man, who was regarded as having brought Russia to the verge of ruin and defeat, was interpreted in a highly unfavourable way by the population.

As far back as August 29th, o/s, 1914, the Supreme Commander's Chief of Staff informed General Soukhomlinoff of the exact expenditure of munitions, begging him to take the necessary measures for having the output increased. The armies of the South-Western Front had to drive the enemy from Lublin and to pursue him through Galicia, and by the end of August the stores of these armies were exhausted. On September 4th, o/s, 1914, the Chief-of-Staff addressed the Chief Administration of the Artillery with the information that the Grand Duke Nicholas considered it imperative to strain every effort in order to allow of the expenditure of one and a half million of artillery cartridges a month. Taking into consideration that the fight was on two fronts, the intensity of battle could only be kept up if the above-named supply were guaranteed. General Soukhomlinoff is accused of delaying and undertaking nothing.

At about the same time General Joffre sent a telegram to the Russian War Minister enquiring the state of our artillery supplies. General Soukhomlinoff's answer, dated September 16th, informed the French General that all necessary measures were taken, and no anxiety need be felt on that score. This reply led the French Government into error, and was an act of treason against Russia. Soukhomlinoff knew perfectly well that the ammunition of the Russian army was far from sufficient. He had received several urgent wires on that account from Headquarters, but he continued to reassure the Tzar and the Allies, all the time leaving the Russian army with insufficient munitions. Even the higher military dignitaries were left in ignorance of the real state of things. For instance, General Ivanoff entered upon his Carpathian campaign fully convinced of being supplied with a continual flow of munitions.

With terrible losses the heroic efforts of the Imperial Guards and of the Siberian regiments succeeded in driving the enemy away from Warsaw, and our victorious army proceeded to Galicia, over the Carpathians up to the frontier of the enemy's territory. Then it was suddenly ascertained that the Russian army was destitute of arms, of the means with which to wage war. Every cannon could only fire a limited number of shells. Four cartridges only to every gun could be allowed daily, and unarmed soldiers had to proceed to the attack. Through culpable malpractices the Russian army was betrayed. It was a thrust in the back that obliged the victorious armies to retreat. The Russian War Minister had failed in the task allotted to him.

The soldiers remembered this when, in the last days of February, 1917, o/s, they were ordered to shoot their disarmed fellow-citizens in the streets of Petrograd, they turned their rifles against the rotten system of the old regime.

At the instigation of the Grand Duke Nicholas, a special commission, under the presidency of the Grand Duke Serge Mikhailovitch, was organised with the object of providing the army with the necessary quantity of munitions. During the space of three months nothing was done!

Everyone knew, more or less, that under cover of the war and under the protection – nay, even with the concurrence – of the Chief Military Administrators, a mad juggling of milliards was going on, but no one thought it was done in such a cynical and stupid manner! The accusation against General Soukhomlinoff is that living on his pay, and possessing no private means, he suddenly became the owner of a large fortune, amounting to about a million of roubles: that he had always been inclined to have business transactions with shady customers, but since his second marriage he was surrounded with all kinds of adventurers and suspicious individuals, German and Austrian spies conspicuous among their number. It is further alleged that Soukhomlinoff's best friends were the Altschillers, a well-known Austrian family, who for many years past had been established in Kiev, and later on transferred to Petrograd. Altschiller senior was the chief of the Austrian spying organisation, and the close intimacy he and his family carried on with General and Madame Soukhomlinoff is said to have been very much to his advantage. Altschiller senior is credited with knowing everything that happened at the War Office, even the purport of the most confidential conversations between the Tzar and Soukhomlinoff. Orders and commissions were willingly given to these people, or to their agents, resulting in dilatoriness, or in their execution proving useless. Once a great quantity of munitions arrived at the front which would not fit the guns and rifles for which they were sent!

When M. Makeroff was Minister of the Interior, some time before the war, he warned General Soukhomlinoff against the Altschillers, but the War Minister stood up for them, saying he knew the family in Kiev, where he had spent several years as Governor-General, and guaranteed their perfect trustworthiness. Altschiller senior absconded a few weeks before the war was declared and his son was arrested, as were likewise many other of Madame Soukhomlinoff's doubtful friends. The General was called to the rescue, and, instead of thinking of the war needs, he spent hours of valuable time in insistent endeavours to have his friends set free.

All this proved such condemnatory evidence against the former Minister of War that a Senatorial revision was ordained to investigate his dealings. The official verification of documents disclosed appalling facts. A warrant was granted to search the General's private abode, which resulted in his arrest and incarceration in the Fortress of St. Peter and St. Paul in the early spring of 1916. A painful scene occurred in the course of the arrest. Madame Soukhomlinoff, who had been intensely excited during the search, had a terrible attack of hysteria, caused by the unexpected turn things were taking. The General likewise was unnerved.

After recovering from the first shock, Madame Soukhomlinoff laid herself out, with wonderful energy and adroitness, to retrieve the fallen fortunes of her husband. She hastened to interview Rasputine, enlisted the sympathy of Madame Vyrouboff, obtained an audience of the Empress Alexandra, and, throwing herself at the latter's feet, implored her intercession in favour of her calumniated and injured husband. The trial was suspended, and the papers ceased giving any communication connected with the case. Subsequently there appeared a short notice about the former War Minister's serious mental illness, and the names of several well-known nerve-doctors were mentioned as attending him. After that no information was given, but everyone knew that General

Soukhomlinoff had been released, and was comfortably quartered in his luxurious apartment!

The news of Soukhomlinoff's liberation passed from mouth to mouth, and produced the most sinister impression on people's minds, especially on those connected with the army. It was well known that this act of weak indulgence towards a man whom the whole nation accused of being criminal, was due to Rasputine's influence with the Empress. It was she who had compelled the Tzar to set free the man who was the primary cause of Russia's reverses. A wave of bitter indignation passed over the whole country, and the Empress was openly accused of being in connivance with the gang of German agents. This insensate act of folly in releasing from prison General Soukhomlinoff undermined the people's trust in the Tzar, and laid the foundation-stone to the approaching revolution.

A few words about Madame Soukhomlinoff's antecedents must be added to give a clear impression of the woman so seriously implicated in the accusations against her husband. Madame Soukhomlinoff, a Jewess by birth, is the junior of her husband by many years. She commenced her adventurous career as a typist in a solicitor's office in Kiev. It was here she made her first husband's acquaintance, through copying some important documents for him. M. Boutovitch was a prosperous landed proprietor, and the clever typist, Mlle. Gashkevitch, dexterously insinuated herself into his confidence and affections. It was a splendid match for a penniless young woman, but the marriage was not a success. Madame Boutovitch, meanwhile, now that she had married into the gentry, moved in the higher circles of society in Kiev, where she came into contact with the Governor-General, who was at the time a widower. Pretty little Madame Boutovitch fascinated him, and when she appealed for his influence to help her to get a divorce from her unwilling husband, the Governor-General used his power to free the young woman from her bonds. By the time it was obtained, the amorous old General was as wax in her hands, and in November, 1909, soon after he had been appointed War Minister, he married her.

There was an attempt on the first husband's part to prove the divorce illegal, for the reason that several documents had been kept back. The affair was hushed up, but will all come out at the approaching trial. The former President of the Upper Chamber, M. Stcheglovitoff, who was arrested on the first day of the Revolution, is accused of having suppressed some important papers relative to the divorce case of M. and Mme. Boutovitch. At that time M. Stcheglovitoff was the Minister of Justice and the Procurator-General. It was M. Altschiller who conducted the divorce case on Mme. Boutovitch's side, and Colonel Miassoyedoff was her adviser and principal helper.

General Soukhomlinoff was rearrested during the first days of the Revolution, and has again taken possession of his cell in the Fortress. Now it is quite comfortless, whereas a year ago, owing to the successful intercession of his wife, it was turned into a little study. The floor was carpeted, a comfortable easy-chair imported, and his bed was luxurious in its comfort. A few days subsequently Madame Soukhomlinoff was arrested likewise and taken to the Fortress. Their trial will be a sensational one. The Grand Duke Serge Mikhailovitch, General Polivanoff (who at one time was General Soukhomlinoff's assistant and eventually his successor), the ballet-dancer, Madame Kchessinsky, the late War Minister, M. Gutchkoff, and many others are included amongst the numerous witnesses who will appear.

Spying and treachery seemed in the air. Petrograd was full of German agents, only one could not lay hands on them. Most of the suspicions seemed to lead up to the Palace of Tzarskoe Selo. The Empress was accused of having a wireless installation secreted in the Palace, which gave her the opportunity of sending and receiving wireless communications from her German relatives. However, the search made after the Empress Alexandra's arrest proved this aspersion, at least, to be false. Notwithstanding the minutest examination all over the Palace, including roof, garrets and countless lumber-rooms, nothing of the kind was found.

The Grand Duchess Marie Pavlovna, the widow of the Grand Duke Vladimir and a Princess of Mecklenburg-Schwerin by birth, was likewise seriously suspected of Germanophile inclinations. All the old stories of her youthful days were ferreted out from the oblivion to which they had hitherto been committed: how in the reign of Alexander III she had been detected in political correspondence with Prince Bismarck. The visits she made to her hospital-train operating at the front were regarded with uneasiness by the officers of the General Staff. Her arrivals, they said, were always the precursors of reverses on our front.

Openly criticising the attitude of the Empress Alexandra, the

Grand Duchess endeavoured to outshine her, and displayed a marvellous energy. Her hospital-trains and other organisations were spread into an extensive network. But the strange part was that the majority of the officials attached to them bore German names, or were robust young men, mostly scions of rich merchant-families, who preferred such work to joining the active army. If they were by chance called upon to enter the ranks manfully, a wire from the Grand Duchess to a certain general smoothed away all difficulties, and these heroes of the white feather remained unmolested.

In the spring of 1916 there arose some dissension among the staff of the Grand Duchess's stores at Minsk, and several officials left, not wishing to be mixed up in unpleasant complications that might occur, for it was soon blazed abroad that Marie Pavlovna's train stationed at 'Stolbtzy' swarmed with German spies, and very shortly afterwards the train was sent to the rear of the army.

The following names seem strange in association with a Russian army fighting the Germans. The principal military authorities of one of our most important fronts are: The Chief of the Military Circuit of Minsk – *General Baron Raush von Traubenberg*; his assistant – *General Muller*; the commandant – *Count Dunten* (whose brother, the owner of an estate in Livonia, had gone over to the Germans and was fighting in their ranks); *Engineer-General von Cube*, the representative of the Empire's Studs – *General von Zander*; the Chief of the Garrison – *General Baron von Dellingshausen*. Further on in 'Orsha': *the Commandant Seidler* and *the Stationmaster Holmberg*. Another Commandant in close vicinity bore the name of *Baumgarten*. The rest of General Baron Raush von Traubenberg's Staff, consisted of *Crossman, Scalon, Kauger, Horschelmann, Hubner, Behr, Schultz*, etc.

Many of the above-mentioned officers may have been loyally disposed towards Russia, and associated with Russians their political integrity would, in all probability, not have been open to suspicion. It was this startling conjunction that gave so unpleasant an impression.

A few months later another international Russian lady made an unexpected appearance in Petrograd. This lady came from Italy, where she had lived for many years. Madame Q. had been a very pretty woman, and in the reign of Alexander II she was one of the leaders of smart society. She had, at all times, been on terms of the greatest intimacy with the members of the Austrian Embassy. The late Baron Ehrenthal was a devoted friend of hers, when he was the Councillor of the Austrian Embassy. When he left, she transferred her friendship to the new Austrian Ambassador, Prince Liechtenstein.

Madame Q. had always been on intimate terms with M. Stürmer, and at one time she had pulled all the available wires, in the hope of having him appointed as the Russian Ambassador in Vienna. Madame Q. was extremely wary in her movements; still her unexpected arrival gave people food for spreading all kinds of appalling rumours. Her sister-in-law belonged to the intimate coterie of the Grand Duchess Marie Pavlovna, where Madame Q. was graciously made welcome. In one of M. Miliukoff's orations during the January sessions of the Duma, he mentioned this lady's sojourn in Petrograd and her increasing influence in instilling pacificatory notions into people's minds.

People commenced talking of M. Sazonoff's resignation and of his being succeeded by M. Stürmer at the Foreign Office. The public at large did not credit the possibility of this contingency, but the initiated knew better . . . they knew likewise that the impending change was inspired from the shores of the Spree.

Chapter V

THE END OF A TRAITOR

THE great change in the Chief Command of the Russian armies was effected at the end of August, 1915. The Grand Duke Nicholas was appointed Viceroy in the Caucasus and the Tzar took the Chief Command upon himself. Most of the Ministers were set against this change, especially M. Sazonoff, for he was doubtful of the impression this change would make on the Allies. In military circles, however, the opinion was in favour of the Tzar. With all his popularity amongst the soldiers, the Grand Duke Nicholas was not much liked by the army leaders. He was too arbitrary in his commands and prone to listen to tale-bearers. Hearing of some supposed misuse, without examining the pros and cons of the question, he would fly into one of his violent fits of passion, uselessly storming at an imagined culprit. Headquarters was full of intrigues and all kinds of misuses. Most of the generals were at loggerheads, and thought more of their petty jealousies than of their work. Too many women were about, some of them were suspected of being German agents and several of the Grand Duke's rash decisions were, so it was surmised, inspired from Berlin, without his being aware of it. The atmosphere wanted clearing, and our persistent reverses, succeeding so quickly upon our brilliant successes, made the change a very acceptable one in the eyes of the army.

People did not know that Rasputine was at the bottom of this change, and that, pressed by him, the Empress had insisted upon it.

A gradual change seemed to come over the Tzar, he was subject to fits of depression, and his regained robustness and animation were giving way to dejected apathy. The Empress made herself

Rasputine's mouthpiece, and insisted upon the most absurd and dangerous measures. The monarch was harassed by his wife's demands, which often went against his own convictions; but the Emperor was as wax in her hands, he could never withstand her long. General Alexeieff confessed that in the 'Stavka' the visits of the Empress were dreaded, and some calamity generally followed them. Her influence over the Sovereign was as complete as it was fatal.

A spell seemed to have been cast on the mental faculties of the Tzar. He was being led blindfolded to an abyss. Tzardom was crumbling slowly but surely, and it was the Empress's acts that were sapping the monarchy. The Government seemed to be dancing a mad war-dance at the very edge of a precipice. A strange juggling of Ministers was going on, which discredited the Cabinet. No confidence was felt, and the symbol of power was sinking. The united Ministry existed no longer: nominations were made without consulting the Prime Minister, and the Ministers were chosen from various camps, with opposite views and convictions. Rasputine and his favourites were felt at every step, their resistance or their insistence interfered with everything. . . and it was the Russian Government that was carrying out their iniquitous plans.

General Polivanoff had succeeded General Soukhomlinoff at the War Office. At one time he had been the latter's assistant, but was removed in consequence of the startling revelations, which the member of the Duma, M. Gutchkoff,[1] had made to the Tzar a couple of years before the war, concerning the misuses reigning in the War Office. General Soukhomlinoff suspected his assistant of being the informer.

At this juncture, General Polivanoff was unmistakably the right man in the right place, for, though somewhat gruff in manner and far from being a courtier, he had the recommendation of a high standard of integrity, was wonderfully energetic and had the gift of organisation. Thanks to him our foundries and manufactories commenced to work with redoubled zeal and, in an astonishingly short time, our army was amply provided with ammunition. Hopes revived, success seemed certain, when suddenly without any visible motive the Tzar's Ukase appeared, appointing General Schuvaieff to the post of Minister of War. The

1 The present War Minister.

news of his discharge was conveyed to General Polivanoff in the following manner. He had sent some papers for the Sovereign's signature to the Stavka. When the signed documents were returned, the General found between the leaves a fully drawn-out Ukase of his dismissal and General Schuvaieff's nomination. A highly flattering Imperial rescript to General Polivanoff appeared simultaneously in the papers.

General Schuvaieff had up to this administered the Intendancy, and had proved himself extremely competent. His honesty was beyond doubt, but he was an old man and, although he worked hard, he had neither the strength nor the energy of his predecessor. About seven or eight months later, shortly before the Revolution, General Belaieff succeeded Schuvaieff, again without any visible reason to justify the change. The new Minister was not a popular man, nor were his abilities outstanding. He was a convinced routinist, and his predilection for formalism did not slacken even when urgency and speed were imperative. Official papers had to be copied and recopied as many as eight times for the most trivial reasons, the Minister insisting on adding or excluding valueless words which could not modify the tenor of the text. Officers were threatened with discharge if a slight printer's error occurred in printed documents. The Minister's activity was principally centred on such immaterial details. Fortunately the Revolution intervened and this Minister was removed.

The discharge of the Minister of Foreign Affairs in May, 1916, was a blow that fell heavily on everyone, and was a surprise to the Minister himself. M. Sazonoff was in Finland at the time, enjoying a short rest-cure, when the news of his dismissal reached him. The diplomatic representatives of our Allies were thunderstruck, and Russian politicians were lost in amazement at this sudden resolve of the monarch to part with his Minister of Foreign Affairs. No one was able to account for it. But when it was known that M. Stürmer was to step into his place, wonder changed to dismay. M. Stürmer's reputation was definitely established and he inspired no confidence in anyone. Only the Empress and her satellites rejoiced, for they thought M. Stürmer would pave the way to secure the much longed-for Peace, no matter at what price.

In the Ministry of the Interior one Minister chased another; it was a regular game of leap-frog. These continual changes became ludicrous. One Minister would, for instance, ordain the revision of some province. The official, to whom this confidential mission was entrusted, would leave Petrograd provided with necessary instructions, but, when he returned, another Minister had been in the meanwhile appointed. The Ministers themselves felt so insecure as to their position that some of them did not take the trouble to move into the state apartment allotted to every Minister, or if they did settle in their new abode, they kept on their former apartment in case of an emergency.

In the spring of 1915, at the insistence of the Grand Duke Nicholas, the Ministers of the Interior, M. Maklakoff, and of Justice, M. Stcheglovitoff, were dismissed because they were retrogressive. This measure was taken to conciliate the Liberals, who were gaining the upper hand. M. Maklakoff's successor in the Home Office was Prince Stcherbatoff. The Prince, though a gallant gentleman and a man of untarnished honour, was no statesman and possessed no experience of the technical side of administration. After a few months he was succeeded by a member of the Duma, M. Alexis Khvostoff, the leader of the Right. It seemed a very wise choice, for Mr. Khvostoff is a man of ability and strength of purpose. Great hopes were entertained of him. Unfortunately he favoured the Jesuitical maxim that the end justifies the means. This proved his stumbling-block. The circumstances of his downfall are as follows. About twelve years previous, a monk of the name of Illiodore played a conspicuous part during the time of the first Revolution. He was a born leader, and his influence over his fellow-citizens in Tzaritzine was unbounded. Being, however, of a somewhat turbulent nature, his acts had excited conflicts with the authorities. Various opinions were held of the monk; some had an exalted idea of him, others quite the reverse. The Empress, always inclined to take up such monastic individuals, wished to see him, and she and the Tzar gave him their support in several cases of dissension with the superior Black Clergy.[1]

Illiodore had been a friend of Rasputine's, for he had frequently met him in the course of their pilgrimages. At the commencement of Rasputine's career Illiodore had helped him and done a great deal to bring him into prominence, but, when he found out the

[1] In Russia the Prelates and Priests belonging to monastical orders are called the 'Black Clergy', whilst the 'White Clergy' is composed of Priests, who are laymen. The latter can enter the married state, but only once in a lifetime.

real nature of Rasputine, he turned upon him and denounced him with the violence inherent in his nature, making a bitter enemy of the favoured staretz. Fresh conflicts arose between the unruly Illiodore and the Holy Synod, and he was persecuted for all kinds of misdoings. The Empress had withdrawn her protection, and, dreading the consequences of Rasputine's rancour, Illiodore fled to Norway, where, feeling safe from malevolent molestation, the vindictive monk devoted his leisure in wreaking vengeance on his foes, and commenced writing a book revealing Rasputine's true character, the cynicism of his doctrine, giving full details of his profligate life, disclosing facts of his intercourse at Court, confirmed by letters and documents, which he asserts were stolen from Rasputine. The book was published under the title *The Holy Devil*, and was vehement in its denunciations. Just before the book was to be issued, and dreading the impression that such a work, full of lashing sneers and condemnation, would have on the reading public, it is said that M. Khvostoff, wishing to prevent its publication, sent a confidential man to Norway, provided with the sum of 50,000 roubles to buy the manuscript from Illiodore.

Unfortunately M. Khvostoff chose a man he had known in Nijni Novgorod during his residence there as Governor, a certain journalist, Rjevsky, in whose skill the Minister trusted, convinced he would manage this delicate business successfully. Instead of which, Rjevsky spent several days rioting in the most dissipated way, bragging about the confidential mission entrusted to him and attracting the attention of the secret police. Rjevsky was arrested on the frontier of Sweden, searched and on him was found a large sum of money. He was prevailed upon to give a quite different account of his mission.

Rjevsky confessed to have been sent by M. Alexis Khvostoff to the monk Illiodore to organise the murder of Rasputine, and thus save Russia from his pestilential domination. The money was given to him to further this plan. There was a great outcry amidst Rasputine's flock of ardent followers: the Empress clamoured for rigorous measures. M. Khvostoff was obliged to resign. M. Stürmer took the portfolio of Minister of the Interior, exchanging it a few months later for that of the Foreign Office. When this happened, M. Alexis Khvostoff's uncle, M. Alexander Khvostoff, who had succeeded M. Stcheglovitoff a year ago in the Ministry of Justice, was induced to accept the portfolio of the Interior, and was one of the best ministers of this difficult period. But he proved a serious obstacle in M. Stürmer's way, preventing the latter from freely carrying out his programme. The Prime Minister complained to the Tzar that it was impossible to work with M. Khvostoff, and the latter received his discharge in the most sudden and unexpected manner.

The growing exasperation, however, reached its climax when it became known that the new Minister of the Interior was to be M. Protopopoff. This nomination broke the record of the Government's vacillation. No one knew what to expect next. M. Protopopoff is personally known in England. He arrived in London in 1916 at the head of the Russian deputation from the Duma. He is a man of considerable wealth, and is the owner of a large estate in the Government of Simbirsk, and of a cloth manufactory in its vicinity. His reputation was not of a high standard, and he had more critics than friends. He was considered clever, proficient in intrigue, with a good head for business, though somewhat crafty in his dealings and utterly unqualified for such an important post. He has a peculiar charm of manner, fascinating at the outset, which gains him a certain shallow popularity. He had been the assistant of the President of the Duma and belonged to the 'Octobrist' faction; but he had entirely discredited himself in the eyes of the Duma, and of the right-minded public by his indiscreet interview in Stockholm with a German diplomatist on the possibilities of peace. Secret though the communication had been, the gist of it appeared in the German press, and was not calculated to impress favourably either the Russians or their Allies.

M. Stürmer, M. Protopopoff, General Woyeikoff and Madame Vyrouboff, inspired by Rasputine and headed by the Empress, were henceforth to rule the country, and everyone knew they were stretching out their hands to grasp the olive branch, so eagerly extended to Russia by Germany. The price the nation would have to pay for this was a question to which they were supremely indifferent.

It was little over a year ago that Doctor Badmaeff introduced M. Protopopoff to Rasputine, and the latter was beguiled by the voice of the charmer and the similarity of their opinions. When he left, the staretz was loud in his praises: 'There's a head for you!' he exclaimed; 'he takes the shine out of our Ministers.' This was the moment when the fate of M. Protopopoff swayed in the balance. The whole course of his life was changed, for until then he was quite unknown in Court circles.

In the course of a few days M. Protopopoff was invited to visit Rasputine, the latter introduced him to Madame Vyrouboff, and through her agency he became known to the Empress. His insinuating manners and brilliant conversation pleased Her Majesty. To all intents and purposes he seemed a man who could be useful, and he soon became a member of the Sovereign's intimate coterie. The other courtiers looked on this intrusion with displeasure, and even the Tzar saw in M. Protopopoff an outsider suddenly sprung into favour like a jack-in-the-box. When the idea was suggested to him in the early autumn of 1916 to choose M. Protopopoff for the vacant post of Minister of the Interior, the Tzar laughed the idea to scorn. 'What kind of a Minister could he make?' he said; but he was overpersuaded. The embryo statesman used all his arts to fascinate, the Empress set forth her most conclusive arguments, M. Stürmer insisted on the advisability of this nomination. The idea seemed gradually to appear less preposterous, and finally the Tzar was prevailed upon to yield.

As soon as his appointment was an accomplished fact, M. Protopopoff, who had belonged to the Octobrists and was considered Liberal and Progressive in political spheres, resolutely turned over a new leaf. He became ultra-reactionary, having recourse to the most exasperating repressions.

The opening of the Duma session was fixed for November 5th. Until then there was a lull before the storm, but the air was full of electricity.

The anxiously expected first session was a tempestuous one. The greatest distrust of the Premier was manifested. He was accused of double-dealing, and when he left the assembly he was followed by the cry: 'Doloy, doloy!' (Away, away). That same evening M. Stürmer started for Mohilev to give His Majesty a full report. M. Protopopoff did not make a public speech, but during private parliamentary debates, held behind closed doors, he proved an amazingly weak antagonist, incapable of defending a single argument, and unable to stand up firmly for any idea.

Several vigorous speeches were pronounced from the Duma tribune. They were so bold in their accusations that the press censor suppressed them. This only enhanced their significance and hundreds of typed copies were circulated among the people.

M. Miliukoff was pitiless in his condemnation of the Empress for her support of the plan, originated in Germany, of a speedy and separate peace, regardless of circumstances, conditions, or national honour. He quoted passages from different German newspapers, in which 'die Friedens-partei der jungen Tzarin'[1] was freely discussed. He was very outspoken in referring to the 'Dark Powers', which surrounded the throne, and had lately assumed such overwhelming dimensions. Other orations followed, eloquent in their aggressiveness against the Government and the Tzar's entourage. The speeches of MM. Kerensky, Schulguine, Purishkevitch, Count Bobrinsky, etc., were vehement in their denunciation. The dubious attitude of the German Grand Duchesses was mentioned, and the baneful Germanophile agitation going on in some of the leading salons in society was alluded to with the most outspoken frankness. No names were mentioned; but everyone knew who was meant.

M. Purishkevitch, up to quite lately of the Right party, and a staunch Monarchist, concluded a speech with the words directly addressed to the assembled Ministers: 'If you are not varlets, all of you, you must go to the Tzar and beg him on your knees to deliver the country of Rasputine and his disastrous influence!' Accusatory speeches were likewise delivered in the Upper Chamber: the most brilliant amongst them was that of Prince Eugene Troubetzkoi.

Meanwhile M. Stürmer returned from the Stavka. His resignation was accepted, both as Premier and as Minister of Foreign Affairs. No other course was possible on account of the attitude taken up by the Duma towards him, but to emphasise the favour which he continued to enjoy with the Sovereign, the distinguished Court post of 'Chief Chamberlain' was granted to him. The choice of the new Premier fell on the Minister of Ways and Communications, Senator Alexander Trepoff, a clever and energetic man and a staunch Monarchist. M. Pokrovsky, who later on was characterised in one of the Duma speeches as being of 'crystal purity', was appointed Minister of Foreign Affairs.

The expected discharge of M. Protopopoff was not forthcoming, but this was explained as the desire in high quarters not to give in too much at once. It was, however, firmly believed that this concession would likewise be made to public opinion, and that a change would be made for the New Year. A means had even been found by which the Empress could keep such a valuable partisan at Court without incurring the Duma's interference. M. Proto-

1 The peace party of the young Tzaritza.

popoff was to be appointed as Chief of the Imperial Chancery for the reception of petitions. But an unforeseen event upset all expectations, creating the greatest perturbation all over the country, especially in Petrograd and in Tzarskoe Selo.

On December 17th, six words in the evening issue of the *Exchange Newspaper* caused this commotion: 'Gregory Rasputine has ceased to exist!'

The news spread like wildfire all over the town that Rasputine had met with a violent death in one of the mansions of the capital. The most amazing details were given, but no one knew exactly what had happened. The newspapers began by giving hazy, yet transparent, accounts; but even these were stopped. The name of Rasputine was not to be mentioned and no details to be given, only the bare facts of his death and the subsequent finding of his body were divulged to the public.

The circumstances which led up to this tragic occurrence are as follows. A strong resentment was felt in high spheres against the ascendancy assumed at Court by such a wretched miscreant as Rasputine. Repeated attempts had been made to open the Tzar's eyes to the true state of things, but every effort shattered against the supremacy of the Empress Alexandra's power. The Dowager Empress Marie had spoken seriously to her son on the subject in the autumn of 1916, when he visited Kiev. Both his sisters told him plainly that the position the Empress Alexandra permitted Rasputine to occupy, and the things going on at the Court, gave rise to the most egregious tales being spread among the army and the people. These conduced only to the abasement of Sovereignty, and sowed the most fatal seeds of ridicule and distrust. Several of the Grand Dukes, the Tzar's brother, Michael, included, warned him of the serious turn events were taking. All was in vain!

There had been a plan mooted of inducing the Tzar to divorce the Empress. The dissolution of his marriage would have saved the throne, and put an effective stop to this awful 'Rasputiniad', but the monarch had always put his family affections before his duty to the country. He would not hear of such a thing, and both the Sovereigns were highly indignant that such an idea could be seriously contemplated. The Grand Duke Nicholas Mikhailovitch, who was always inclined to be a 'frondeur', prepared a written statement, which he personally brought to Tzarskoe Selo and read out to his cousin the Emperor.

The Grand Duke was extremely outspoken, and did not hesitate to call a spade a spade. He told the Tzar that he was responsible to the Romanoff family for the safety of the dynasty. When he mentioned Rasputine and his pernicious influence, the Emperor interrupted him in an irritated manner:

'That is only Purishkevitch's nonsense,' he said.

After having attentively listened to all his cousin had to say, the Emperor took the written statement and showed it to the Empress, who flew into a violent passion and tore it up in indignation.

About the same time occurred the episode between the Empress and the wife of a member of the Upper Chamber, Princess Wassiltchikoff, by birth a Princess Mestchersky. The Princess wrote pointing out to the Empress the danger of her perpetual interference, cautioning her as to the peril into which she was leading the Empire. The name of Rasputine was not mentioned in the letter. But the warning did more harm than good. The Princess was guilty of a serious breach in writing to a Sovereign without observing any of the usual forms. The letter was written spontaneously on several sheets of notepaper torn from a letter pad, hurriedly put into an envelope and slipped into the pillar-box. The Princess confessed that she wished to say what she had said, but had not the courage to read it over. It would have been much wiser to have left the serious part of the letter untouched, at the same time softening some of its harshness, and observing the forms etiquette requires in addressing a crowned head. This flaw in the Princess's armour was used against her.

The Empress was furious, and considered the way she had been addressed by a subject of the Tzar as a gross impertinence towards his Consort. She complained to the Emperor, showed him the sheets of block notepaper, and pointed out the way she was addressed, laying no stress on the tenor of the letter. The Sovereigns agreed to act rigorously, especially as the Empress had been lately receiving many anonymous letters full of recrimination. Princess Wassiltchikoff was sent out of Petrograd to her estate. Her husband accompanied her and, soon after the incident, received his discharge: he was a member of the Upper Chamber by appointment, not by election.

All these danger-signals were left unnoticed; the Empress, reassured by her favourite associates, did not believe in the existing peril.

Shortly before these events a plan of the Empress had been discovered which caused the members of the Imperial Family grave anxiety. The part Catherine II played in Russian history had from the first appealed to the Empress's imperious nature. When the question was broached as to what name she should assume as the future Empress of Russia, the Princess suggested *Catherine*, but the name was disapproved of by the Dowager Empress, and Alexandra was substituted. The idea had been suggested to Her Majesty that the best way to obtain unlimited power would be to get the Emperor into such a state of debility that he would have to be set aside in favour of the Tzessarevitch, and she would be proclaimed the Regent during her son's minority. She could then direct the course of Russian politics in the way she pleased.

Madame Vyrouboff was only too anxious to play the part of Princess Catherine Dashkoff, who had so skilfully helped the wife of Peter III to overthrow her husband and proclaim herself Empress of Russia. With the support of Rasputine, M. Stürmer, Protopopoff and some others, it was thought this bold plan could be successfully carried out. This is said to explain the various stories of philtres and herb-infusions with which the Tzar had been drenched under pretext of giving him new strength, health and the blessing of God.

The Empress forgot two things: first – the time we live in is widely different from the period of the reign of Peter III, over a hundred and fifty years ago. What was possible then would scarcely succeed now. The second omission was the immense popularity of the Empress Catherine who, from the first day of her foot touching Russian soil, had steadfastly endeavoured to ingratiate herself with the Russians, and gain the hearts of her future subjects. Whereas the Empress Alexandra was frankly detested by the Russian nation, and from the very first had done everything she could to repel popularity.

Gatherings were held in private palaces, as well as in aristocratic mansions to deliberate on the critical position of the country brought about by the reprehensible extravagance of one woman. The last conference took place in the hospital-train of M. Purishkevitch. What passed during this consultation is not exactly known, for all those implicated in the plot were extremely cautious in their *partial* revelations. Even at the present moment, when all danger of reprisal is over, they object to have the veil torn off which shrouds the ghastly secret of that fatal night. The conclusion was arrived at that Rasputine and his viciousness were the plague-spot of Russian existence and, as no exhortation helped to put a stop to this wanton farce, the fellow must be forcibly removed out of harm's way. Three of the participants – the Grand Duke Dmitry Pavlovitch, Prince Felix Youssoupoff junior, and M. Purishkevitch – tossed up as to who should fire the shot. The hazard of the die, it is said, fell to the lot of Prince Youssoupoff.

The Prince decided to give a supper party on the night of December 16th, o/s, in the sumptuous apartment he inhabited in his father's mansion on the Moika Quay. Ladies were present at the festivity, but except the three above-named participants the names of the other guests have not been divulged. By some means Rasputine, who had become very suspicious of late, had been decoyed into accepting an invitation to be present. Subsequently his daughter stated that her father had been very eager to go to the party. At a little past midnight the staretz was fetched in a motor by an elegant young man, supposed to be Prince Youssoupoff. A lady was waiting for them in the car. After revelling for some hours, during which the libations had been very generous, when most of the guests had left, at about six in the morning, shots were heard coming from the Youssoupoff Palace. The police hurried up to enquire the reason for this shooting, but were told that nothing was the matter, only a dog having been shot, and the corpse of a beautiful retriever was found in the adjacent garden.

It has been said that Prince Youssoupoff's hand shook in aiming the pistol, and that his first shot missed, thus giving Rasputine time to draw his revolver and fire, but as he was drunk he only succeeded in killing the dog. Purishkevitch then came to the rescue, and the general impression is that his shot delivered the country of Rasputin. A little later Rasputine's dead body was carried into a motor-car, which stood ready waiting before the palace portal. Prince Youssoupoff stepped inside, M. Purishkevitch took the place of the chauffeur (the Grand Duke Dmitry Pavlovitch had gone home), and they drove to the islands and threw the body into an ice-hole of the Neva.

The news of Rasputine's disappearance caused a tremendous commotion. The Chief of the Police was in the last stages of despair, M. Protopopoff on the verge of lunacy, and the Court circle staggered. When the Empress was told, she was speechless with dismay.

Her first words proved prophetic:

'We are done for,' she cried; 'now we shall also perish!'

Her Majesty gave imperative orders that Rasputine's body was to be found, and for several days the ice was broken and a thorough search instituted, until the frozen corpse was found and identified. By the order of the Empress, it was carried to the chapel of a veteran asylum close by. Madame Vyrouboff motored over from Tzarskoe Selo and was loud in her lamentations. Prayers for his soul were held in that lady's apartment in the presence of the Empress, her daughters and some of the most ardent admirers of the deceased. The body was embalmed and sent to Tzarskoe Selo, where it was buried in a remote part of the park. The funeral took place at the dead of night; no one knew exactly the whereabouts of the grave, but during the days of the Revolution the spot was discovered, the grave dug up and the coffin taken to Petrograd, where it was finally burnt.

During those ominous days the following telegrams were sent by the Empress to her husband in the Stavka:

December 13th, three days before the murder:

> Very disturbed not to know details of rumours. Remember what I wrote to you last week.
>
> ALIX.

December 17th an urgent wire was sent.

> Can you send Woyeikoff directly? Need his advice concerning our friend who has disappeared since last night. We continue to hope in the mercy of God. Felix and Dmitry mixed up.
>
> ALIX.

December 17th in the evening.

> K.[1] does all that is possible. Up to now found nothing. Felix was stopped at the moment of starting for the Crimea. I wish you were here.
>
> ALIX.

December 18th in the morning.

> Nothing is known until now. Questions to people have

---

1 K. stands probably for General Kurloff.

availed nothing. It is to be feared the two boys have done the worst.

ALIX.

December 18th in the evening.

Give orders to Maximovitch to forbid Dmitry in your name to leave the house. Dmitry wished to see me today. I refused. We are especially mixed up. Body not found yet.

ALIX.

December 19th.

Thanks for yesterday's wire. Found in the river.

ALIX.

Chapter VI

THE UPHEAVAL

ON the third day after Rasputine's murder, the Emperor returned from Mohileff. In Tzarskoe Selo all was confusion and consternation. Madame Vyrouboff, in the throes of unconsolable despair, incited the Empress to wreak vengeance on the authors of this tragic event. Her Majesty's distress at the loss of a devoted friend was mingled with dread of some overhanging calamity to her family, for she was convinced that in some mysterious way Rasputine's existence was interwoven with their own happiness.

Instead of receiving his immediate discharge for not having foreseen or prevented Rasputine's violent death, M. Protopopoff found his way to the Empress's heart by the desolation he manifested at the terrible fate of the staretz. On first seeing Her Majesty he fell on his knees exclaiming: 'What a loss the country has sustained, the wonderful man exists no longer!' This rather theatrical way of tackling the mournful subject was, strangely enough, appreciated by the Empress, and she clung to M. Protopopoff as to a legacy left by the departed.

The Emperor had his hands full. He was harassed by his womenfolk. The Empress's vindictiveness found full scope. She insisted on the Grand Duke Dmitry and Prince Youssoupoff being tried by court martial. The Empress Marie, on the other hand, was anxiously interceding for the culprits. The Grand Duke was by the Empress's wish put under house-arrest, but he was not once examined, or even questioned, as to the events of that fatal night, and although he craved an audience, both from the Emperor and the Empress, he was denied an interview. He was the object of ovations during the days of his arrest. Everybody who was anybody left cards at his palace, and his numerous friends, including his fellow-officers of the Horse Guards,[1] called to express their sympathy.

The Grand Duke told the Commander of the Horse Guards that he thanked God that his hands were stainless of bloodshed, but the Empress would not listen to any extenuating circumstances and, very shortly after these events, the Grand Duke was sent to the Persian front and forbidden to communicate with anyone, either by letter or by telegram, during his journey. The Emperor's adjutant, Count Koutaisseff, was to accompany him to his journey's end and enforce the Imperial Command.

Prince Youssoupoff was sent to his estate in the Government of Kursk. He likewise was forbidden to have any communication with the outer world, either by letter or by telegram. On hearing of their son's disgrace, his parents hurried to join him and share his exile. The young Princess Irene Youssoupoff hastened from the Crimea and, accompanied by her grandmother, the Dowager Empress Marie, arrived at the country seat fixed upon for her husband's exile. The Dowager Empress Marie, after a short stay with the Youssoupoffs, returned to Kiev, where a reassuring telegram of the Emperor awaited her:

> Thanks for telegram. Prosecution will be immediately stopped. Embrace you.
>
> NICKY.

Thus of the three alleged participants in this political murder, the only one that was left free and unmolested was M. Purishkevitch.

The exile of the Grand Duke Dmitry to the Persian front produced a profound impression on the members of the Imperial Family. They were disgusted with the Empress for insisting upon such severe measures with a young man whose guilt was not proved, whose health was known to be delicate and unable to stand the Persian climate. A joint letter was written to the Tzar and signed by His Imperial Highness's grandmother, the Dowager Queen Olga of Greece; his father, the Grand Duke Paul; his sister, the Grand Duchess Marie Pavlovna junior; the Tzar's brother, and by all the Grand Duchesses and Grand Dukes present.

1   The Grand Duke Dmitry Pavlovitch is an officer of the Horse Guards.

Written in a conciliatory tone the letter reminded the Sovereign of the affection he had always lavished on his cousin, whose guardian he had been and who had been brought up under his care. The delicate state of his health was pleaded, and the hope expressed that His Majesty would show mercy and not leave his cousin to perish in a climate he would not be able to stand.

Two or three days passed before the response came, consisting of a few curt words:

> I wonder at your insistence, although I know that many of you are guilty likewise. A murder cannot be left unpunished.

Three days after Rasputine was killed, the Grand Duke Paul returned from the front to find his son arrested. The young man gave his father his solemn word of honour that he was not guilty of the murder, and the Grand Duke proceeded to the Palace of Tzarskoe Selo to plead his son's cause. The Emperor received him standing, avoided looking at him and seemed agitated. Amongst other things the Grand Duke asked: 'What are you doing? Where are you leading the country to? It is time for you to pull yourself together and put a stop to this fatal "petticoat-government".' The Tzar promised to release Dmitry Pavlovitch from arrest, but the next day the Grand Duke received the following letter:

> Dear Friend Paul,
>
> I regret not to be able to release Dmitry from under house-arrest until the preliminary enquiry has been concluded. I have given orders for it to be hurried on, and that Dmitry should be carefully guarded. All this is extremely hard and painful, but who is in fault that he got mixed up in this trouble? I pray to God that Dmitry should come out honest and untarnished.
>
> Yours in heart,
> NICHOLAS.

The Grand Duke Nicholas Mikhailovitch was the next member of the Imperial Family to incur disfavour. He wrote a separate letter to the Tzar, in which he was very outspoken and unsparingly accused the Empress of bringing ruin to the country and to the dynasty. His opinion was that the only solution at the moment would be a divorce. 'Remember the fate of the Emperor Paul' was his final exhortation. The Sovereign retaliated by sending Nicholas Mikhailovitch for two months to his country seat in the Government of Kherson.

The existing state of things could not last: indignation was felt in all ranks of society. The strange doings at Court had set the aristocracy and the most devoted monarchists against the Sovereigns. The people, who heard the most garbled tales, were shaken in their allegiance. Displeasure and distrust reigned in the army. The antagonistic feelings towards the monarch and his Consort were equally shared by people belonging to the Right and to the Left parties. But the Empress would not see the coming danger, and her confidence blinded the Tzar. Things were bound to come to a climax. His estrangement from his mother was a heavy trouble to Nicholas II, the more so that he forbore to show his wife the extent of his grief. The following are the telegrams the Dowager Empress received from her son at Christmas and on New Year's Day:

> December 25th. Very sad not to be together. We had a small tree for the children. Embrace you and Olga fondly.
> NICKY.

> December 31st. With you in thought. Hope with all my heart the New Year will bring you health and joy. Fond embraces for you and Olga.
> NICKY.

His wife's and children's names, as may be noticed, are not included in these festive greetings.

New Year's Day passed and the expected discharge of M. Protopopoff did not occur, although he had a hair-breadth escape, when the Prime Minister Trepoff came to the Stavka to acquaint the Sovereign with his programme for 'saving the country'. The Tzar entirely agreed with the views M. Trepoff expounded.

'But,' said the Minister in conclusion, 'for the welfare of the country, for your own happiness, I cannot consent to be at the helm while M. Protopopoff remains Minister of the Interior.'

The Tzar looked worried.

'But what am I to do with him?' he asked.

'Give him his discharge,' was the reply.

Visibly impressed, the Tzar reflected for a few moments, then, stretching out his hand to M. Trepoff, he replied: 'Let it be as you desire.'

The Prime Minister left the Stavka with a lightened heart, but he lost sight of the fact that it was the Empress Alexandra and her camarilla who were the rulers of Russia. As soon as M. Protopopoff heard of his impending dismissal, he took the necessary steps to ensure the rumour reaching Madame Vyrouboff. The necessary wires were immediately pulled, and M. Protopopoff retained his portfolio.

M. Trepoff resigned and was not pressed to take back his resignation. A member of the Upper Chamber, Prince Nicholas Golitzine, was appointed to succeed him.

No one could have been more surprised at this nomination than the Prince himself. Upright and honourable, he had never made the least pretence at being a statesman. He endeavoured to dissuade the Tzar, and frankly owned his complete incapacity for filling so responsible a post. In fact, as Prince Golitzine told a friend, if anyone else had disparaged him in a similar manner, he would have considered it his duty to knock him down. But nothing availed and he was obliged to accept.

Prince Golitzine was entirely the Empress Alexandra's choice; he had once reported to her upon some matters connected with the Red Cross. She liked his soft, unassuming ways, and thought he would be pliable to her wishes. Meanwhile M. Protopopoff was doing all he could to render himself indispensable to the Empress. At his suggestion spiritualistic sittings were arranged, at which Senator Dobrovolsky, the last Minister of Justice of the old Government, acted as medium. Rasputine's spirit was evoked and consulted. Closely examined about the guests present on that tragic night at Prince Youssoupoff's supper party, the spirit named Madame Derfelden (the step-sister of the Grand Duke Dmitry Pavlovitch) and insisted on her being arrested. That was sufficient. The next day Madame Derfelden was apprised that she was forbidden to leave her house. Her apartment was searched, all her letters taken, but nothing compromising was found. Her arrest lasted about a fortnight.

The Duma was to reopen its sessions on February 14th, o/s, 1917. It was rumoured that the reopening would be indefinitely postponed, in which case a huge strike was to be retaliation. It was likewise expected that the workmen would arrange a great demonstration before the Duma. But the reopening took place on the day fixed. The gallery and the diplomatic loge were crammed with auditors, who were doomed to disappointment as the session was extremely dull. Prince Golitzine did not make any declaration, and most of the speeches were moderate to dull, the whole interest centring on the Minister of Agriculture, M. Rittich's brilliant oration, about the supply of food for the army and the country. M. Purishkevitch appeared the next day and made an incendiary speech upbraiding the Government and accusing the Ministers.

The air was full of electricity. People foresaw that something would happen. It was feared that Rasputine's murder was not sufficient, that another tragedy would follow. The Empress continued to repulse every friend or partisan, and was steadily sowing the seeds of hatred amongst her husband's subjects, especially among the army, where the most bewildering tales were spread of her predilection for the Germans and her prejudice against the Russians. On her visits to the war hospitals, her attitude called forth the most bitter feelings of animosity; indeed, these hostile sentiments had of late been so manifest that Her Majesty ceased them, and even suspended her daily visits to Tzarskoe Selo.

When the Empress entered a ward, she nodded her head stiffly, a forbidding look set on her face. She seldom addressed anyone, but in exceptional cases her repertory of questions was invariably the same: 'At which battle were you wounded?' 'Which part of your body is hurt?' 'Does it give you much pain?' These visits were always a source of disappointment to the wounded warriors. Her coldness stabbed them more cruelly than the sharpest weapon of the enemy. Her aloofness they were convinced was the outcome of the contempt she felt for them.

On one occasion there was a painful scene. The Empress asked a soldier where he had been wounded. The soldier happened to be garrulous and entered into details of how they had put the enemy to flight.

'Which regiment was it?' queried the Tzaritza.

'The Hessians, Your Majesty.'

'The Hessians never flee before the enemy!' remarked the Empress haughtily. Then, pale with wrath, her lips compressed, she walked out of the ward, leaving everyone in consternation. The miserable soldier burst into tears, and agitation reigned in the ward. Nearly every patient had to receive a sedative to soothe him from the effects of the Empress's dramatic departure.

A disagreeable incident occurred in August, 1916, in Her Majesty's own hospital for officers. Rasputine liked to visit the hospitals and talk to the soldiers, but the officers detested him and considered his presence an intrusion. The Empress knew this, but paid no heed. On this particular day Rasputine announced his intention of visiting the officers' hospital. Some of the courtiers tried to dissuade him from his purpose, but he insisted. Madame Vyrouboff accompanied him, showing him over the different wards. But the officers decided to treat the unwelcome guest with silent contempt. Those who were convalescent went out into the garden; the others pretended to be asleep. This mute greeting incensed Rasputine and he remarked spitefully:

'They lie there as if they were dead: well, dead they soon will be!'

One of the causes of the wounded warriors' displeasure with the Empress was that Her Majesty spoke German in their presence with one of the doctors. This infraction of the established rules excited the soldiers' bitter indignation; for boards were put up in all public places, bearing the legend, 'One is requested not to speak German.'

The young Grand Duchesses, however, continued their daily visits to the different hospitals, talking gaily with the officers and soldiers; but never touching on any war episode, the topic nearest to every warrior's heart. One day, it was just before Roumania joined the Allies, one of the officers was bold enough to put some questions alluding to this event. The Grand Duchess Tatiana (her mother's favourite daughter) got very red and answered with some confusion: 'Mamma has forbidden us to speak about the war with you.' Another time, in answer to some disparaging remark about the Germans, the same Tatiana remonstrated: 'You must not forget Mamma is a German.'

During the concerts given periodically in hospitals, the Empress made a perfunctory appearance, entering without looking at anyone, and going straight to her chair in the first row. After half an hour's stay, she would retire in just the same manner, without having spoken to anyone. This treatment gave great offence and was taken for disdain. The Empress would unflinchingly render the most menial service to a wounded man, but she would never give him a smile, or gladden him with a kind word, yet it was the smile and the graciousness that would have been appreciated, and would have made the men her devoted slaves for life.

Shortly after Rasputine was killed, the day was fixed for the annual Christmas Concert in the hospital of the youngest Grand Duchess, Anastasia Nicolaïevna. The Tzar's daughters, who led a secluded existence, seeing little of the enjoyment of life, were always delighted to attend these musical evenings, and the wounded warriors appreciated their presence and liked to watch their approval of the performance. The senior sister of mercy apprised the Grand Duchess on the telephone of the day and hour, expressing the hope that she and her sisters would honour the concert with their presence. 'We shall be delighted to come,' was the ingenuous reply, 'only I must ask Mamma's permission.' A little later a tearful voice was heard through the receiver: 'Mamma says we have our own grief, and that this is not the time for pleasure.' The soldiers' gratification was sacrificed to Rasputine's memory!

Some time prior to these events, an eminent French surgeon, Dr. C., returned to Petrograd, after twenty-two months spent in German captivity. The doctor was invited to Tzarskoe Selo, and received a most gracious welcome from the Tzar. The Empress, who was present at the interview, did not depart from her usual dignified stiffness. In the course of the conversation over a cup of tea, the Tzar plied the surgeon with questions concerning the hardships endured. The Empress did not break her rigid silence.

'Tell me honestly, Doctor,' queried the Emperor, 'in which country are our prisoners treated the most rigorously? In Germany, Austria, Turkey, or Bulgaria?'

'In Germany, Sire – there can be no doubt about the question.'

'I knew beforehand what the answer would be,' scornfully remarked the Empress in English, mistakenly thinking the worthy Frenchman did not understand the language.

When the sisters of mercy returned from their inspection of the concentration camps of Russian prisoners, they were received in Tzarskoe Selo by the Empress Alexandra. She listened austerely to the melancholy report of Sister Schenkevitch, but did not seem affected at the recital of the misery endured by our captive soldiers. Madame Schenkevitch complained that the parcels sent to them from home were not delivered.

'What can be done, the distance is so great?' remarked the Empress indifferently.

'But the parcels sent from Austria and Germany reach their destination,' observed the sister deprecatingly.

'The Austrians and the Germans are likewise human beings,' was Her Majesty's sneering retort.

'Still,' rejoined the sister with spirit, 'the English and French Governments have found means to ensure the safe delivery of the things they send to their captive soldiers.'

An angry flush suffused Her Majesty's face, and, after a few unmeaning words, she closed the interview.

The sister's urgent request that a detachment of Russian nurses and a priest be sent to each concentration camp was disregarded. On leaving the Palace the sisters wept with mortification.

In Kiev these sisters of mercy received a delightful welcome from the Dowager Empress. She listened with tears in her eyes to the account of all the misery and painful scenes they had witnessed. Her Majesty was begged to use her influence so that an army chaplain and Russian sisters be sent out to relieve the spiritual and physical needs of the captives. The Empress looked very sad. 'I would do anything,' she said, 'to bring comfort to those unhappy prisoners, but I have no power; I can do nothing!'

On December 26th a strange accident happened, which gave rise to the most extravagant rumours being repeated from mouth to mouth. The Empress, after a long interval, went to her own hospital to distribute the Christmas presents. She was sitting before a table strewn with all kinds of things and neatly made up parcels. Madame Vyrouboff stood behind her. Each officer approached, took his present from Her Majesty's hand, bowed low and withdrew, making room for the next recipient.

About noon an officer entered from a side door, bowed low to the Empress, and retreating a few steps suddenly fired his revolver, hitting Madame Vyrouboff in the palm of her left hand, which was shot through. The Empress jumped up, put her arm round her wounded friend, and, thus supporting her, left the room, without even an exclamation having passed her lips. The hall filled with officers and hospital attendants; the culprit was detained, but he steadfastly denied his guilt, saying it was an accident. After some deliberation, the officer was set free, but he was sent out of Tzarskoe Selo.

Some people maintained that the culprit was no officer, but a political enemy of the Sovereign, who had put on uniform to get into her presence. His ultimate fate was the subject of various conjectures. It is difficult to believe that the attempt was an accident, but was it meant to kill the Empress, or Madame Vyrouboff? The affair was hushed up, although every inhabitant of Tzarskoe Selo heard about the incident an hour after its occurrence, and from there the news spread like wildfire all over Petrograd and Moscow. A few days subsequently the Empress received a typed letter full of the most determined threats, including a vulgar caricature of Rasputine. All typewriters thereupon were removed from the hospitals, and from that day the Empress entirely ceased her visits to the wounded. At the time, it was said that Count Fredericks insisted upon her keeping away from the Court hospitals.

About this time the Grand Duchess Victoria Feodorovna returned to Petrograd from Yassy, where she had been staying with her sister, the Queen Marie of Roumania. She asked for an audience with the Emperor, and in the course of conversation touched upon the intense unpopularity of the Empress with the army, because of the German policy she was credited with fostering. The Tzar fired up, taking up the cudgels in defence of his wife:

'What has Alix got to do with politics? She is a sister of mercy, devoted to the wounded, whom she nurses with rare self-abnegation. She receives heaps of letters, expressing heartfelt gratitude. You are quite mistaken, Alix is highly esteemed by the people.'

It is truly said that there are none so blind as those that will not see; none so deaf as those that will not hear.

The Tzar left Petrograd a few days after the reopening of the Duma, proceeding direct to Headquarters. The Tzessarevitch did not accompany him this time. His little friend, the cadet Makaroff, who had been invited to spend the Christmas vacation in Tzarskoe Selo, had sickened with measles, and it was feared that the heir might have caught the infection. The conjecture proved true; for in the course of a few days the Tzessarevitch was taken seriously ill. He was separated from his sisters, but, although all precautions were taken, the four Grand Duchesses, as well as Madame Vyrouboff, all took the disease.

The strikes commenced on February 21st, o/s. Three days later they developed into revolutionary manifestations. On the 24th the tramway communication was stopped, and from the 25th no newspapers were issued. Long processions carrying red flags filed down the principal streets clamouring for bread. The disturbances had originated because, according to a recent arrangement, bread was sold only at certain hours, and the customers were admitted into the shop by turns. Until their turn came they had to stand outside forming long queues of half-frozen creatures, waiting sometimes for over two hours in the bitter cold to get a few pounds of bread. It was quite revolting, and proved a deplorable want of organisation, for we had bread and continue to have it in abundance.

People of experience, who occasionally had glimpses behind the scenes, state that these superfluous and fatal queues, as if famine was staring us in the face, entered into the plans of MM. Stürmer, Protopopoff and Co. They meant to exasperate the people and provoke riots with loud cries for 'Peace'. This would have facilitated their course of action and enabled them to put forward *'the unanimous will of the nation'* as an imperative reason for the conclusion of a separate peace. On the February 26th the disturbances took on a decidedly political colouring.

Notwithstanding the prevailing conviction for weeks previously that ominous events were approaching, and the obvious proofs that the revolutionary preparations were being feverishly pushed on, the arrangements of resistance and defence on the part of the Government were preposterously inadequate. The Commander of the Petrograd Military circuit, General Khabaloff, a man without either daring, initiative or energy, delayed all attempts to subdue the insurgents, until they had organised their forces to threatening proportions.

For some incomprehensible reason M. Protopopoff had gained the reputation of extraordinary strength of purpose, and his skill was relied upon to suppress the insurrection; but, when the climax came, M. Protopopoff proved a broken reed. His plan consisted of spreading a network of machine-guns all over the city: on the roofs of houses, in lumber-rooms, in lofts, attics and all kinds of unthinkable places, ordering the police, when the time came, to shoot from these ambushes. But what could these shots do against the combined forces of armed workmen and soldiers, except bring down vengeance on the unfortunate police, who after all were only obeying orders.

In a few hours the police were destroyed, their chief, General

THE UPHEAVAL

Balk, arrested and the subaltern officers and policemen either massacred or imprisoned. When the regiments were ordered to march against the workmen, they refused to move and turned their rifles against their commanders, and those officers who wanted to prevent their joining the forces of the workmen. One regiment after another went over to the Revolutionists. Such regiments as the Preobrajensky's, the Semenovsky, the Ismailobsky, the Volynsky, etc., openly declared themselves as partisans of the Revolution. When he saw he had no control over his men, the commander of the Semenovsky regiment shot himself. The colonel of the Volynsky regiment was killed by his own soldiers. Some terrible tragedies were enacted in these days of violence and horror. Fortunately the Duma intervened.

The last act of the old Government had been the dissolving of the Duma on February 25th until some time in April. The members of the Duma were considered victims of the tyrannical Government, and the insurgents willingly accepted the lead of M. Rodzianko (the President) and of several other members. This prevented a great deal of bloodshed, and kept the mobs from the arrested Ministers, who otherwise would have been lynched. All those who were arrested were brought to the Tauride Palace and incarcerated in the Ministers' Pavilion, whence later on they were transferred to the Fortress of St. Peter and St. Paul.

The Tribunal on the Liteyny was burnt to the ground, many of the magistrates escaping only with their lives. The headquarters of the secret police and several police stations were burnt down; many Crown buildings and private mansions were also burnt, sacked and pillaged. The military Hotel Astoria was completely demolished; the beautiful mansion of Count Fredericks entirely destroyed, with all the lovely artistic furniture and priceless collections it contained. No palace was touched, except the one belonging to the Grand Duchess Marie Pavlovna, where the wine-cellar was broken into and rare old wines, worth about a million roubles, destroyed.

In the first flush of triumph the insurgents did a very foolish thing, which they regretted when it was too late. They opened all the prison doors and let out swarms of prisoners, instead of liberating only the political captives. It happened that the prisons contained comparatively few political delinquents, but numbers of burglars, and dangerous thieves and hooligans. Thousands of them were let loose on the town at a time when they need have

THE FALL OF THE ROMANOFFS

no fear of the police. Masquerading as soldiers, they were responsible for many acts of robbery, pillage and even murder. M. Rodzianko and M. Gutchkoff telegraphed to the Tzar, informing him of what was going on, but though the first message reached His Majesty, General Woyeikoff had thought fit to suppress the second, in spite of its urgency.

The Palace of Tzarskoe Selo during those days of anxiety was practically a hospital. The Tzessarevitch was very ill, and his temperature so high that at one time his life was in danger and the report of his death was circulated. The two elder Grand Duchesses were in bed, and the youngest, Anastasia, was sickening for measles. Only the third daughter, Marie, was well; she was the last to develop the illness, and her case was a very severe one. The position was dramatic in the extreme.

On the morning of February 25th, the Empress sent a telegram to the Tzar about the health of the children and Madame Vyrouboff, ending:

> Until now everything is quiet in town today.
>
> ALIX.

On the same day in the evening Her Majesty wired:

> Not at all well in town. To avoid false rumours, I want the old man[1] to announce officially that three of the children are taken ill with measles, and that the illness is taking its normal course.
>
> ALIX.

February 26th, in the morning, another telegram was sent containing information about the children and Madame Vyrouboff's health, concluding with the ominous words:

> Very anxious about the town.
>
> ALIX.

That same evening the following telegram, obviously in English cipher, was sent:

> Unicode vicinia vicissim continue. Vesras weak seems affore cadmites better quickly for two days, think vetulus necessary veretrum weak.

---

1 The Empress means Count Fredericks.

{80}

The words 'vicissim', 'vesras', 'vetulus' and 'veretrum' were
private code words between the ex-Empress and the ex-Emperor.
The message as clearly as it can be decoded ran: 'Vicissim (? revolutionary outbreaks) continue. Vesras (some minister or official)
wishes to see you. What date do you arrive? Better quickly for two
days. Think vetulus (? some measure to suppress the revolutionary outbreaks) or strong man necessary. Veretrum (? some minister or official) weak.

Again on February 27th, in the morning, she wired:

> The revolution has attained terrifying dimensions since
> yesterday. Aware that other parts have joined. News worse
> than ever.
>
> ALIX.

The same day two hours later:

> Concessions indispensable. Strikes continue. Great part
> of the troops gone over to the revolutionists.
>
> ALIX.

February 27th, evening:

> Lili has spent the day here and has stayed the night. No
> motors or carriages. The Tribunal is on fire.
>
> ALIX.

Till then everything had been calm enough in Tzarskoe Selo,
but on February 28th the soldiers of the garrison marched up to
the Guildhall and declared their intention of joining the revolutionary movement. A gathering was held in the Town Hall;
representatives of the nobility, the Zemstvo, delegates of officers
and likewise of the revolted garrison were present. The Commandant of the Palace, Prince Poutiatine, was present at the meeting,
and assured everyone of his sympathy with the Revolutionists
and his Liberal views. His declaration was coldly listened to, but
he was left unmolested. He returned to the Palace, which soon
afterwards was surrounded by troops, and the servants warned
that if a shot were fired the Palace would be bombarded with
cannon.

The Empress came out to them stern and collected: 'I beg you
not to shoot,' she said. 'My children are very ill. I am here only in
the capacity of their nurse.' With these words and a haughty bow
she withdrew. Her words were taken as implying surrender, and

not a shot was fired. Later in the day the Empress sent for the Grand Duke Paul, and begged him to go to the front and fetch people devoted to them. 'We must save the Empire above all things,' she said. 'The throne is in danger', but the Grand Duke declined the errand, convinced of its uselessness.

A manifesto, granting a complete Constitutional Government, with a responsible Cabinet, was in the interim being composed in the Palace of the Grand Duke. The Tzar was to sign it, and meanwhile the signatures of his brother Michael, his uncle Paul, and his cousin Cyril were affixed. This manifesto was sent to the Duma and delivered to M. Miliukoff. After this had been done the Grand Duke Paul went to the Empress. It was the 1st of March, o/s.

'Where is my husband? Is he alive?' was the greeting of Her Majesty. 'What is to be done to settle the disturbance?'

The Grand Duke informed her of the contents of the manifesto and she approved of them. Two days later the Grand Duke came to tell her of the Tzar's abdication. The Empress was in complete ignorance. His Imperial Highness showed her a printed news-sheet issued by the Revolutionary Committee, which contained the manifesto of Nicholas II's renouncement of the throne.

'I don't believe it,' exclaimed Her Majesty. 'It is all lies, news-paper inventions. I believe in God and in the army!'

But, alas! Alexandra Feodorovna was mistaken in her faith, for God had turned away and the army had betrayed them!

Chapter VII

THE TZAR ABDICATES

THE Tzar had left Headquarters on February 28th, and was hurrying to Tzarskoe Selo. He was accompanied by Count Fredericks, General Woyeikoff, Admiral Niloff, General Narishkine, Colonel Mordvinoff, and his usual attendants; but the Imperial train was prevented from reaching Tzarskoe Selo and, after being shunted on to a branch line, proceeded to Pskov. This enforced change of plans painfully impressed the Sovereign.

'What is to be done!' he asked in perplexity.

'Open the front of Minsk to the Germans,' proposed General Woyeikoff, 'and let their troops repress the Revolutionists.'

'No, I would never betray my country,' remarked the Tzar.

On the platform at Pskov, General Russky met the train. The Tzar was looking strained and worried, and the General gathered from his expression that he knew the worst.

'I have decided to grant a responsible Ministry,' were his first words after the usual greeting.

General Russky did not venture to express his opinion that the moment had passed for such measure, so he said nothing. The Emperor was expecting the visit of the President of the Duma, who had promised to come to Pskov. In the meantime the General called up M. Rodzianko on the telephone and, after hearing of the gigantic strides the Revolution was making, he telegraphed to the Grand Duke Nicholas and to all the army leaders. Each replied that in his opinion the only thing the Tzar could do at the present moment was to abdicate.

At ten o'clock the next morning General Russky presented himself before the Tzar with the report of what he had heard from M. Rodzianko, the Grand Duke Nicholas and Generals Alexeieff,

Brussiloff and Ewert. The Tzar listened with grave attention, manifesting no outward sign of emotion, except a slight twitching of the lips and the nervous pulling of his moustache.

'I am ready to renounce the throne,' he said; 'but I should like to do so in the presence of M. Rodzianko.'

When the General informed him that M. Rodzianko was not coming to Pskov, the Tzar seemed to lose his last illusion. After this he became very silent, and spent most of the day and part of the night in drawing up manifestos. The one conceding a responsible Ministry being useless, it was succeeded by two others: one in favour of the Tzessarevitch Alexis, the other in favour of his brother Michael. In the intervals the Tzar walked about the station enclosure, fearlessly leaving the train, without anyone of the suite accompanying him, walking up and down the platform in deep thought.

At ten o'clock in the evening of March 2nd His Majesty was informed that two members of the Duma, M. Gutchkoff and M. Schulguine, had arrived and wished to speak to him.

The following is an account of M. Schulguine's description of the interview:

'The necessity of the Tzar's abdication was unanimously recognised, only the putting of this resolution into execution had been delayed. M. Gutchkoff and I decided to go to Pskov, where, according to intelligence received, the Emperor had stopped. We arrived at 10 o'clock in the evening, intending to have a preliminary interview with General Russky, who was apprised of our arrival. As soon as our train stopped, however, one of the Tzar's adjutants entered our compartment, with the intimation that His Majesty was expecting us.

'I felt extremely nervous, and the fact that I should have to enter the presence of the Sovereign, unshaven, dishevelled, without the possibility of changing my clothes, made me uncomfortable, even at such an important moment. As we entered the saloon-carriage, the Emperor rose courteously and shook hands with each of us, looking perfectly calm and collected. Count Fredericks, General Russky, General Woyeikoff and a general whose name I do not know,[1] were present.

'The Tzar asked us to be seated. M. Gutchkoff began to speak, I was a silent witness of this historical scene. I must confess I was

1 Probably General Narishkine.

afraid that Gutchkoff would be harsh and pitiless in his words to the Tzar, but that was not the case. Gutchkoff spoke lengthily – well, and even eloquently. The past was not touched upon at all; he endeavoured only to point out what an abyss we had come to. He spoke without looking at the Sovereign, his right hand leaning on the table. He did not see His Majesty's face and I suppose this made it easier for him to speak to the bitter end, for he said everything that had to be said, concluding that the only solution would be for the Tzar to abdicate in favour of his little son, the Tzessarevitch Alexis, appointing the Grand Duke Michael as Regent.

'General Russky leant forward and said to me in a low voice: "That is already decided."

'When the General had said these words, the Tzar commenced to speak. His voice and manner were much calmer and more businesslike than M. Gutchkoff's, who was rather carried away by the greatness of the moment.

' "I have been thinking deeply all yesterday and today," said the Tzar, "and I have resolved to renounce the throne. Until this afternoon I was ready to abdicate in favour of my son, but I have since come to the conclusion that I have not the strength to part with him." Here the Tzar made a slight pause, adding: "I trust you understand this feeling? I have therefore decided to abdicate in favour of my brother."

'The Tzar ceased speaking, as if expecting an answer. I then remarked that this contingency took us unawares, as we had only foreseen his abdication in favour of the Tzessarevitch Alexis. I therefore asked to be permitted to have a quarter of an hour's conversation with my colleague. The Tzar readily assented to my request. After this I do not quite remember how the discussion was again resumed. We conceded the point regarding the Tzessarevitch. M. Gutchkoff said he did not feel himself called upon to interfere in paternal sentiments, and considered any pressure in that direction inadmissible.

'It seemed to me that a faint gleam of satisfaction passed over the Tzar's features. I remarked that his resolution, however contrary to the decision we had previously come to, had many points to recommend it. For, as matters stood, the unavoidable separation would create an extremely doubtful situation. The little Tzar would be continually thinking of his absent parents, and might in his heart harbour a grudge against those who had parted him from his father and mother. The question arose, could the Regent take the required oath of fidelity to the Constitution for the underaged Emperor? Such an oath would be indispensable in the present circumstances, in order to avoid the repetition of a dual responsibility. Having arrived at this understanding, the Tzar went into the next compartment to draw up the manifesto, containing his abdication. Before leaving the saloon-carriage, he turned once more to us.

' "Are you certain," he asked, "that my renunciation of the throne will suffice to appease the country?"

'Our reply was to the effect that we did not foresee any other complications.

'After some time the Tzar returned and handed us the documents, written on several sheets of block notepaper.'

The manifesto read:

'*Manifesto by the Tzar Nicholai II abdicating the throne.*

'To prevent the enslavement of our country by foreign enemies we are still fighting a War which has already been proceeding for three years, and God has now seen fit to visit a still further trial on our sorely tried Russia.

'The indication of internal unrest among the people threatens to reflect very unfavourably on the War to protect our frontiers.

'The fate of Russia, the honour of our heroic army, the happiness of our people and the whole future of our Fatherland make final victory vital to us.

'Our cruel enemy is exerting his final efforts against us and already the hour draws near when, thanks to our army in company with our Allies, the enemy will be brought to his knees.

'At this decisive moment of the fortunes of Russia, we find it our bounden duty to take such steps as will enable our people to attain to that unity of purpose and power indispensable for the earliest possible conquest of the enemy, and in accordance with the advice of the Imperial Duma we abdicate from the throne of Russia and renounce the high powers attached to the office.

'Not wishing to part with our beloved son, we pass the succession in favour of our Brother, His Highness Prince Michael Alexandrovitch, with our blessing on his accession to the throne of Russia.

'We command our Brother to govern the country in strict accordance with the wishes of the Ministers to be chosen by the people and that he swear this oath for the sake of our dearly loved Fatherland.

'We command all true sons of the Fatherland to fulfil their sacred duty, obedience to him as Tzar in this dire moment in the troubles of the people, and to help him, in company with the people's representatives, to guide the Russian Empire to victory, happiness and success.

'So may God help Russia.

'(Signed)   NIKOLAI.

'PSKOV, 15th March (2nd March), 15 hours 3 minutes, 1917.
'(Countersigned) Minister of the Imperial Court,
'General Adjutant, COUNT FREDERICKS.'

M. Schulguine was struck with the tone of nobility prevailing in the text, which, as he frankly confesses, made him blush for the tenor of the renunciation act that they had brought with them to Pskov. M. Schulguine only wished the word 'public' inserted before 'oath', but the Emperor put in 'inviolable'.

The original text of the Abdication Act was printed in type on a thick telegraph-form. The signature of Nicholas II was, as is usual in such cases, covered with varnish. Count Fredericks, with the consent of His Majesty, affixed his counter-signature. The other copy, written on the leaves of block notepaper, likewise duly signed, was given into the keeping of General Russky. Provided with this precious document, M. Gutchkoff and M. Schulguine bowed themselves out and, hurrying into their own train, returned instantly to Petrograd.

M. Schulguine adds that the rest of the interview seems to be shrouded as by a mist. How did they take their leave? Did they, or did they not, shake hands with the ex-Tzar? All seems a confused jumble, but he retained the impression that no ill-feeling was felt on either side, and that they parted cordially.

Half an hour after having signed the Abdication Act, the ex-Tzar and his suite quitted Pskov and returned to the Stavka (Headquarters). One of the details that to all appearance impressed the Tzar most painfully, was the news that the soldiers of his own bodyguard had gone over to the Revolutionists.

There are some who regard it as unfortunate that M. Gutchkoff should have been the one to go to Pskov. It was well known that no love was lost between him and the Tzar. It was the Tzar's dislike for M. Gutchkoff that resulted in his not remaining President of the Duma, and this in itself was surely sufficient reason why someone else should have been entrusted with so delicate and tragic a mission.

The plan of the Duma was to persuade the Tzar to separate from his wife for a time. This he was prepared to do, and, furthermore, arrange for the Empress and her daughters to go to England on a visit, which would have lasted until the war was over. He would likewise have met the wishes of his subjects and granted a responsible Ministry. At the last moment, however, everything seemed to happen with such bewildering suddenness that there was no time for negotiation.

M. Gutchkoff and General Russky are said to have been responsible for the idea of abdication as the way out, and there are many among the more moderate factions who do not hesitate to blame them.

March 1st is a fatal day with the Romanoff dynasty. It is impossible not to remark upon the coincidence of dates. It was on March 1st that the Imperial train was prevented from reaching the capital. This proved the hopeless turn events were taking, and, although the Abdication was signed on March 2nd, the latter was decided the day before. Thirty-six years ago on this very day the present Tzar's grandfather, Alexander II, was killed by a bomb thrown into his sledge by the revolutionist Ryssakoff.

A curious story is related in connection with this date. A couple of months before these disturbing events, the Empress Alexandra, whilst on a visit in Novgorod, went to see an old staritza, Marie Mikhailovna, who had attained the rare age of a hundred and sixteen years. For thirty years she had not left her cell in the convent. The venerable nun received Her Majesty sitting up in bed, for she was too weak to rise. The Empress bent forward and the staritza told her something that no one else heard, but which visibly impressed the Sovereign. Then she added in a louder voice: 'Don't be afraid for Leshinka (derived from Alexis), he is quite safe, no one will hurt him, but tell the Tzar to beware of the 1st of March.'

The Empress left the cell of the aged staritza a prey to intense agitation. A month later the staritza died, and the Empress sent a cross of white flowers to Novgorod to be deposited on her grave.

General Ivanoff, at the head of a considerable force, was in the meantime on his way to Petrograd to subdue the insurrection. He had reached the station of Wiritza, not far from the capital, where two members of the Duma were awaiting his arrival. The soldiers arrested the deputies, but as soon as the General heard of this, he gave orders to have them set free, and received them in his compartment. They explained to him the true position of affairs. The army at the front could not be weakened, and the forces at the General's disposal were hardly adequate for a struggle with the garrison of Petrograd.

No orders from the Tzar awaited the General in Wiritza, for His Majesty, wishing above everything to avoid useless bloodshed, had given up the idea of repressing the revolutionary movement with violence. After a few moments' reflection, General Ivanoff decided on retreat, and returned with his troops to the Stavka. Nevertheless, General Ivanoff was later arrested, and it is only due to the Procurator-General Kerensky that he was liberated, after a few days of imprisonment.

Thus ended the contest between Absolute Monarchism and Socialistic Democracy. The chain of autocratic despotism was broken.

The French have surnamed the Russian Revolution a 'smiling' one, because the inevitable bloodshed was limited, and the numbers of victims comparatively small. The acute period lasted about three days, but they were terrible days! The streets were unsafe, shooting was going on in all directions, and one lived in the perpetual fear of one's house being burnt down, or the apartment one occupied invaded, sacked and pillaged.

After the Tzar's abdication was announced, the violent agitation seemed to calm down and order was gradually restored. To secure power, the Socialists joined the Labour Party and the Council of the Soldiers' Deputies, and were steadily getting the upper hand. They protested against the Grand Duke Michael's ascending the throne. M. Rodzianko and several members of the Duma adjourned to the Grand Duke's Palace and, placing the former Tzar's manifesto before him, told him that there was a division among the people, and that the Labour Party was against his becoming the Tzar of Russia. The Grand Duke accordingly abdicated likewise and declared he would only consent to be the constitutional monarch of Russia if after the war the whole nation should elect him their Sovereign.

M. Kerensky, who was present, shook hands with the Grand

Duke, saying: 'I never thought I should ever take the hand of a member of your family with as much cordiality as I now take yours.' The army at the front was disappointed at this decision, for the Grand Duke Michael is sincerely loved and respected by the soldiers, who, during these last years, had come closely in contact with him.

The text of the Grand Duke Michael's abdication ran:

> 'A difficult task has been laid on me by the wish of my Brother abdicating the Imperial throne in my favour during the period of an unprecedented war and unrest among the people.
>
> 'In common with the whole nation my wish above all others – the happiness of Russia – I have unalterably decided that I will only accept the high powers offered me in the event of its being the wish of the whole people, who also choose with undivided voice through their representatives in the Representative Parliament, decide the style of Government and the new laws of the Russian Empire.
>
> 'Therefore with God's help I ask all Citizens to obey the Provisional Government established by the efforts of the Imperial Duma, which is endowed with unlimited powers, until that moment in which in the shortest period, on the basis of unfettered and free election by the people, is elected a House of Representatives and by their choice the form of Government to show the will of the people.
>
> '(Signed)   MICHAEL.'

After his abdication the Grand Duke Michael sent in his resignation. His example was followed by all the members of the Imperial Family.

Most of the Ministers and statesmen of the old Government were arrested; several of the former administration also shared the general fate. The Minister of the Interior, M. Protopopoff, eluded arrest for a day or two, but seeing the impossibility of escape, he gave himself up. Coming to the Duma on the evening of March 1st, he approached a student, saying: 'I am Protopopoff; I have come to put myself at the disposal of the Duma.' The student escorted the former Minister into M. Kerensky's presence. Before being put under arrest, M. Protopopoff expressed a desire to communicate something to M. Kerensky in private.

What passed between the two men is not exactly known, but it was supposed that the former delivered the plan of the capital's defence. This resulted in the positions of all the machine guns being easily discovered, and useless bloodshed saved. It was also noised about that M. Protopopoff offered to give M. Kerensky the proofs of the Empress Alexandra's treachery to Russia, and of her transactions with the German Government.

The temporary Committee of the Duma, under the Presidency of M. Rodzianko, hastened to form the new Cabinet. Prince G. E. Lwoff was appointed Prime Minister and Minister of the Interior. Prince Lwoff, though an ardent Radical, belongs to one of the oldest aristocratic families in Russia. Better known in Moscow than in Petrograd, he has always enjoyed great popularity in Liberal circles, and his reputation for true patriotism, loyalty and integrity is known all over the country. During the Russo-Japanese War Prince Lwoff spent many months in Manchuria giving help to the wounded. When the period of political disturbances in 1905–6 was at its height, Prince Lwoff took a prominent part in several Liberal organisations, and joined the Constitutional Democratic party, the members of which are called 'Cadets'. He was a member of the first Duma, is considered a man of superior intelligence and marvellous energy, and is gifted with a remarkable oratorical talent. He is an authority in all agrarian matters, and was one of the founders, as well as the President, of the Zemstvo Confederation all over Russia. Since the war the Prince resumed his activity in relieving the sufferings of the wounded, and many times visited the different fronts. He was always looked upon askance by the Government, who not so very long ago would not confirm his election as Mayor in Moscow.

Professor Miliukoff was appointed Minister of Foreign Affairs. He was a member of the third and fourth Dumas and the principal leader of the Constitutional-Democratic faction.

After taking his degree in the University of Moscow, M. Miliukoff, as assistant professor, gave lectures on Russian history at the University. He also lectured and gave lessons in provincial towns, but his work did not find favour in the eyes of the old Government, and the young professor had to give up his occupation and become a wanderer. He lectured at the Bulgarian University in Sofia on the history of the world, and was one of the publishers of *Mir Bojy* (God's World). He was sentenced to six months' imprisonment for having presided at a students' political assembly. In the year 1902, M. Miliukoff went to America, where he lectured on the Slavonic question. In London he worked in the British Museum, lectured at one of the higher colleges in Paris, visited all the Slavonic countries, and returned to Russia in 1905.

Carried away by the wave of Revolution which at that time overflowed the country, he took an active part in many Progressive confederations and became the soul of the party of National Liberty. Being one of the best orators of the 'Cadets', he frequently spoke in public of the desirable programme for reconstituting the nation on democratic lines. He was one of the publishers of *Narodnaia Svoboda* (National Liberty) and *Svoboda Naroda* (Liberty of the People), and finally became the publisher and one of the most important collaborators of the *Retch* (Speech), the organ of the 'Cadets'.

M. Miliukoff at once took a leading part in the Duma. In his speeches he relentlessly attacked the politics of the Russian Foreign Office. His speeches were always listened to with attention, and he was the first publicly to accuse the Empress of underhand transactions with Germany. M. Miliukoff speaks well, but he is not a brilliant orator; his speeches savour too much of lectures and are rather monotonous in intonation. M. Miliukoff has reached the age of sixty. His son was killed in the first year of the war.

For many years an acute political feud reigned between M. Miliukoff and M. Purishkevitch, at that time an ardent Monarchist, and one of the staunchest pillars of the Right faction. Their opinions were continually clashing, and M. Miliukoff and his pungent speeches drew from M. Purishkevitch his most sarcastic sallies. The two deputies always avoided each other in the lobbies, and the first time they shook hands for several years was on the occasion of the Duma's gathering, two days after the War-Manifesto had been proclaimed. This act was in reality a patriotic manifestation, in which the members of all parties and factions joined. M. Purishkevitch, who is rather inclined to theatrical effects, approached M. Miliukoff with outstretched hand and the words: 'At last we can meet on common ground!'

The youngest Minister of the first Cabinet was M. Kerensky, the 'good genius' of the Russian Revolution, as some people call him. He must be about thirty-six. He was Minister of Justice and Procurator-General and later Premier. He was born in Simbirsk in a middle-class family; his father was the Director of the Gymnasium in Tashkent, where his son received his preliminary education, subsequently entering the University of Petrograd. He became a barrister of some renown, especially in Socialistic circles, for he continually took upon himself the defence of political criminals.

After being elected a member of the fourth Duma, M. Kerensky joined the Labour Party. He is an impressive orator and his ardent eloquence carries one away. Being a convinced Socialist, some of his speeches defending the interests of the working classes attracted not only public attention, but aroused the ire of the Government. He was to be made legally responsible for one of his last orations, but the revolutionary tide turned the current of events. M. Kerensky is a born leader, his influence over the members of the Labour Party and those of the Council of Soldiers' Deputies has been quite wonderful. As a matter of fact, he was the only link between the first Government and the Labour Party.

The War and Marine Minister, M. Gutchkoff, who is fifty-four years of age, is a scion of a wealthy merchant family from Moscow. Gifted with remarkable brain-power and energy, his whole life forms a chain of adventures. After taking his degree at the University of Moscow, M. Gutchkoff went abroad to complete his education. When the disturbances broke out in Asia Minor, he hastened to that country intent on protecting the defenceless Armenians. In 1891, during the famine, he went to the Government of Nijni Novgorod to help as a food-distributor. Subsequently he enlisted as a volunteer in the Boer army and was wounded in the leg.

From the Transvaal he returned to Moscow, and for some time devoted himself to the municipal affairs of his native town. He became a member of the town council and was elected a director of the Moscow Discount Bank. But the insurrection in Macedonia drew him to the Balkan peninsula. He stayed for some time in Bulgaria, and afterwards travelled about India, visited Tibet, etc. When the Russo-Japanese war broke out he went to Manchuria in connection with the Russian Red Cross Society. After the retreat of the Russians from Mukden, M. Gutchkoff remained behind to look after the wounded that could not be moved, and was taken prisoner by the Japanese.

His release from captivity in 1905 coincided with the revolutionary disturbances in Russia. He lost no time in joining the Progressive movement, and, when the confederation of October

17th was founded, it elected him president. M. Gutchkoff took an active part in the electoral struggle in connection with the first Duma, but the 'Cadets' carried the day and this prevented M. Gutchkoff from being elected either to the first or second Dumas. Nevertheless he continued to fight for his party, and, for this purpose, issued a newspaper, *Goloss Mosky* (The Voice of Moscow).

In 1907 he was elected a member of the Upper Chamber, but he soon gave up his seat, being elected to the third Duma, where he considered his influence would be greater.

As a member of the Duma he assumed the leadership of the 'Octobrists', and twice he was President of the Duma, but on each occasion only for a short time. He was the President of the country's Defence Commission and presided for a long time in the Central Military Industrial Commission. He has entered closely into the technical organisation of military and naval power.

Many months before the war commenced M.Gutchkoff exposed the shortcomings and misuses of the War Ministry, and pointed an accusing finger at Colonel Miassoyedoff, boldly giving utterance to his conviction of the latter's treachery. The affair was hushed up thanks to General Soukhomlinoff's interference, and the traduced colonel sent a challenge to M. Gutchkoff, which the latter accepted. A duel was fought, but subsequent circumstances proved only too clearly how right M. Gutchkoff had been in his suspicions. Had he been listened to at the time the valiant Russian army would have been spared much disaster.

Since the war commenced, a great part of M. Gutchkoff's astonishing energy was displayed at the different fronts, in organising all kinds of establishments for giving relief to the wounded and succour to the soldiers. His vigour and activity never abated during the long and weary months of warfare.

Twelve years ago Count Witte proposed to M. Gutchkoff to enter the Cabinet he was forming as Minister of Commerce and Industry; but the offer was declined because the late M. Peter Dournovo occupied the post of Minister of the Interior, and M. Gutchkoff disapproved of his methods.

The Minister of Ways and Communications, M. Necrassoff, is still a young man: an engineer by profession. He at one time occupied the chair of statistics and bridge-constructions in the Technological College of Tomsk. M. Necrassoff has always been in favour of academic autonomy and, after the disturbances among the students in Tomsk, he was delegated by the Professorial Corporation to the Prime Minister, to report to him the real circumstances of the case and indicate the reforms necessary to secure the success of scholastic matters. The new Minister belongs to the 'Cadets', and was a member of the third and fourth Dumas, taking an active part in all matters concerning finance and communication. A few months ago he was elected the second assistant of the President of the Duma.

The Minister of Public Instruction, M. A. A. Manouiloff, the former Rector and Professor of the University in Moscow, is well known as a distinguished political economist, not only in Russia, but also abroad. His most important work is *The Lease of Land in Ireland*. Professor Manouiloff's opinion on the land-property question is, that estates should not be freehold, but that the land should belong to the country and be given in usufruct for a certain number of years.

The Minister of Agriculture, M. Shingareff, is by profession a doctor, and the author of several clever works on Sanitary Statistics. He was a member of the second, third and fourth Dumas, and was considered one of the most gifted orators among the 'Cadets'. His speeches on some of the more important proposals were most remarkable for their wisdom and depth of insight.

The Minister of Finances, M. Terestchenko, is a man of intellect, perfect breeding and great wealth. One of the most distinguished men in Kiev, he is an active member of the society of sugar-refiners in Russia, and was the President of the Military-Industrial Committee of Kiev. When a Central Committee was formed in Petrograd, M. Terestchenko became one of its members, and several of his speeches were severely critical of the existing system of providing food for the army. M. Terestchenko shared the opinion of M. Gutchkoff and M. Konovaloff, that the representatives of the working associations should have been represented on this committee's organizations.

When M. Terestchenko accepted the portfolio of Finances, one of his first acts was to insist on his predecessor, M. Bark, being let out of prison. It was indispensable for him, declared M. Terestchenko, to be initiated by M. Bark into the system hitherto employed of governing the Crown's finances, but he did not consider it dignified, as the representative of the temporary Russian Government, to receive instructions and explanations from a prisoner. M. Bark was instantly set free.

M. Konovaloff, the Minister of Commerce and Industry, acquired a thorough knowledge of his subjects as a manufacturer himself, and during the time of M. Gutchkoff's illness he directed the works of the Military-Industrial Committee. M. Konovaloff was a member of the fourth Duma and belonged to the Progressives. As an orator he made a mark by his speeches on matters concerning the press and commerce.

M. Roditcheff, who was appointed Minister of Finland's affairs, is an experienced politician. He has been a member of all the four Dumas. He is past sixty years of age.

M. Roditcheff belongs to the landed gentry of the Government of Tver, and was the initiator of the famous address to Nicholas II presented on his ascending the throne twenty-two years ago. It expressed the hope that the young Sovereign would grant a Constitutional Government to the country. By profession a barrister, M. Roditcheff was known for some years as a lawyer. His ultra-Liberal opinions occasionally got him into trouble with the old regime. M. Roditcheff is one of the most important leaders and principal orators of the 'Cadets', and always took an active part in the pre-electoral agitation of his party. He was prevented from signing the Wiborg declaration, after the dissolution of the first Duma, by being at that time in London at the International Parliamentary Congress; thus escaping the rigours of the Russian Government.

The State Controller, M. Godneff, by profession a doctor, was a member of the third and fourth Dumas. In 1905 he took an energetic part in forming the 'Confederation of the 17th of October', and since he was elected he has joined the 'Octobrists'. M. Godneff is sixty years of age. He is an honest man of sense and intellect, and is considered a clever orator.

The Procurator of the Holy Synod, M. Lwoff, was a member of the last two Dumas. He presided over the Commissions concerning matters of the Greek Orthodox Church. After taking his degree in the University of Moscow, where he studied historical philology, M. Lwoff entered the Clerical Academy as a free auditor. One of the creators of the Confederation of the 17th of October, M. Lwoff also belongs to the Octobrists.

The above-named twelve statesmen constituted the first Revolutionary Government, to which was entrusted the arduous task of wading triumphantly through the countless difficulties and complications started by the Revolution and maintained by the masses, who do not comprehend anything of politics and are intoxicated with the success they achieved and the power that has suddenly come into their hands. The struggle with the Labour Party and the Council of the Soldiers' Deputies required not only brain-power and strength of purpose, but tact and skill in gaining their confidence and making them understand what is evident to the more enlightened minds. M. Kerensky fulfilled all these requirements. The Labour Party believed in him, trusted his motives, and were willing to be led by him.

The Revolution has for the first time given the fate of the Russian people into their own hands. It is a severe test to the Russian democrats, which will prove their constructive and governing capabilities. They will have to pass a strict and rigorous examination, which will show the world if they have acquired the right to govern their country and wield power over the nation. It is a weighty responsibility they have assumed, and the nation is anxiously awaiting the proofs of their ability.

The principal task would be for the masses to join forces and centre their strength in defending their national independence. At such an historical moment, when the enemy is nearly at our door, it is not the time for discussion, for wrangling and bickering. The organs of the Democratic Socialists are much to blame. Instead of striving to unite the different parties, they publish provocative articles calculated to inspire class division. If the Russian people wish to glean the reward they have richly earned by overthrowing absolutism, which they feared was once more leading them under the yoke of Germanism, they must likewise completely destroy the spell that socialistic maniacs are casting over them. They must rally all their strength and energy to fight the German enemy to the bitter end, and prove to their Allies that an alliance with free and mighty Russia is desirable from every point of view.

Chapter VIII

RUSSIA'S EVIL GENIUS

T HE Palace of Tzarskoe Selo was filled with gloom and sickness. The Tzessarevitch, though convalescent, was still very weak: the young Grand Duchesses had also contracted the measles in a severe form and were very ill. But fate had still more terrible trials in store for the unfortunate Imperial Family.

The Government had decided to deprive the abdicated Tzar and his Consort of their liberty. Delegates from the Duma were sent to Tzarskoe Selo. On enquiry when the Empress could receive them, the Chief Marshal, Count Benckendorff (the brother of the late Russian Ambassador in London), informed them: 'Not before ten o'clock.' At the hour fixed the emissaries presented themselves at the Palace, and were ushered into one of the private reception rooms.

The Empress entered dressed in a plain black dress buttoned up to the throat. She was pale, but perfectly self-possessed. When she was apprised of her arrest, she bowed acquiescence and the only word she uttered was to ask if she might have the required medical attendance from town for her children. This was accorded her, with the stipulation, however, that one of the sentinels in charge would have to be in the room during the doctor's visit. The former Sovereign inclined her head and left the apartment. The courtiers and attendants remaining in the Palace were likewise to consider themselves under arrest, and all were forbidden to communicate with the outside world. The only one who protested was Count Apraxine, attached to the person of Her Majesty. The Count preferred to leave the Palace and go to his own home.

Two members of the Duma were sent to Mohilev to escort the

ex-Tzar to Tzarskoe Selo. After his abdication, the Dowager
Empress Marie came from Kiev to Mohilev and spent four days
with her son. When the delegates arrived, Nicholas II was in his
mother's train, where he had lunched with her. The Imperial train
was in readiness and when the ex-Tzar was informed of the
emissaries' arrival he took an affectionate leave of his mother and
went on to the platform, where the Headquarters Staff, with
General Alexeieff at their head, was assembled to see him off. It
was a pathetic moment! There was a hush as Nicholas II went up
to each one present and took a cordial leave of him. Admiral Niloff
wished to accompany his Imperial Master, but on being prevented
he went up to him, wrung his hand and kissed it; the Emperor
hastily stepped into his train.

The Dowager Empress stood at the window of her compartment, a silent witness of what was going on.

The Marshal of the Court, Prince Dolgoroukoff, General Narishkine and Colonel Mordvinoff accompanied the Tzar during this
historic journey. The members of the Duma did not see their
'prisoner'; a sense of delicacy kept them in their own compartment.

The calm of the Tzar, which did not forsake him for a moment,
was outward only. To those who knew him well it was obvious
that he was deeply moved.

He had not expected the turn events were taking, or he might
have made terms with M. Gutchkoff and M. Schulguine, who had
required only his abdication. As a matter of fact it was not the
Government that took the initiative of this extreme measure. It
was the Labour Party that insisted upon the arrest.

His Majesty conversed with his suite about the illness of his
children, the quick movements of the train, the progress of the
war, but only once did he touch upon the events of the day. When
he heard of Count Fredericks' and General Woyeikoff's arrest, he
said:

'I am sorry for them, they are not in fault.'

His manner was perfectly tranquil, as amiable and courteous
as ever; only the glance of his eyes into distance betrayed the
heavy tension of his mind.

Ten minutes before the train stopped at Tzarskoe Selo, the
Emperor took leave of all his attendants, giving each of them the
fraternal kiss, and thanking them for their devoted service. After
the Russian custom, they kissed the Emperor's shoulder; many of

them wept. The moment the train stopped, the Emperor hastily stepped out of his carriage, and, with his hand held up in salute, he silently and rapidly passed along the platform and jumped into the motor-car, followed by Prince Dolgoroukoff. Arrived at the Palace, he hastened to the Empress, who was waiting for him in their private apartment. She threw herself into his arms exclaiming:

'Forgive me! Forgive me! It is I who have brought you to this.'

But the chivalrous Tzar would not hear of this, and affectionately reassuring her replied:

'I alone am to blame.'

Since then, it is rumoured that this humble strain of mind has passed, and Alexandra Feodorovna has been heard to upbraid her husband in English for having given in too soon, and rashly signing the Abdication Act.

It was Nicholas II himself who told his little son of the change in their prospects, explaining to the boy that he was no longer the Tzar. The Tzessarevitch wept bitterly, adding: 'And I also shall never be a Tzar!'

As soon as Madame Vyrouboff was well enough, she was arrested, removed to Petrograd and incarcerated in the fortress. The arrest of the aged Count Fredericks had the effect of making the old man so ill that he had to be sent to the Evangelical Hospital. Admiral Niloff was set at liberty after a few days' arrest. General Woyeikoff is in the fortress. His attitude as a prisoner is as self-assertive as ever. On his journey to Petrograd, after his arrest, he is said to have spoken of the Imperial couple in terms that he, above all others, should not have used, giving way to accusations that he ought never to have uttered.

The newspapers, relieved of the censor's yoke, proved once more the gulf that exists between the English and the Russian Press, and the difference of mental calibre of the Russian and British journalists. The Russian Press lost all sense of proportion. It was as if a hurricane of abuse had been hurled at the Romanoffs, past and present. Myriads of writers dipped their pens in venom and gave utterance to quite useless and disgusting details, most of which were false. For instance, all the papers spoke of the Emperor's intemperate habits. This statement is flatly refuted by all those who know him intimately.

The English General W., who was a constant inmate of the Stavka, and had daily intercourse with the Sovereign, frequently sharing his repasts, declares that in all these months he never once saw the Emperor in a state of inebriation.

Nicholas II had quite ceased to drink wine since the war.

The Empress was vilified, covered with mud, and even her innocent young daughters could not be left unmolested. The poet, Lermontoff's beautiful words were forgotten:

'The Temple abandoned, is still a temple,
The fallen Idol, still a god.'

Only a few newspapers were moderate in their accounts. The following acrostic eloquently shows how people felt towards the Empress Alexandra:

Romanova	Romanoff
Alexandra	Alexandra
Svoim	by her
Povedeniem	conduct
Unitchtojila	destroyed
Tron	the Throne
Imperatora	of the Emperor
Nicolaia	Nicholas

The capitals of this sentence form the word 'Rasputin'.

Various interviews were published. Some of the members of the Imperial Family showed a deplorable lack of taste in imparting all kinds of superfluous confidences to promiscuous reporters. Others there were who, formerly, would never have dared to utter a word of admonition to the Tzar and who now publicly declared how often they had warned and advised him, but alas! always in vain!

The cup of calumny, misrepresentation and insolence was filled to overflowing. The traditional donkey kicks were not wanting either. People seemed to forget that the actual faults and errors were quite sufficient, that it was no use adding imaginary ones.

The chief responsibility of the dynasty's downfall lies at the door of the Empress Alexandra. It is always a fatal sign when people cease to look up to their Sovereign, but, in her extravagances with Rasputine, Her Majesty overstepped the limit. Her tactless attitude towards the Russians, her surprising fancies, and, above all, her strange behaviour since the war, caused the gradual decline of the Tzar's popularity, and put an end to the country's former veneration for the throne and the Sovereigns and, finally, caused the Revolution. The nation repudiated the Tzaritza, because the Tzar would not do so. The Emperor was the victim of his loyalty to his wife.

Admiral Niloff relates the following story which intensifies the responsibility of the Empress Alexandra, and clearly designates her as the chief culprit who caused the Revolution and the overthrow of the Tzar.

Nicholas II had quite decided to grant to the country a full Constitution with a responsible Ministry. The manifesto was composed by himself, and it was to be given out on his name-day, December 6th (19th), 1916. Up to the last moment the Empress Alexandra was kept in ignorance of this resolution, but somehow, probably through General Woyeikoff, she was apprised of what was going on. Entering her husband's study, and finding the manuscript manifesto on his table, she took it up and tore it to pieces, and succeeded in prevailing upon the Tzar to give up his intention.

If the Emperor had not listened to her and had maintained his decision, the Revolution would have been averted by one stroke of the pen!

The Russian people accuse the Empress of bringing ill-luck to everyone who comes near her. Since her arrival in Russia, she has been fatal to her family, the Nation, the Court, and the monarchy. The following facts prove her fatality:

At the time of her birth, the accident occurred to her brother, who was killed by a fall from a window.

As a small child she caused the death of her mother by infecting her with diphtheria.

She came to Russia when death was brooding over the Romanoffs.

Her betrothal was solemnised on the threshold of death.

The Coronation festivals in Moscow were marred by the terrible catastrophe of Hodynka.

The precipitate peace with Japan was concluded under her pressure.

The Russian retreat from East Prussia in the autumn of 1914 is attributed by the people to her influence.

The ikons the Empress sent to the garrisons of Kovno and Ivangorod arrived on the day preceding their surrender, a precursor of evil.

And last, but not least, her occult occupations with Philippe,

Papus and lately with Rasputine, which were interpreted by the people as sorcery and witchcraft.

Politicians accuse the Empress of persistently interfering in affairs of State, and using her influence with the Tzar to promote her own plans to the detriment of the country.

This story is a sample of her continual interference in matters that she should have left alone.

One of the shadiest individuals, M. Manassevitch-Manouiloff, who for many years managed to play an obscure but influential part in the spheres of the secret police, and a somewhat important position in the world of journalism (he was a member of the staff of the *Novoe Vremia*, and the *Vetdhernee Vremia*), about a year ago, whilst attached to the service of M. Manassevitch-Manouiloff, was accused of blackmailing one of the banks in Moscow, and was arrested. Owing to the protection of Stürmer, Rasputine and *tutti quanti*, he was set at liberty on bail, but his trial was not hurried on, and it was whispered that this was done by the desire of high spheres. The Minister of Justice, Makaroff (the predecessor of Dobrowolsky – both are incarcerated in the fortress) had to resign because he fixed the day of the trial, which was again put off on some slight plea.

After the Revolution the proofs were found of the pressure the Empress had brought to bear on the Tzar to prevent this trial. The following telegrams were sent by Alexandra Feodorovna to the Emperor at Headquarters:

December 14th, 1916.

> I beg you to stop immediately, by wire, the trial of Manouiloff. It commences at 11 o'clock in the morning and will be pitiless. I wrote to you and to General Batiouschine concerning this circumstance, and asked you point-blank to stop the affair. This is absolutely necessary to your happiness.

> ALIX.

December 15th, 1916.

> Thanks from the depths of my heart for your dear letter. Forgive Sana.[1] I am so thankful that my telegram of yesterday influenced your noble order.

> ALIX.

1 Sana is Madame Vyrouboff's younger sister, Mrs. Pistohlcorse.

After Rasputine's murder the trial did take place, and Manas-sevitch-Manouiloff was sentenced to several years' imprisonment. The putting off of the first trial caused a great deal of talk, displeasure and criticism.

The Empress never sympathised with France, and all her endeavours were directed to sever the Franco-Russian Alliance and bring about the renewal of the Three Emperors' Alliance, which would have been a serious rebuff for France. If the war had not intervened, this Alliance of the Emperors would have been ratified and announced to the world! M. Clemenceau warned the French Government of the Russian Empress's intrigues against France.

That was before the war; since then her conduct has been such as to throw the gravest doubts upon her loyalty to the country her husband reigned over. From the day of the first battle between the Russians and Germans, the Russian army was imbued with the conviction of the Empress's intrigues with Berlin, and there are officers who maintain that the proofs exist showing that all treacherous plans against Russia are traceable to Tzarskoe Selo. It seems hard to realise that a mother could range herself against her own son, and one so ardently beloved as the Tzessarevitch, and it remains to be proved whether or no Alexandra Feodorovna was aware of the machinations of some of her courtiers. It is affirmed on convincing authority that, if the Revolution had not frustrated the Empress's plans, peace would have been concluded with Germany in a very short while, to the evident detriment of the country and that of our Allies.

The Empress is likewise accused of giving the Tzar philtres, which Rasputine procured for her, to weaken his brain and blunt his memory. This accusation, savouring rather of the Middle Ages, is not solely due to the fertile imagination of the people, but is based on accusations made by several members of the Imperial Family and some of the generals of the Tzar's entourage.

The Emperor is branded with the reproach of being culpably weak, of letting his wife rule him and his Government, of considering her wishes before the country's well-being. In his wife's presence the Sovereign had no opinion of his own.

She took the lead in any discussion or argument, and contrived to make him waver in his most firmly conceived resolutions. Her will was his law. The most heinous imputation against the Emperor is the protection he accorded to General Soukhomlinoff, who is accused of being a traitor to his country, by virtue of his readiness to fall in with Alexandra Feodorovna's wishes concerning a separate peace, which would have brought shame to the country and have alienated us for ever from our Allies.

Was it guilt on the part of the Sovereigns or only error?

Public opinion inclines to the belief that it was error on the Tzar's part, but guilt on the Empress's! Time will show the correctness of these impressions.

The first member of the Imperial Family to recognise the new state of things was the Grand Duke Cyril. He marched up to the Duma at the head of the Guards' equipage, and had himself announced to M. Rodzianko. A few hours later the President of the Duma and several of the members adjourned to the Grand Duke's palace, and were received by him on the threshold of his abode with Royal honours. The Grand Duke Cyril was likewise the first to hoist the red flag over his palace. This caused some wonder among the upper classes, for, except the Imperial Standard, Russia has her national three-coloured flag, which would seem more suitable on palaces and state buildings than the scarlet emblem of Revolution.

After the Tzar's abdication, the Government decided to recall the Grand Duke Nicholas from the Caucasus and reinstate him as the supreme Commander-in-Chief. In fact the deed was done, and the Grand Duke was on his way to the Stavka, when the Committee of the Workmen's Delegates and the Council of the Soldiers' Deputies, egged on by the socialists, protested against the measure. If the truth were known, it was the fear of the Grand Duke's popularity with the army, and that it might impel them to proclaim him Tzar of Russia, after having been led by him to victory, that caused the Labour Party to insist on the revocation of his appointment. M. Kerensky upheld them, threatening not to remain in the Cabinet if the Grand Duke took the chief command. The Government was in a disagreeable plight, but it was overruled by M. Kerensky and the Social Democrats who unfortunately are getting the upper hand. It was somewhat incoherently explained that the Grand Duke's nomination was due to a misunderstanding, and had been made by the old Government. The Grand Duke was requested to give up his vice-regal position in the Caucasus, and has since retired into private life on his estates in the Crimea.

A letter of the Grand Duchess Marie Pavlovna to her son Boris, which General Tchebykine, one of the most loyal and devoted monarchists, was to take to the Grand Duke in person, caused the arrest of the Grand Duchess, her son Boris, General Tchebykine, and of several officers in attendance upon the Grand Duke Boris.

The tenor of the letter was to the effect that the hopes of the Romanoffs centred henceforth in the Grand Duke Nicholas and that it would be wise, if he became the Commander-in-Chief, to predispose the army in favour of his ascending the throne later.

A short while before the disturbances commenced, the Grand Duchess Marie Pavlovna had left Petrograd for the Caucasus. For the present she remains there, undergoing her arrest in her villa in Kislovodsk. The Grand Duke Boris is at his palace in Tzarskoe Selo.

The Government's idea was to embark Nicholas II and his family on one of the Imperial yachts and convey him under the escort of M. Kerensky to England, where the ex-Tzar would have been safe, but the Social Democrats once more interfered, stating that the Sovereigns knew too many military and state secrets and, whilst the war lasts, this would be detrimental to Russia. They also insist on knowing the amount of guilt attached to each, and that will only be revealed in the course of the forthcoming trials of the Ministers.

Military men state that the reason for General Brussiloff's successful Galician campaign a year ago was due entirely to the fact of the date being carefully concealed from the Empress. The General parried her enquiries by answering that his army was not in readiness, and he could not think of setting forth before the end of June, whereas the attack commenced in the middle of May.

In the commencement of the year 1916, when for some reason General Russky had been temporarily set aside, the Grand Duchess Marie Pavlovna junior, who was working as a sister of mercy in the hospital of Pskov, wrote to her father, the Grand Duke Paul, requesting him to speak to the Tzar and tell him the grave error he was making in removing General Russky, for the army trusted him and was displeased at his removal. General Russky had often been victorious in the battlefield, and could lead them once more to victory. Those were the professed sentiments of the soldiers, which had reached the ears of the young Grand Duchess. Her father wrote a letter to the Tzar, apprising him of these facts, and including his daughter's letter from Pskov. The

Grand Duke's letter was intercepted by the Empress, and it was she who sent an answer to this appeal in the following terms:

> I have read your letter and am glad it did not reach Nicolai Alexandrovitch. Let the old man have a rest. We shall call him back when necessary.
>
> ALEXANDRA.

Nothing, not even the appointment or withdrawal of a general in the army, happened without the connivance of the Empress Alexandra.

Amongst the arrested statesmen of the old Government who are now incarcerated in the Fortress of St. Peter and St. Paul, are the former Minister of the Interior, M. Maklakoff. He was badly maltreated by the crowd, and was in such a state of desperation when brought to the Duma that he would have committed suicide had a revolver been at hand. There are the Minister of Commerce and Industry, Prince Shahovskoy, the War Minister, General Beliaeff, Admiral Kartzeff (he lost his reason and had to be sent to an asylum). The former Prime Minister, M. Goremykine, was set free after a two weeks' arrest on account of his venerable age.

Other prisoners are a member of the Upper Chamber, Stechinsky, Senator Krasheninnikoff (a former judge, known for the severity of his sentences in political cases), Senator Beletzky (the Commandant of the Palace in Tzarskoe Selo), Prince Poutiatine (his assistant), Colonel Welitchkovsky, General Grünwald, Senator Dobrocolsky, General Habaloff, the Police Prefect, General Balk, Senator Klimovitch, to name only a few.

The Prime Minister, Prince Golitzine, was arrested for only a few days. In the provinces there were likewise many arrests, and the excesses committed were even greater than in Petrograd. The Governor of Tver, M. Nicholas Bünting, was killed, and the Governor of Vologda, M. Crighton, had his leg broken, and his wife's hair was pulled out in handfuls. In Helsingfors and in Cronstadt the excesses amongst the sailors were terrible, but one knows nothing definite of what happened there.

The incarcerated statesmen of the former Government are accused by the socialists of a deeply laid plan to widen the frontiers of Russia. Because of this alleged Imperialistic avidity, the war is continued and the blood of the Russian people is being shed in torrents, for reasons best known to themselves. It suits the policy of the socialists to forget that the war was not desired by the Russian Government, and the 'Right' was extremely averse to a conflict with Germany.

As a matter of fact this is what is alleged to have occurred. Long before the war commenced, General Soukhomlinoff, incited by personal motives of greed, exerted his energy to weaken the country. On the chance of a possible armed strife with Germany, he took care to facilitate the enemy's ingress by dismantling and blowing up several forts on the Russian side of the Prussian frontier, which had they existed would have strengthened the defence of the Russian positions. The western forts of Warsaw were likewise destroyed and the work of destruction entrusted to a German firm, thus forging another link in Soukhomlinoff's accusations, that of paying millions of Russian money into German hands to accomplish this nefarious design.

Soukhomlinoff kept two German spies in his close vicinity, Miassoyedoff, the Prussian, and Altschiller, the Austrian agent. Both of them had free access to the War Office, and to the Minister's private study. No secrets were withheld from them, and it is said the General's private banking account increased in the same measure as the intimacy grew.

The interior roots of the country were steadily sapped by a systematic undermining of one of the greatest moral mainsprings of the Government – the dispensation of justice. The independent judges were removed, criminal trials, based on forgeries, perjury and provocation, were artificially created; no respect was shown to the existing laws. The former Minister of Justice is accused of having wilfully tampered with the *corpus delicti* of the following trials: the Wyborg declaration (after the dissolution of the first Duma), the indictment of the Armenian patriots, two accusations of the socialistic members of the former Duma, the supposed attempt on Count Witte's life, the murders of Tollos, Henzenstein and Karavaeff, as well as according full pardon to false witnesses, burglars and thieves, if they wore on their sleeve the badge of the 'Russian People's Alliance'. The members of this association were considered by the former Government as pillars of the country, and their staunch allegiance to the monarchy rendered them unimpeachable in all other respects.

Those responsible for all this looked with a jaundiced eye on the progressive friendship between Russia and France. All their endeavours contributed to detach Russia from the alliance with France, for they considered that an alliance with a republican government could only bring harm to the monarchical principle. All manifestation of freedom of thought were suppressed during the war, and strenuous efforts were made to direct public opinion in favour of a separate peace.

M. Stürmer was always considered a staunch monarchist. A German by birth, he is accused (but it remains to be proved) of having remained in the Kaiser's pay, impeding the country's defence-organisation, directing his tactics to incite public opinion against the Allies, hoping by adhering to this policy to attain the desired goal – a separate peace with his fatherland.

The German Kaiser was the idol of the fanatical partisans of monarchism; they saw in him the surest support of absolute power. In their prejudiced eye war with Germany seemed a calamity, threatening disaster to the dynasty and to the order of things in this country. This was the keynote of their policy, and explains their equivocal attitude during the war. Needless to add that these ultra-monarchists formed the great minority of the party, for most of the 'Rights' were glad of the opportunity to shake off the German yoke, and welcome the hope of a future close alliance and political friendship with our splendid Allies.

The members of the Right were likewise displeased with Nicholas II. They harboured resentment against the monarch for not giving them the moral support to which they considered themselves entitled because of their staunch partisanship of royalty and loyalty. The Monarchists blame Nicholas II for having given his consent in 1905 to the convocation of the State Duma, which is quite alien to the Russian national spirit, departing from the principle that every monarch belonging to a dynasty elected by the nation (like the Romanoffs) is the temporary holder of power, which he is obliged to transmit to his lawful heir in the same form and extent as it was given over to him by his ancestors. The Monarchists affirm that the autocratic Tzar, Nicholas II, in creating the semblance of a Constitution, and having thereby for ever limited the Imperial autocratic power, revoked the only organic law of the country, which he had not the right to modify unless the will of the nation distinctly expressed it.

In 1613 a deputation consisting of representatives of all classes of the Russian nation convoked the Boyar Michael Romanoff to Moscow, where he was invested with the unlimited autocratic power of Russia's ruler. Thus was the will of the nation which Michael Romanoff accepted in the presence of its representatives, taking the solemn oath, for himself and his descendants, to be the autocratic Tzar of All Russia. Consequently the indications are manifest of a treaty morally binding to both sides.

If, say the Monarchists, in the year 1905 the Sovereign commenced to have doubts as to the desirability of effecting a change in the form of government, His Majesty ought to have followed the old Russian custom bequeathed to the country by history and tradition; that is, he should have convoked a 'Zemski Sobor' in Moscow, in the same manner as it was done in olden times, consisting of deputies from the people, nobility, merchants, clergy and peasants. Only from such a Zemski Sobor in Moscow – the heart of Russia – could it be competent to bring about a change in the form of government, if a change was found advisable.

The Monarchists further affirm that a true national 'Zemski Sobor', composed for the most part of representatives of the heart of Russia, which up to this have only been slightly contaminated with revolutionary and socialistic propaganda, would have been certain to pronounce itself in favour of the periodical convocation of a Zemski Sobor, as a help to the Sovereign's rule. The Sobor would have discussed new laws and given the Tzar support and true information of all events and happenings amongst people of the vast Empire of Russia. The Zemski Sobor, however, would have remained exclusively deliberative, leaving the autocracy of the Russian Tzars unmolested.

The Duma, consisting of representatives of unstable groups of the populations of towns and provincial 'Zemskos' (Country Courts), is not considered by the Monarchists adequate to represent the country. They point out, not without foundation, that the four Dumas, during a decade, have not given the country a single statesman, and the essays which have since been made to give Ministerial nominations to members of the Duma (Khvostoff and Protopopoff) or even to form a Cabinet from members of the Duma have not been successful.

Many of the atrocities of the Revolution have remained ignored, for there were no newspapers in those days, and the Social Democratic Party forbade the mention of names of people who had been faithful to the old Government and had shown fight. Some were killed without any aggression on their part. General Count Stackelberg was killed under the following circumstances. He and his wife (Countess Stackelberg is by birth a Countess Schouvaloff) were at home in their house on the Millionnaia. Several soldiers, accompanied by a gaping crowd, came to fetch and escort the Count to the Army and Navy Assembly to take his oath under the new Government.

In his wife's presence, General Count Stackelberg gave up his revolver and consenting to follow his escort left the room and went out into the hall, which was full of people. A stray shot was suddenly fired into the ceiling, at the very moment of the Count's appearance. Was it an accidental shot, or was it fired with malevolent intention? This remains shrouded in mystery, but the shot produced a panic.

An awful scene of confusion ensued, amidst which the Count and an old retainer were killed, the house pillaged and ransacked, the cellar broken into, and the most atrocious orgy followed. The Countess fled on foot, with barely a wrap round her shoulders, and took refuge with friends. When she returned the next morning to her house, the body of her husband had vanished and could not be found for several days.

Countess Kleinmichel was amongst the arrested. She spent several days in the Duma, though later she returned to her own house, where for many days she was considered under arrest. For long years past the Countess had the reputation of being a political agent of Germany. She is a clever, highly cultured woman, a skilful leader of Society, and her conversation is extremely fascinating. She can be charming when it is necessary, sweet as honey, but she can also be just the reverse on occasion. The Countess is enormously rich, and this is at the root of the suspicion she inspires.

When the former Minister, M. Plehve, was the Director of the Police Department, the Countess, who at that period was not the fashionable leader she has since developed into, was, so it was said, under the surveillance of the police. Since that far-removed time, the fortunes of the Countess have undergone a wonderful change: from a social nobody she blossomed into the first hostess of Petrograd. Her house is one of the most luxurious in Petrograd, her receptions as brilliant as they are frequent. Her salon was the rendezvous of foreign diplomats and Russian statesmen, and her intimacy with Count and Countess Pourtales, Count and Countess Dohna-Schlobitten was never concealed.

A few days after the war commenced, the rumour spread all over the town that a search had been made in Countess Kleinmichel's house, evidence of her guilt found, and the Countess taken to prison; some of the more gruesome scandalmongers averred even that she had been hanged. All these tales were false, but the Countess, whose Germanophile proclivities were known, remained henceforth the object of suspicion and was one of the first to be arrested.

On February 28th the Countess had a small dinner party. Prince and Princess Kourakine, Countess Kotzebue-Pilar von Pilchau and her daughter, Baron and Baroness Schilling and some other guests were invited. The dinner commenced cheerfully enough, the conversation naturally centring on the threatening development of political events. After the fish had been served, a somewhat lengthy pause ensued. Suddenly a scared footman entered, saying that the kitchen was full of soldiers come to search the house; they were meanwhile eating the food prepared for the guests, and there was nothing left to serve.

The impression of this announcement was sensational. A panic took hold of everyone present. There was a general 'sauve qui peut', even the hostess quitting her house. For some days she took refuge in the Chinese Legation and had a board put up in the hall of her house with the following inscription printed in large letters: 'The Countess Kleinmichel has been arrested and taken to the Duma.' But she could not hide for ever; stratagems did not help, and she was finally arrested.

Some of the newspapers have declared that the Countess was an intimate friend of Alexandra Feodorovna, but that is untrue. I do not believe the Empress ever saw her to speak to, and the Countess, whose tongue is sharp and mordant, always alluded to the Empress and the goings-on at Court in an extremely mocking way. It was only during the last two or three seasons preceding the war that some of the members of the Imperial Family have occasionally accepted Countess Kleinmichel's invitations, without ever having been intimate with her.

Madame Narishkine, née Countess Toll, was arrested likewise, but after a conversation with M. Kerensky, she was set at liberty.

The effect of her husband's arrest, and the anxiety his fate inspired, had a terrible result on Madame Stürmer. She was in a desperate plight, for her servants had left her, in consequence of the repeated searches that had been made of the apartment and among her husband's things. She remained alone, uncared for and unattended, in a large unheated apartment. The solitude and the helplessness got on her nerves; but the last straw was a letter in which some officious friend informed her that her husband was certain to be sentenced to fifteen years' penal servitude. That was too much to bear, and she cut her throat with her husband's razor. Fortunately her groans were heard and she was taken to the hospital in time to have her life saved although her head for ever will remain crooked, for she cut several tendons and sinews. Her one care is that her husband should not be informed of this occurence.

Without having the least sympathy for M. Stürmer, one cannot help feeling deeply sorry for his unhappy wife. The friends of her prosperous days abandoned her, and even the many people who owe their success in life entirely to her husband never thought it necessary, at this terrible crisis of her life, to go to her and sustain her by their moral support and sympathy. It was with some difficulty, that a sister of mercy was found willing to stay with Madame Stürmer and nurse her. *Sic transit gloria mundi!*

General Riemann and his wife were arrested on their way to Norway. Twelve years ago General Riemann was a colonel in the Semenovsky Regiment and the right hand of General Mine.[1] Their activity in subduing the riots of 1905–6 is still vindictively remembered.

The sudden political development of the workmen's strikes frightened many people into taking effective precautionary measures. The famous ballet-dancer Madame Kshessinsky was among the number. The gifted artiste had for many years been the friend of the Grand Duke Serge Mikhailovitch, and she feared, not without reason, that her house might become the scene of riot and excess. She therefore chose to disappear, and effected her eclipse in the most skilful manner. Without any preliminary preparation, she and her son, a boy of fourteen, his tutor and the dancer Vladimiroff, left the house directly after dinner, ostensibly for a constitutional. Madame Kshessinsky had no luggage except a small handbag. She told the unsuspecting servants that they would be back for tea and ordered the samovar for 10 o'clock. But the servants waited in vain, and when their mistress did not return they went to the Commissariat (which takes the place of the former police-station) and reported her disappearance.

When calm was more or less restored, Madame Kshessinsky

1 General Mine was killed in Peterhof about a year or two subsequently by a young woman, Tchesnokova.

came to the Commissariat and declared that the rumour of her disappearance was an erroneous one, that she had only gone to Finland for a change of air, and had spent a few days in one of the well-known health-resorts. During her absence her house had been broken into by evil-doers, who had robbed her of everything they could lay hands on, and had ruined the rest. Madame Kshessinsky estimated her loss at the sum of half a million of roubles.

The house is for the present uninhabitable, with its broken windows and doors. It became the refuge of the notorious Lenine. From the balcony of the house he lectured the populace, expounding the most anarchical theories, encouraging the people to murder and pillage, inciting their suspicion of the new Government, and holding up the French revolution of 1793 as a model to be followed.

This Lenine[1] has quite recently come to Russia from Switzerland, where he emigrated to. The astonishing fact is that he chose to return to Russia *through Germany*. The German authorities welcomed his passage with alacrity and gave him every facility to reach Russia safely. This makes wise people suspicious. This dangerous firebrand was more dangerous than ever at the moment when the passions had not abated and were easily brought to boiling point: was he not an emissary of Germany intent on provoking fresh disturbances and producing more bloodshed? M. Lenine was actively engaged in forming a new party, which he called 'the party of the Communists.'

The downfall of the monarchy has caused the upheaval of everything all over the country. The very basis of social life is destroyed; the former system and the old organisations exist no longer. Russia is in an embryo condition, and the question is, what direction will the new development take, where are the country and its Government being led to? The Revolution and its consequences were brought on by the masses, but the flame was lit from above. The Duma was the first to lift the banner of revolution, but the way was paved for them in still higher spheres, and the shot that killed Rasputine on December 17th, 1916, was the first shot fired into the monarchy of Russia.

1 Some people who know all about Lenine's antecedents state that *Lenine* is a pseudonym; that his real patronymic is von Lehmann, and that he is a German.

Chapter IX

THE BLOOD OF THE ROMANOFFS

DELIVERED of the Romanoff dynasty, people are inclined
to look upon the past with scepticism, and the question
arises involuntarily:

'What right has the Imperial Family of usurping the Russian
name of Romanoff, when their origin is clearly German, and not
a drop of the Romanoff blood flows in their veins?'

The last scion of the Romanoff dynasty, the Empress Elisabeth
Petrovna, died in 1760, and even she was not flawless, for she was
Peter the Great's illegitimate daughter, born out of wedlock and
acknowledged after the Tzar's marriage with Catherine Scavronsky, the child's mother, known eventually as Catherine I.

Catherine Scavronsky was a young woman of obscure origin
who married a Swedish soldier. During the war between Russia
and Sweden, after the surrender of Marienburg (1702), she was
taken captive. Prince Menshikoff saw her and was enraptured
with her beauty, but when he saw the infatuation of his Imperial
master, he gave her up to the Tzar, and she lived with him for
many years, followed him in all his campaigns, and bore him
several children. Eventually Peter the Great married her and had
her crowned in Moscow in 1724.

It was Catherine Scavronsky who, in 1711, saved the Tzar from
the captivity he was held in by the Turks, on the shores of the
river Pruth. She was so skilful in her dealings with the enemy
that, by giving up all the jewels she possessed, she succeeded in
driving a bargain with the Great Vizir and bribed him to retreat.

Peter I never forgot that he owed his safety and the escape from a distressing position to the firm stand she took and the clever way she managed the affair. It was in her honour, and to commemorate this valiant feat, that the Tzar founded in 1714 the Order of St. Catherine for ladies.

When the Empress Elisabeth was getting on in years, she sent for the son of her eldest sister, the Grand Duchess Anna Petrovna, married to the Duke Frederic of Holstein Gothorp, intent on making him the heir to the throne. The young Duke Peter of Holstein Gothorp came over to the capital. In the course of time he became a member of the Greek Orthodox Church, and was henceforth known as the Grand Duke Peter Fedorovitch. The future Tzar appreciated the prospect of reigning in Russia, but he never concealed his contempt for his future subjects and his devotion to Germany. The Grand Duke was married to Princess Sophia Dorothea of Anhalt-Zerbst, who, on being received into the bosom of the Greek Church, adopted the name of Catherine, subsequently known as Catherine II, the Northern Semiramis. There was only one son from this marriage, the future Emperor Paul, the ancestor of the dynasty of future Russian Emperors.

From a physiological point of view the few drops of Romanoff blood that flowed in the veins of the Emperor Paul were inherited from his paternal grandmother. But Russian historians state that Paul was not his father's son. Some regard him as the son of Prince Saltykoff, others of Prince Poniatovsky. There is still another version of the infant's birth, which, however, has never been proved by facts. It is that the Grand Duchess Catherine gave birth to a still-born daughter. The Empress Elisabeth, in the hereditary interests of the throne, had it secretly removed and replaced by a healthy boy. This would explain the reason why the Empress Elisabeth surrounded the first days of her grand-nephew's birth with such mystery, and the dislike, amounting to aversion, that his mother felt for him.

In the reign of Alexander I, a Finnish peasant family was designated as that from which the future Emperor Paul was taken and brought into the Palace. The father of this Finnish family was the living image of the late Tzar, and was positive in his belief that the Tzar had been his brother. The face of Paul I was extremely plain-featured and coarse; he had absolutely nothing in common, either with the Empress Catherine, Saltykoff, or Poniatovsky. But, even admitting this story to be a legend, the

Emperor in that case remained a Holstein Gothorp and not a Romanoff.

As a matter of fact the origin of Paul I was never definitely established. But be he Holstein Gothorp, Saltykoff, Poniatovsky, or even an obscure Finn, he was the stock from which descended the dynasty of Russian Emperors who have ruled Russia for one hundred and sixteen years. Modern historians incline to draw a parallel between the reigns of Paul I and Nicholas II. Paul I was the first monarch of the so-called Romanoff lineage to fall; Nicholas II was the last Tzar of the overthrown dynasty. Both Sovereigns fell with startling celerity, only the circumstances of the last Emperor were more fortunate, for he was surrounded by human beings of the cultured twentieth century, with moderated feelings, far removed from the inclination to put into action the famous gold snuff-box of Nicholas Zouboff, or the scarf of Prince Jashvill.

M. Burtzeff, in his book of historical references, reverts to the murder of the Emperor Paul as the starting-point of Russia's emancipation movement, which lasted over a century, ending in the final overthrow of the monarchy. The partisans of independent liberty therefore deny that the Russian Revolution is newly fledged, but consider that it has entered upon its hundred and seventeenth year. One hundred and sixteen years, individually taken, is a long span of time, but in the life of a nation the term is inconsiderable. That is why, like the rest of Russia's progressive developments, her revolution must likewise be regarded as immature. In looking back to a hundred years ago, one can only marvel at the rapid emancipation of mind, and at the awakened political conciousness. History repeats itself occasionally, and a certain analogy between the Courts of the two dethroned Sovereigns must be acknowledged. The Court of the Emperor Paul was eminently German. His Consort, a Princess of Würtemberg by birth, the Empress Marie, was thoroughly imbued with German views, tastes and proclivities. She was surrounded by German courtiers, and all her endeavours were directed to further German interests, political as well as commercial. Intrigues against France and Great Britain were going on the whole time, and found the strongest support in the Empress Marie Feodorovna. Petticoat government was the order of the day at the Court of Paul as it was at the Court of Nicholas, with the difference that in the present instance the Empress Alexandra led the show, whilst at Paul's Court there was a multitude of petticoats.

The principal influence of that bygone time belonged to Her Majesty's lady-in-waiting, Mlle. Nelidoff. Her power was strengthened because her Imperial mistress sided with her, and both ladies formed an alliance to support each other. When Mlle. Nelidoff was supplanted by Mlle. Lopoukhine (married subsequently to Prince Gagarine), the Empress manifested her displeasure by a protracted period of sulks.

Here ends the similarity, for, although the writers of the present hour try to establish a moral likeness between the two Sovereigns, their arguments cannot stand the test of logic and truth, and are inspired by principles of personal hostility: Paul's nature was a warped and fantastical one, he was liable to ungovernable fits of passion, bordering on insanity, with rare flashes of kindness and generosity. He was jealous and envious, which sentiments he nurtured towards his mother, the Empress Catherine II, and his heir the Tzessarevitch Alexander. Even his wife's popularity caused him displeasure.

Paul was coarse and brutal, a bad husband and an indifferent father; whereas Nicholas has a chivalrous nature – he is kind, generous and gentle-tempered. He has not a spark of envy or jealousy in his disposition, and his devotion to his wife, his mother and his children is beyond all doubt. The only feature the two monarchs have in common is the suspiciousness inherent to both. The want of mental stamina and strength of will were the Tzar Nicholas's undoing. Paul succumbed to the revolting vagaries of an undisciplined nature, which manifested itself in irresponsible acts of wanton cruelty.

The Emperor Paul was strangled by Count Pahlen when he was on the verge of discarding his wife and imprisoning the Tzessarevitch Alexander, in whom he constantly saw a dangerous rival to his power. The strange favour the Emperor Paul accorded to his barber, Koutaissoff, is an instance of his eccentricity. This simple uneducated man of the lower classes was enriched by the Tzar, and suddenly uplifted to be an important Court functionary. He was granted the title of Count, and is the ancestor of the present Count Koutaissoff. The ex-barber wielded a strong influence and pulled the wires of many intrigues that were going on in the Sovereign's vicinity.

The Emperor Nicholas II is reproached for his lack of emotion and moral receptiveness, and for his utter indifference to outward impressions. But people forget that the former Sovereign received the training of a gentleman who scorns to wear his heart on his sleeve for ravens to peck at. But the average Russian, be he ever so learned, has only a vague conception of the rules and requirements of breeding. A well-bred gentleman, who exercises self-restraint and does not flourish his inmost feelings before the public is misunderstood; but a man whose sentiments are less under control would appeal to them. The ex-Tzar comes nearer the British public-school idea.

One of the most irreconcilable antagonists of the dethroned Sovereign says in a recent article about the Empress: 'Alexandra Feodorovna is an interesting type for future psychologists, historians and dramatic authors. She will give them ample food for their hypotheses; a German Princess, educated in England, on the Russian throne, a convert to a peasant's religious sect, and an adept at occultism. Such a phenomenon occurs seldom in the pages of history, and is met for the first, and fortunately the last, time on the throne of Russia. Alexandra Feodorovna is a more complicated and dangerous personality than her husband, and Russia can be considered lucky to have escaped so cheaply. She is made of the substance that those terrible, tyrannical Princesses of the XV–XVII centuries in the Western countries of Europe were made of; those Princesses who united in their personality the despot Sovereign, bordering on the witch and skirting the fanatical visionary, who were completely in the hands of their reactionary advisers, their wizard-doctors and their insinuating wily confessors.'

The same writer, who cannot be accused of being charitably inclined towards the former Empress, certifies that he has read several of her letters to Rasputine, but that not one of them gives the slightest foundation for the ugly slanders that have been heaped on this most fatal and unfortunate of women. The writer says that not for a moment does he believe these calumnies, which are spread and supported by vindictive rumour, and which will be credited for a long time to come. He is convinced that the Empress's infatuation for the staretz Rasputine originated from a purely mystical point of view, but he adds that for Russia's felicity it would have been better if she had succumbed to the many frailties which were attributed to Catherine II, whom the Empress Alexandra admired and wished to emulate. This quotation gives the keynote to the public opinion of the Empress Alexandra.

The Emperor Alexander I had been carefully trained by his grandmother, the Empress Catherine II, who took both her elder grandsons, Alexander and Constantine, from their parents and had them educated under her own eye. A pronounced strain of mysticism was inherent in Alexander's nature, and was strengthened and intensified by his close friendship with the Baroness Krüdner of well-known fame. These mystical propensities of Alexander I engendered the legend, which even now is implicitly believed by the people, that Alexander I did not die in Taganrog in 1825. Another was buried in his stead, and the Tzar disappeared from the world, living henceforth as a hermit in the wilds of Siberia, under the name of 'Feodor Kuzmitch', where he died after attaining a venerable old age.

Alexander I inaugurated his reign with many liberal acts. Those whom his father had banished were permitted to return, he suppressed the censorship, diminished the taxes, suspended confiscations, granted Poland a constitutional government, etc. But during the last years of his life his ideas changed, he became retrogressive and revoked many of his liberal acts. Although Alexander I earned the surname of 'the Blessed', he is more appreciated by foreign historians than by the Russian biographers. The latter give him the character of insincerity and dissimulation. His reign was a peaceful one as regards the inner life of the country. Russia was so taken up at the time with the Napoleonic wars that she had no time to give to dreams and aspirations. The young generation, however, was hoping to change the existing order of things, but their conspiracy was discovered in the first days of Nicholas I's reign.

Nicholas I was his brother's junior by seventeen years. Except her two elder sons, who had been estranged from her from their birth, the children of the Tzessarevna, Marie Feodorovna (the wife of Paul), were all daughters. She therefore welcomed with rapture the advent of a son. When the Empress Catherine II came to see her new grandson, she was struck by the wonderful beauty of the young Nicholas, and even hesitated to leave him with his mother, but in the moment, whilst his fate was in the balance in his powerful grandmother's hands, the unconscious babe set up a disconsolate wail, and the disgusted Empress hastened to give him up to his mother, whose favourite child he became.

The Empress Marie Feodorovna had a thoroughly German tuition given to her son Nicholas, and to his younger brother Michael. Their bringing up and education were confided to Princess Lieven and Count Lamsdorf, and the two younger brothers had not the same educational advantages as their elder brothers, Alexander and Constantine. Subsequently the Grand Duke Nicholas married Princess Charlotte of Prussia, this alliance only strengthening his German proclivities. He loved Russia passionately, and was sincere in his endeavours to protect the country's interests, but he acted according to his lights, and he was honestly confident that only a close alliance with Germany could bring Russia security and prosperity.

In his reign Petrograd swarmed with Germans and their influence was omnipotent. Nicholas I was a convinced autocrat and legitimist. Any attempt at insubordination inspired him with deep indignation, and he ruled the nation with a rod of iron. His prejudice against France was an established fact, not that he disliked the Frenchmen, but he disapproved of their turbulence and revolutionary inclinations. He inherited his mother's prejudice for the Bonapartes and regarded Napoleon as a usurper and an upstart.

Political disturbances marred the dawning days of his reign, but he kept down the unruly element with a heavy hand. Still the seeds of revolution were sown and the unruly sprouts were shooting up. In the reign of Alexander II the revolutionary movement made gigantic strides, but Alexander III forcibly met it by a series of repressive measures.

After his death the emancipation movement progressed steadily for twenty-two years, gradually gaining strength, whilst the Government, on the contrary, was slowly weakening. The Duma helped to mature people's minds, taught them to argue with the Government and publicly criticise its actions. The devastating war with Germany brought things to a climax, and the insolvency revealed by the military preparations was the last blow to the old regime, and gave the necessary impulse to the impending revolution.

The Allies may have felt some displeasure with the Russians for thus suddenly overhauling the existing system of government and dethroning the reigning monarch. The moment may have seemed to them unpropitious for such a momentous change. They may have argued that Russia might have waited till the war was over before bringing about the change that shook the whole nation from one end of the country to another. But if the Allies had witnessed all that went on in Russia for the last three or four months, they would have agreed that not a moment was to be lost, that an immediate revolution was the only solution, the one way to get Russia out of the quagmire, where the Empress Alexandra and her satellites had landed her.

Her Majesty was determined to bring about an independent peace with Germany. It is impossible to understand what secret motive made her strike out this dangerous line of policy. It was against the nation's wish and interest; it imperilled the throne of her husband and son. Admitting even that she was not fond of Russia, her devotion to her son is above all suspicion, and an ambitious woman like the ex-Empress Alexandra would scarcely willingly sacrifice her son's future to her allegiance to Germany. It is a mystery that only the future will solve. But the irretrievable fact remains *that Alexandra Feodorovna wanted peace at all costs*, and was resolved to bring the war to an end in the shortest possible time, regardless of the detriment to the Allies.

The Tzar was against this plan, but would not have been firm enough to sustain a long resistance. His wife and her Germanophile friends would have persuaded him that his sacred duty to the country demanded the sacrifice of his pride and the cessation of bloodshed and strife. Reluctantly perhaps, but the Tzar would ultimately have given in. What would have happened after this premature conclusion of peace? What would have become of the country in these humiliating circumstances? France and England would have been for ever alienated. All the bloodshed and misery would have been in vain. The nation's aim would have been pitilessly frustrated, for isolated Russia could have no other course open to her than that of once more fraternising with the detested Germans. They would have been forced to submit to the Teuton's commercial thraldom and have their lands, their banks, their own industries once more controlled by Germans, those same Germans who for years sponged upon Russia, but deserted her in her hour of need and proved her bitterest enemies; for they used the knowledge they had gained to bring harm to the country that had accorded them such wide hospitality.

Is it to be wondered at, when one thinks of this danger, that when the thunder-cloud was darkening Russia's horizon, the nation revolted and decided to throw off the yoke of Tzardom?

The first Revolutionary Government was a transitory one, and it is only after the war that the form of Russia's future government will be decided by votes of a National Assembly. There is no use in deluding oneself with false hopes. The present state of mind of the populace points out clearly that Holy Russia will be transformed into a Republic, at least for some time. The Social Revolutionists and the Social Democrats will vote for a Republican Government, and they will do their best to enlist the peasants on their side by promising them an increase of land, giving out the cry 'Zemlia y Volia' (Land and Liberty).

Their plan consists of taking the land from the gentry and dividing it equally amongst the representatives of nobility and peasantry, thus destroying utterly the domains and ancestral lands, even the entailed ones, belonging to the members of Russian aristocracy and untitled nobility: the land belonging to the Imperial appanages and to the members of the Imperial Family being divided in a similar manner. The private property of the Emperor and of the Imperial Family is also to be confiscated.

People with well-balanced minds, real patriotism and true love of their country dread the result of these socialistic reforms, and hope for the restoration of the monarchy on improved and renovated foundations. They are convinced that any attempt to make Russia republican would be suicidal, proving that the Social Revolutionists and Social Democrats have gained the upper hand, which would mean woe to the country. If that contingency arises, Russia will out-Herod Herod in her democracy. She will give points even to Mexico. Too much liberty is not good for the Russian people. They want a firm hand to keep them straight.

The following instance, which is based on fact and not on rumour, is a convincing proof of the truth of this statement. After the excesses at Cronstadt, which cost the lives of so many gallant officers, a deputation of sailors came to the War Ministry, and in the absence of M. Gutchkoff was received by his assistant. The sailors came to implore that a chief might be appointed to them as quickly as possible, for they felt the anarchy that was going on at Cronstadt would lead to chaos.

'Whom can we appoint?' the Minister's assistant asked. 'You have killed so many of your admirals and superior officers, and have had the others arrested. Our choice is very limited.'

He then named several well-known admirals. Some of the objections formulated by the sailors were: 'No, this one is too kind-hearted.' 'That one is not strict enough', and so on, adding: 'We want a commander who will be very strict, but just and impartial.'

If these sailors are to be believed, many of those who incited them to excesses during the tragic days in Cronstadt did not belong to them, but were only masquerading as sailors. The question involuntarily arises: 'Were they Revolutionists or German agents?'

The captivity of the Imperial prisoners is becoming very restricted. Only a few rooms have been left at their disposal, and the intercourse of the ex-Tzar and his wife and children is limited to one interview a day. They are prohibited to converse in any foreign language, and they may take only one daily walk in the park. A sentinel is posted at every door, and no letters are delivered to the prisoners. The ex-Tzar has requested that Divine service should be held on Sundays in the private chapel of the Palace. This wish has been acceded to. It must have caused him intense suffering to listen to the liturgy for the first time and not hear the Tzar and his family prayed for. Instead of which a prayer was said for the present Government.

On the first Sunday, the children being still on the sick-list, Nicholas II and his Consort were the only members of the family who attended the religious service. They stood in the middle of the church, facing the altar; the Mistress-of-the-Robes, Madame Narishkine, the Chief Marshal, Count Benckendorff, and the Marshal of the Court, Prince Dolgoroukoff, stood behind them. The sentinel officers filled the further end of the church. When prayers were said for the country and the Government the ex-Tzar bent his knee.

No visitors from outside are admitted to the Palace. The captive inmates are completely isolated from everyone, and the courtiers who attend the ex-Sovereigns share the same fate. An incident occurred that caused the removal of the Palace Commandant, Kotzebue. One of the sentinels reported that the Commandant had taken charge of some letters mysteriously confided to him. The enquiry instituted revealed that incriminating letters were addressed to Prince Kotchubey and written by Count Benckendorff and Prince Dolgoroukoff, asking the Prince and Countess Elisabeth Schouvalov to look after their affairs and sell some shares for them, for in the existing circumstances they could do nothing for themselves. That was all; but rumour magnified the affair into an attempt to liberate the ex-Tzar and give him the chance of leaving the country.

The only time the arrested ex-Tzar asked to infringe the regulation of not sending any letters or telegrams was to send a wire to General Williams at Headquarters, with whom the former monarch had always been on the friendliest terms. The request was granted, and the following telegram was sent to Moheler:

The children are recovering. Self feeling better.
Greetings.

NICHOLAS.

The soldiers of the 12th Army brought under the Government's notice the question of the advisability of incarcerating the ex-Tzar in the Fortress of St. Peter and St. Paul. The Minister of Justice and Procurator-General, M. Kerensky, explained to the soldier delegates that the ex-Tzar is as well guarded as possible. Any attempt at flight could only end in failure, and that more rigorous measures applied to the former Sovereign would create displeasure among the Allies. When the 12th Army heard of this interference imputed to them, they were aghast and sent a formal denial duly witnessed and signed. In this they protested against the suggestion that they had insisted on the ex-Tzar's closer confinement, declaring their full trust in the arrangements of the Government and certifying that the soldiers professing to have been delegates of the 12th Army were impostors.

The significant changes that have recently occurred in Russia have found a sympathetic response in the democratic feelings of the Americans. They have sent the Committee of Workmen's and Soldiers' Deputies their most ardent good wishes and promises of unlimited credit and help of all kinds, but should they touch a hair of the dethroned monarch's head, the Americans will have nothing to do with them. If this proviso be true, the Americans can only be congratulated on their good feelings, which appeal to the hearts of every true Russian. The rule of Nicholas II has proved inefficient; he is not wanted as a monarch, but the great majority of his former subjects wish him no harm; on the contrary, a feeling of intense relief will be felt when he and his family are set free and will have safely quitted Russia.[1]

1 Since this was written the ex-Tzar and his family have been transferred to Siberia as a precautionary measure against reaction.

Preparations for the enquiry into the actions of the arrested Ministers are being hurried on. The three first will be the trials of Soukhomlinoff, Stürmer and Protopopoff. Their trials will be sensational, and will reveal many abuses and shortcomings of the old regime. The trials of Stürmer and Protopopoff may gravely implicate the Sovereigns, and it is thought probable that the ex-Tzar and Alexandra Feodorovna will be exposed to the ordeal of bearing witness in public. The enquiry into Protopopoff's actions has given crushing proofs of his culpability, and has established the fact that his interview a year ago in Stockholm with the German diplomat, Warburg, was inspired by the Germanophile Court party. That fatal colloquy was not a simple search for information, but was destined to serve the purposes of the Court and of the inner enemies of the country.

A strong rumour has lately been current that Protopopoff will hardly be able to stand his trial. In the doctor's opinion he is suffering from progressive paralysis. It is strange that no one noticed previously that he was not in a normal state.

The trial following those of the ex-Ministers named will be that of the former Minister of Justice, subsequently the President of the Upper Chamber, M. Stcheglovitoff.

M. Stcheglovitoff is a man of great intelligence, endowed with a strong will, a narrow mind and great capacities for work. For several years he occupied the post of Minister of Justice. He acted energetically according to his lights, but his methods were ultra-retrogressive. If the interest of his cause was at stake, he would not hesitate, it is said, to shuffle the cards according to his wishes. When the Grand Duke Nicholas Mikhailovitch was lately interviewed about his impressions of recent events, he was asked: Whose influence, except that of the Empress, had such a preponderance over the Tzar as to induce him to use such retrogressive measures as has lately been the case? The Grand Duke, who would have done well in this instance to remember St. Paul's axiom that, if speech is silver, silence is golden, answered spontaneously: 'Stcheglovitoff, we even gave him the nickname of Vanka-Cain.'[1]

Stcheglovitoff's arrest is in a great part due to the Jews, who are wreaking revenge on the former Minister for the Beylis trial

1 Vanka is a derivation from Ivan, employed by the lower classes. M. Stcheglovitoff's name is Ivan.

in the last months of 1913 in Kiev. The Jewish party is a very strong one in Russia at the present moment. But to all interests and purposes, so it is rumoured, there is no tangibly incriminating action in his past career which could cause a condemnatory verdict.

It seems incredible that those who desired peace before a decisive victory had been achieved over Germany were so irresponsible and blind as not to foresee into what distressing conditions they were involving the country.

The war with Germany has lasted nearly three years.

The superior technical preparation of our enemies, and the wide use made of these technical means of destruction, called forth in Russia the necessity of developing the war-appliances to an enormous extent, requiring a great monetary outlay. As Russia's financial resources were inadequate, the Government had recourse to loans, and at the present moment the nation's debt amounts to 45 milliards of roubles. These will require the yearly payment of three milliards for interest. Taking into consideration that the country's yearly Budget was three milliards of roubles, it is evident that the yearly expenditure will henceforth be doubled. But if one adds to this the cost of reparations, restorations, idemnifications, pensions, etc., rendered necessitated by the war, another milliard will have to be added. If in augmentation of these seven milliards one counts the cost of improvements, which the growth of culture will require, such as public instruction, the sanitation of towns, the making of new roads, etc., the country's future Budget must be estimated at ten milliards. The strain to live up to such an expenditure would be heavy indeed, without a highly developed industrial labour.

The exportation of Russia's raw materials, such as grain, leather, wood, etc., as it was done before the war, has proved ruinous to the country. Enormous as Russia's riches are, they cannot last for ever without being restored. The former system was like a grand sale, like living on one's capital. This must be remedied and the industrial organizations widely enlarged. The question arises, how is this to be accomplished without gaining a complete victory over Germany?

Germany has a large national debt likewise, and the burden will be heavier to bear because her population is inferior to Russia's. She will therefore seek to pay her debt at the expense of others. The means to do this successfully, barring annexations and indemnities, will be the establishment of trade of the most cultivated products on the most profitable terms. The development of commerce and industry in Germany is a vital question of her future well-being. The proof of her safety in the time to come lies in the monopoly of commerce, and in being the sole provider of her neighbours with products of her industry. Her first aim in Belgium and in Poland is to destroy all the existing manufactories.

Sixty per cent of German wares were sold in Russia prior to the war. When the war is over she will wish to increase her export, and if Russia is not victorious, if Germany's militarism is not crushed, she will not let Russia create her own industry. The country will be gradually exhausted in favour of Germany, the people will suffocate under the burden of taxes, all the earnings will go to pay the National Debt. What but her wonderful industry helped France forty-six years ago to pay Germany the required contribution and blossom out into one of the richest countries?

This war has proved that success is on the side of the more cultured countries, and if Russia is not victorious she will never be able to develop the indispensable culture which has been lacking in the country for so long. People who wish the war to end in a draw, without giving Russia any benefit, forget that for the successful development of commerce an issue into the Mediterranean and into the oceans is imperative. The conclusion one comes to is that, if we do not beat Germany, Russia's progressive development will be seriously impeded.

Apart from this economic side of the matter, there exists a moral one. Not only the conclusion of a separate peace, but even the discussion of possible conditions, is an act of treachery towards our noble Allies.

Has the anxiety been forgotten that was felt during the first days of the war, when the question was: would Great Britain join the Allies or not? Then there came the elation when it was known in Russia that England was going with us against Germany. This very anxiety and the subsequent gladness proves that the nation fully understood the importance of Great Britain's decisive step.

This is the reason why the old Government was so easily overthrown. The country felt that the war was carried on in a half-hearted way, without the vigorous energy it required. That is why Nicholas II found no one to defend his throne. This is the justification of those who did not stand up for their Tzar!

A curious legend is spread amongst the Russians in connection with the Tzar's crown. It is believed that no Sovereign who has been crowned with this crown will die a natural death whilst he remains Tzar of Russia.

A beautiful emerald shines in the front of this crown. The French sorcerer René (in the reign of Louis XVI) is supposed to have cast an evil spell on this emerald which was subsequently acquired by Catherine II. She ordered the gem to be set in the Imperial Crown. Paul I, the first Tzar crowned in this crown, was murdered. Alexander I died alone and uncared for in a far-off part of the country (referring to the above-mentioned belief that Alexander's death in 1825 was only simulated). Nicholas I died, if tradition is to be credited, by poison, administered by his own hand during the reverses of the Crimean War. Alexander II was killed by a bomb. Alexander III died of slow poison, administered by the German Government, because the Tzar was not amenable to their wishes.[1]

1 Nothing will uproot the belief of the Russian public at large that Alexander III's death was not a natural one. They are convinced that his death was caused by a lingering poison, and not from nephritis, as was given out. They are convinced that the Germans poisoned the Tzar, as they had previously poisoned General Skobeleff, because they were both impediments to German plans.

Chapter X

THE BLACK CABINET

THE Revolution gave the public a glimpse behind the scenes of the former Government and brought out many of its shady sides, revealing the wheels within wheels of the machinery, betraying secrets rigorously kept for over a century.

One of the most interesting disclosures concerns the famous 'Black Cabinet'. Notwithstanding the formal denial of one of the last chiefs of the Postal Department, pronounced from the tribune of the Duma,[1] the Black Cabinet did exist and was discovered in the centre of the General Post Office. The place it occupied has been revealed, and the whole organisation of this mysterious Chamber has been found out, which for over a hundred years proved the safest weapon of search and pursuit. The official name of this section was: 'The Censorship of Foreign Newspapers and Magazines'. The Black Cabinet, originated in the dark period of the Emperor Paul's reign, was founded in the year 1799, under the influence of the events connected with the French Revolution, and was put an end to, on March 15th, 1917, by order of the Provisional Government.

The proceeding of opening letters was accomplished with marvellous dexterity, never leaving the slightest trace. The suspected letters were put into steam-baths and every agent employed in this business was provided with sharp instruments adapted to open an envelope and with a special plastic substance, with the aid of which a few moments sufficed to procure a perfect impression of any crested seal.

The way the letters liable to this secret examination were

1 The words were: 'The Black Cabinet is a fiction.'

delivered and taken out of the Black Cabinet was most cleverly contrived. The Cabinet was placed on the middle floor, close to the elevator in which huge baskets of sorted letters were sent down to the dispatch department to be sent on to the different minor post offices of the town. The prepared basket, containing the suspected correspondence, would be taken off the elevator, and another with the letters already examined put in its place. This was done so quickly that even the man accompanying the elevator did not notice the subterfuge and the stoppage passed unobserved on either of the other floors.

The letters were opened and photographed. After that process, they were slipped back into their respective envelopes and a similar seal affixed to the envelope, if required.

It would be a mistake to think that only the correspondence of people suspected of political delinquencies was subjected to such treatment. The examination extended to all the letters of people whose thoughts and opinions could be of interest to the Tzar, the Minister of the Interior, or the Police Department. This comprised a very wide range, for the Minister of the Interior based part of his power on such documents produced by the Black Cabinet, and for this reason hardly any important personage's letters were left untampered with, not even the correspondence of the Tzar, his relatives or friends, nor that of the other Ministers and statesmen. Such Black Cabinets were established in Petrograd, Moscow, Warsaw, Kiev, Odessa, Riga and Vilna.

The functionaries, to whom this secret work was entrusted, were well paid. For instance the chief of this mysterious section received officially a yearly salary of 2,000 roubles and an apartment on the premises, but he received another 12,000 roubles a year out of the secret funds of the Ministry. The minor officials received not less than 5,000 roubles a year; the watchmen were chosen from among the illiterate. Each functionary, on being admitted for the first time into this Blue Beard's Chamber, had to take an oath never to divulge the existence of the Black Cabinet to a living soul, 'not to your wife, your father, sister, or dearest friends'.

When the Minister of the Interior, M. Plehve, was killed, one of the Emperor's Adjutant-Generals was sent to examine his papers. This is usually done in such cases to avoid any important State documents from falling into wrong hands. Among the numerous papers, neatly docketed and labelled, the General's attention was attracted to two books. On the white pages of one of them were carefully pasted the copies of the Tzar's private letters. The other contained the contents in writing of the Tzar's conversations on the telephone. Both books were given to the monarch, and Nicholas II was extremely indignant at this spying-system applied to himself. His displeasure with the deceased caused him, so it was said at the time, to diminish the pension he had previously fixed for the assassinated Minister's widow.

Alexander III regarded this system as a necessary evil in dangerous times, but, although unable to put an end to the Black Cabinet, he had a strong prejudice against such methods, and personally never availed himself of this means of acquainting himself with the contents of other people's letters.

His father, Alexander II, if wicked tongues are to be believed, was rather inclined to use this machinery for getting a glimpse behind the scene.

The 'Okhrana' (safeguard), consisting principally of the Corps of Gendarmes, likewise exists no longer. The Gendarmerie was the political police; it was their business to survey suspected individuals, watch their movements, and gain an adequate knowledge of their intentions. Gendarmes were posted at every station to look after suspicious passengers. At all the frontier-stations a section of them was quartered, under the orders of a superior officer. They examined the passports of the travellers, and possessing the photographs of most of the political emigrants, as well as a list of their names, it was their business to arrest any individual whom they suspected of not having the right to leave or return to Russia. Colonel Miassoyedoff, of evil memory, was stationed for a considerable time at Wirballen, the German frontier-town. He was personally known to the Kaiser, and was occasionally invited to join the German potentate's shooting parties on his estate in Eastern Prussia. It was here Miassoyedoff was enlisted into the German spying organisation and commenced his treacherous career.

A simple denunciation from the Okhrana sufficed to have a person sent out of town into some far-off region. On the authority of these denunciations, often scarcely verified, a man would be dragged from his house and work, separated from his family and left to vegetate in some remote corner of the country. All depended on the Chief of the Gendarmerie. The two last, General Djunkovsky and Count Tatishteff, were conscientious, but in General

Kurloff's time things were different. It was then that Stolypine was killed. Instead of thinking of his responsibility, during the Count's stay in Kiev, the General spent his nights in feasting and carousing. The inquest, after Stolypine's death, caused the General to pass a very bad quarter of an hour and left him with a besmirched reputation, but that did not prevent Protopopoff from taking him up and giving him the position of his assistant, unofficially it is true, for his nomination, it was feared, would arouse too much indignation. However, his anonymous position was 'Polichinelle's secret', for everyone knew that General Kurloff's activity was in full force and his influence paramount until the days of the Revolution, when he was arrested and put into the fortress to await his trial.

The Imperial Okhrana, which has now been abolished, yearly cost the nation a half a million of roubles.

It is said that the former Minister of the Interior, Maklakoff, during one of his examinations, exclaimed about the horrors of the fortress: 'I never thought it was so awful!' Yet in the days of his power, he had been responsible for many incarcerations. Would it not have been his duty to humanity to investigate the conditions in which the prisoners were obliged to exist?

An amusing story is told of how the Procurator of the Holy Synod, M. Raeff (a friend of the late Rasputine), escaped arrest. When he saw how fatally things were turning out for the old Government and its representatives, he had recourse to stratagem. He took off his dark wig, which came low down on his forehead 'à la Capoul', shaved off his moustache, took out his set of artificial teeth, and, putting on an old coat that had seen better days, he unobtrusively sat down in a corner of the ante-room, unrecognised by his own servants. The soldiers arrived in due time to arrest M. Raeff. They enquired for the Procurator, but were informed by the servants that he was not in the house. They questioned the shabby-looking old man, who answered in a quavering voice that he had himself been waiting for M. Raeff for over an hour, and did not know where he was. The soldiers took no more notice of the insignificant old duffer, and, having vainly searched for the Procurator, they went away, leaving the coast clear for the old man to do what he liked. A few days later, when M. Raeff made his official appearance, the acute moment of the Revolution had passed and he was left unmolested.

Some of the former statesmen, notwithstanding their loyalty,

THE FALL OF THE ROMANOFFS

were worse foes to Tzardom than the most ardent socialists. They incited enmity and hatred against the Sovereign, who never suspected the effect produced by more than one of his Ministers. Power was repeatedly entrusted to undeserving, or unable, hands, and the representatives of Government were frequently to blame for the foolish arbitrariness of their actions. Unfortunately these actions were imputed to the Tzar, and rendered his reign unpopular. The following instance is a proof of this.

After the death of M. Ivan Dournovo, Sipiaguine[1] was appointed Minister of the Interior. Sipiaguine was the scion of a wealthy family of ancient lineage. He was an honourable gentleman of extremely limited intellect, but endowed with a certain adaptability to circumstances. Having proved his utter inadequacy as an administrator during the period of his governorship in Kharkoff, he was nevertheless transferred to Mitau as the Governor of Courland. Here he enjoyed a certain popularity, because he chummed up with the German barons, who knew Sipiaguine to be an ardent sportsman, and got up in his honour magnificent hunting and shooting parties in their ancestral baronial country seats. People were greatly surprised to hear of Sipiaguine's appointment to the post of Minister of the Interior. Modest and unassuming at the outset of his career, he subsequently succeeded in convincing himself (though not others) that he was a born statesman.

In the course of his administration of Interior affairs, one of the Russian democratic journalists was guilty of writing a feuilleton entitled 'The Family Obmanoff', which appeared in the newspaper *Rossia* (Russia). The narrative was harmless enough and rather silly, purporting to describe the Romanoffs. Only one chapter appeared. Sipiaguine's attention was instantly drawn to the hidden meaning of the narrative. Instead of treating the matter as one of extreme bad taste on the part of a writer and publisher, Sipiaguine chose to create a scandal, which attracted general notice at home and abroad.

Thus emphasised, it became a classical production, and the affair earned the fame of a 'cause célèbre', remembered to the present day, instead of passing unperceived by the majority, and in due time committed to oblivion. Had he been wise and exercised common sense, the Minister would have forbidden the continu-

1 Sipiaguine was killed by a shot fired at him by a revolutionist in 1902.

ation of the feuilleton, and warned the publisher that in future he had better take care; but Sipiaguine, in his pompous display of power, suppressed the paper *Rossia*, and sent the author of the incriminating article into exile, surrounding him with an ever-lasting halo of martyrdom. The Tzar was averse to such rigorous measures, but Sipiaguine overruled all objections by pointing out the inadmissibility of treating with too much leniency a case which he magnified into a crime of 'lèse-majesté'.

The unfortunate writer, cut off from his wife and children, prevented from gaining his family's livelihood, spent two wretched years in Siberia and in Vologda before he was allowed to emigrate. He has returned to Russia a soured and embittered man full of hatred, a virulent enemy of Nicholas II, and the author of the most acrimonious articles against Tzardom and the ex-Tzar. The maltreated writer is eager to avail himself of this opportunity to pour out the rankling venom of his hate; but his malevolence – the result of Sipiaguine's blundering – must be condoned, when one remembers how immeasurably he suffered for a comparatively slight offence. His nature is warped, and suffering has not ennobled it.

Many were the shortcomings and the misuses of the old system of Government. It was rotten to the core, and reform was inevitable. It was only the suddenness of the upheaval that startled one. However, success is generally connected with strength, when it is young and fresh, so one must hope that the reformed Government will attain the summits of Glory and Wisdom.

The last Tzar of the preceding dynasty, founded by Rurik, Fedor (1584–1598), was a weakling in body and mind. His father, Ivan IV, had crushed the little spirit with which nature had endowed him. The Tzar was a good and a religious one; his favourite occupation was to ring the church bells, but he was an incompetent monarch. His weakness encouraged iniquities and crimes to be committed and innocent blood to be shed, even the blood of his most faithful adherents, as, for instance, that of Prince Vassily Shuisky. Fedor was a pawn in the hands of his masterful brother-in-law, Boris Godunoff, a clever and ambitious man, but unscrupulous in his deeds.

The reigns of Ivan the Terrible and that of his son Fedor were considered the most sanguinary period in Russian history. Still, the blood shed in that lapse of time is a drop compared with the blood shed during the twenty-two years of Nicholas II's reign:

Hodynka, Tsussima, the Russo-Japanese War, the 9th of January, the carnage in Moscow, the repression of the Baltic disturbances and this devastating war, which the Kaiser started and which the Tzar accepted, sustained by Soukhomlinoff.

There was a fatality in everything the Tzar undertook; through error and mischance the blood that flowed in the last twenty-two years would fill an ocean.

It is curious to trace the ill-luck that all the Hessian Princesses have brought as a dowry to the Romanoffs. The first wife of Paul I was a Princess of Hesse – her husband was murdered. Alexander II's wife came from the same family – her husband was killed. The Grand Duke Serge Alexandrovitch married Elizabeth of Hesse – he met his death in a tragic way. The present Tzar married to Princess Alix of Hesse – he has lost his throne.

Superstitious people, who notice omens and believe in predestination, remember the incident that happened three weeks prior to the Coronation. The Empress's train for that solemn occasion, following the traditional custom, was sent to one of the convents in the vicinity of Moscow to be embroidered. The most skilful gold-embroiderers were chosen among the nuns, who during the period of work were locked up, nobody having access to them except their task-mistress and the Mother Superior. It took many months to put in the innumerable stitches and produce the elaborate designs traced on the rich gold brocade destined to be attached to the crowned Sovereign's sarafan. The train was almost completed, the Mother Superior came to inspect the work, only a few stitches remained to be added, when one of the workwomen sharply pricked her hand, the needle entering an artery: a jet of blood gushed out over the train, and creating consternation among the nuns. The train had to be carefully cleansed, previous to its delivery. Naturally enough, the mishap with her Coronation train was kept from the Empress Alexandra, but the gossip in Moscow was full of this unlucky occurrence.

The fact had likewise been disclosed that Princess Alix in her own country was considered a 'Pechvogel'.[1] When she was leaving Darmstadt, amidst the crowd that came to bid her good speed, the murmur was heard: 'Und nimm Dein Pech mit Dir.'[2]

A revolutionary movement arising exclusively from the lower

1 A bird of ill omen.
2 And take your bad luck with you.

ranks could not have achieved the success of completely overhauling the existing state of things without the support of higher regions, supplied in this contingency by the Duma. Still the primary movement was so cleverly organised that it is hardly to be supposed the plan was worked out only by the workmen and soldiers. German money and German agents were at the bottom of the disturbances; but they overreached themselves, for the Teutons only wished to call forth riots, they never foresaw it would turn into a regular Revolution, causing the abdication of the Emperor and the downfall of the dynasty.

Judging by the articles that appear in the German press, the changes in Russia are not welcomed in the Land of the Kaiser. *Die Warte* is quite candid in expressing her mortification, and frankly laments that the German hopes have been smashed, after all the trouble taken to have appropriate Ministers appointed in Russia and the way paved to attain a separate peace.

The army paper published in Russia, for the benefit of the Russian captives in Germany, does not pronounce the word 'Revolution' and mentions only disturbances, endeavouring to discredit the Provisional Government in the minds of the readers, steadfastly upholding the prestige of Tzarism and the Romanoffs.

To all intents and purposes the Romanoff dynasty has come to an end. A miracle could alone save the throne for them, and in the twentieth century miracles are rare.

Rasputine and ill-luck have destroyed the dynastic rights of the Tzar Nicholas II. His brother Michael's unfortunate marriage[1] would prove a serious impediment, and most of the other members of the Imperial Family have discredited themselves in the eyes of a right-minded public by their indiscreet attitude during the days of the Revolution. Should the monarchy ever be restored in Russia, it will not only be on reformed lines, but probably with a Tzar who will found a new dynasty.

A story is told of an Ambassador of one of the Allied Powers. A Radical Minister called on him to confer as to Nicholas II's departure from Russia. In speaking to the Ambassador, the Minister referred to 'Nicolai Romanoff'.[2] The Ambassador inter-

1 The Grand Duke Michael Alexandrovitch is married to a notary's daughter. Her maiden name was Scheremetevsky. She has been divorced twice, and the Grand Duke is her third husband.
2 Nicholas is pronounced in Russian Nicolai.

rupted him: 'Permit me to ask to whom you are alluding? I do not know any "Nicolai Romanoff".' The somewhat abashed Minister owned that he was speaking of the former Sovereign – 'Oh! you mean His Majesty the ex-Tzar. Whatever happens to him he will always remain an Emperor, and I really cannot allow him to be otherwise alluded to in my presence.'

The members of the Duma who were present at the arrest of the various courtiers testify their admiration. All of them, especially Count Benckendorff and Prince Dolgoroukoff, behaved with wonderful nobility, dignity and tact. M. Kerensky frankly acknowledges that he was deeply impressed by the staunch fidelity they manifested to their Imperial master. The only exceptions were General Woyeikoff, who did his utmost to condemn the Tzar, but only succeeded in inspiring his listeners with disgust; and Madame Vyrouboff. Her attitude, when she was brought to the Duma, was deplorable.

One would have expected such an influential dignitary in the ex-Tzar's environment, as M. Taneief – Madame Vyrouboff's father – to be one of the first to be arrested. Instead of which, he has managed to vanish. No one knows where he is, but it is supposed he escaped abroad. It is considered somewhat extraordinary that not one newspaper has ever mentioned his name in connection with the events of the Revolution, and strange rumours are afloat concerning his disappearance. It is said that Nicholas II had no liking for Taneief, but the Empress favoured him. On the occasion of some jubilee of Taneief's, the Empress Alexandra sent a special wire to Headquarters reminding the Tzar to take a gracious notice of this festive occurrence.

The usual ill-luck that pursues Nicholas II and his Consort made itself felt even in the days of the Revolution. Their children's illness happened at the most inopportune moment. Had this not been the case, directly after the Tzar's abdication, the Imperial Family might have left Russia and been safely conveyed to England. The protracted illness of the children gave the socialists time to rally their forces, and insist on inflicting this superfluous humiliation on crowned heads. M. Kerensky visits Tzarskoe Selo periodically to see that everything is as it should be, and that the ex-Sovereigns are in need of nothing. But with all his good intentions, M. Kerensky is no courtier, and his ways are apt to jar on the Empress Alexandra.

On one of his visits, he entered her presence unannounced.

'What do you wish here?' queried the ex-Sovereign in her most Imperial manner.

'It is I who have come to enquire if Your Majesty has any wish to formulate.'

'I wish nothing from you,' shortly answered Her Majesty, and the Minister had nothing else to do but to bow himself out.

His intercourse with the ex-Tzar is sustained on more amicable terms, and it is said that M. Kerensky is losing his prejudice against the Romanoffs, and has become quite fascinated by the peculiar charm that emanates from the personality of Nicholas II. In the course of one of their conversations the latter told M. Kerensky that he had heard of him, as an eloquent orator and a clever barrister, but he did not suppose that M. Kerensky possessed great administrative experience.

During one of his last visits to Tzarskoe Selo, the Tzessarevitch Alexis came up to M. Kerensky with the query:

'You are a barrister, is it not true?'

'Quite so.'

'Then you must know all about the laws of the country?'

'I think I may venture to say that I do.'

'Well, then you can tell me: Whether or no my father had the legal right to abdicate the throne in my name?'

M. Kerensky was nonplussed. He was puzzled how to frame an appropriate answer. He replied that from the strictly technical point of view such an abdication was not exactly legal.

'Thank you, that is all I wished to know,' was the boy's response.

Another time the Tzessarevitch bitterly complained to M. Kerensky that all the horses, even his favourite pony, had been taken away. The Minister gave immediate orders that the Grand Duke Alexis's pony should be returned and put at the boy's disposal.

The Tzarevnas (the Tzar's daughters) are very quiet. They look grave and subdued, their merry chatter is seldom heard now, and their gaiety and joyous laughter does not fill the place as of yore.

Two months have passed since the Revolution put an end to the monarchy in Russia, but the passions have not abated, and the political ground is as slippery as ever. The excitement is maintained by the harangues, unceasingly poured forth by the new-fangled tribunes, who hold their meetings in the open air.

THE FALL OF THE ROMANOFFS

An incident occurred the other day in the Maly[1] Theatre, which reflects the general agitation and intolerance that characterise the present state of people's minds. The theatre belongs to the popular actress, Madame Souvorine, the only daughter of the late M. Souvorine, the founder of the *Novoe Vremia*. Being the directress of this theatre, Madame Souvorine objected to producing any new comedy in her theatre containing ugly allusions to the Imperial Court, and refused to permit the actors, in the course of the usual performance, to give utterance to sallies tending to vilify the ex-Tzar and his family, and excite the audience's derision.

Madame Souvorine can only be honoured for such sentiments, which prove the innate good feeling of a well-bred lady, but this prohibition was differently viewed by the unruly part of the public, and it raised a regular tempest. Several members of the company, and some of the theatrical retainers, revolted against what they considered an arbitrary attitude, but most of the artistes sustained their directress. The rumour of this friction was dragged before the public. A gang of socialists, led by the indefatigable Lenine, threatened Madame Souvorine with all kinds of reprisals. A scandal was expected on the first occasion of Madame Souvorine appearing on the boards.

The performance on the ominous night had gone on quietly enough. The house was crowded with spectators. Excitement was in the air, the actors' nerves were quivering, Madame Souvorine had a hunted look in her eyes. Just before the curtain rose on the last act, a murmur was heard amidst the audience: 'The Lenintzys have arrived', and numerous uncouth individuals filled the gallery and the back seats of the parterre. A thrill of excitement went through the theatre. The curtain slowly rose, revealing Madame Souvorine in the centre of the scene. A terrible noise greeted her; hisses, yells, whistles and loud shouts of 'Doloy,[2] Souvorina, Doloy!' The unfortunate artiste, pale to the lips, looked helplessly round, and swaying fell fainting on the nearest chair. The curtain dropped, but the vociferation only grew louder. A gentleman stood up on his chair, shouting: 'Shame on you for publicly insulting a defenceless woman! Out with the disturbers.' A regular fight ensued. The representatives of the Militia[3] had disappeared, and the belligerents had thus full scope. The performance had to be

1 Small
2 Away.
3 Which has replaced the police.

suspended, and the money was returned the next day to all the spectators who wished to claim it.

The position at the theatre continues to be extremely delicate. Madame Souvorine is under boycott, and should she appear on the boards the scandal would recommence. The sympathetic artiste is to be coerced into giving up the direction of her own theatre and turn it into an autonomy. Madame Souvorine, however, shows pluck and does not give in, but she will avoid a public appearance on the boards until the end of the season, which is close at hand.

Events have created a vogue for the word 'Autonomy', which is at present the favourite expression in Russia. One continually hears it, sometimes from lips that have only the vaguest idea of its real meaning. It is like the word 'Annexation'. People go about bellowing: 'We don't want annexations', yet, if they are asked what the word means, more than half of them do not know. The Russian people want a good deal of political training before they will be able to take a wise and conscious part in the governing of their country. At present the majority resemble the mujik who wants 'Russia to be a Republic, only with a Tzar.'

It must not be imagined, therefore, that the Tzar's abdication appeased everyone and turned the current of events into a more desirable channel. Russia has not yet got the wheel out of the rut. The Government is struggling against two formidable foes, who play into each other's hands. German influence is felt at every step, with the sole difference that in former times it insinuated itself in high places, whereas now it is gnawing at the bottom. German money is spent in abundance to sustain strife and stimulate the people to fresh riots and agrarian disturbances, inciting them against the Government and the principle of Moderation.

Having thrown off the thraldom of the monarchy, Russia must take care to escape the yoke of the socialists, which would be much worse. It would be like leaving Scylla for a more terrifying Charybdis. The people must be made to understand that the Russian socialists are the most reliable allies of the Germans. At present the country revolves around a completely new and unaccustomed axis, visibly swerving to the left, unable to maintain the proper equilibrium established during the first weeks after the Revolution, leaving the hopes and the ideals of the well-intentioned true patriots far behind.

Fate ordained the members of the fourth Duma to step forward as the leaders of the revolutionary movement. They followed the call because they felt they were saving Russia's honour and dignity, which were being trampled on in the most egregious way.

What was the course of the old Government? Contempt for people's enquiries, total incomprehension of life, no desire to take into consideration the general indignation. It was impossible to endure such a state of things any longer. All measures were tried to bring the rulers to their senses, and induce them to act conscientiously towards the people who were shedding their life-blood in defence of their country. The members of the Duma, belonging to all parties and factions, came forward with admonishing orations, accusing and criticising the criminal indifference manifested by the Imperial Government towards the country's interests. It was a grave mistake to confine responsible posts to the members of the Imperial Family, who were not held responsible for their deeds. In fact, the great error of the old Government was that those who wielded power were not liable to responsibility, and those who could be made responsible did not possess the necessary power to act independently. The hopelessness of the position had become unbearable to everyone, and the unanimity with which the change was welcomed proved that the ripening political consciousness of the people understood where to seek the solution of this critical situation.

The salvation of Russia from threatening danger was the basis of the Revolution in Russia. The leaders only desired the restoration of Russia's good name, the conservation of her entireness, and the guarantee of being able to maintain her future might.

It remains now with the Russian people to prove that they are deserving of the liberty thus acquired, and give the lie to the pessimists who doubt their mental ripeness. They must prove their worth by turning the liberty gained at the price of such sacrifices into a blessing to the nation and not into a curse.

The first duty of the liberated Russian nation towards the country and her noble Allies is to prove the wisdom of her acquired independence, and strain every nerve to bring the war to a victorious conclusion. All other thoughts and aspirations must be postponed until the war is over. After that has been achieved to the satisfaction of all the Allies, the energy of the new Government, be it Monarchical or Republican, must be directed to realise the urgent reforms of the country, redress the former shortcomings, abolish misuses and let the rejuvenated country step forth and develop along her natural lines towards increasing progress and the full realisation of her greatness.

Only in that case will it be said of Russia that she has set forward the clock fifty years, and will now have the opportunity to prove the true mettle of her people.

Chapter XI

THE AFTERMATH

THE first three months after the Revolution wrought extensive changes in Russia, but the consequences of these changes have unfortunately resulted in quite unforeseen events, deeply deplored by the majority of true-hearted Russians. Even those who welcomed the Revolution are distressed at the course these events are taking, for their ideals are smashed and their hopes destroyed. The upper and middle classes are full of anxiety as to the future, and the level-headed part of the masses are displeased at the unexpected development of things in 'Holy Russia'.

The reaction has set in, the glamour of the first days has completely vanished, and the mistakes committed by the leaders of the revolutionary movement have retrospectively become vividly conspicuous. The effects of these errors are increasing daily, and are getting fatal to the future might and well-being of the country. The position of affairs is becoming tragic indeed, for no one knows what is to be done, and no one has the power to stem the socialistic-anarchical current that is invading the country.

Events have proved only too well that the Russian nation is not ripe for self-government. It has not proved worthy of the liberty that was suddenly thrust upon it, and as one of the Ministers boldly expressed it, in one of his speeches to the soldiers and workmen: 'They resemble revolted slaves and not liberated citizens.'

The majority of the population in Russia is represented by peasants, for, be they soldiers, workmen or labourers, they all come from the ranks of peasantry. The putting of the reigning

Tzar aside and keeping the Sovereign under arrest, has caused the upheaval of their most sacred tradition.

The plank on which they stood has suddenly been removed from under their feet, and they flounder in all directions without any moral stay. A peasant was heard the other day formulating his impression of recent events: 'We believed in the might of the Tzar and we looked up to him, but it was proved to us that he acted criminally against our interests, and that he is our foe. After that who can be trusted? The Provisional Government includes "mujiki" [peasants] like ourselves. How can they inspire awe and faith? We can't look up to them, and don't believe in them!'

This is the general opinion of the populace, of what is going on in Russia.

To give the English public the key-note of the present distressing circumstances in this country, it will be necessary to take the reader back to the preliminary days of the Revolution and point out some of the errors committed, which in the first effervescence of enthusiasm were not taken notice of, and describe in their true light some events that have now become known to a few people, but which for obvious reasons have not been imparted to the general public.

The newspapers' accounts of events cannot be trusted. An English gentleman, who is devoted to Russia and has spent over twenty years in this country, affirms that during all these years he has never known the Russian newspapers to lie to such an extent as they have done since their reappearance after their suspension during the revolutionary days.

The events of the last months have proved that the Monarchists were right in their convictions that the security of Russia lay in the invulnerability of Tzarism. It was the symbol the people required, which to them was a sacred one! Now that Tzarism is destroyed, all seems shattered in their eyes, even religion. Nothing seems sacred to them, nothing appeals to their better and higher feelings, no moral standard sustains them under the stress of this subversion. Their morality, their sense of the fitness of things, has completely given way. But even among the lower classes there are people with common sense averse to excesses, who disapprove of the existing state of disorder, disorganisation and confusion, but they keep aloof and are afraid to express their real opinions.

Most of the soldiers when taking an active part against the old

Government were left in ignorance that they were going against the Tzar. For a long while some of the Left members of the Duma had been surreptitiously preparing the people's minds for the coming change, but it suited the purpose of revolutionary leaders to use the force that the soldiers' and workmen's support gave the revolutionary movement, without confiding their real aims to the people they used to attain the goal of their aspirations. The fact of the Emperor's abdication did not disturb the latter's feelings of loyalty, for they were too much intoxicated with the triumph of success and the feeling of importance they had suddenly acquired.

The members of the Duma, who had assumed the direction of things during those eventful days, were obliged to take into due consideration the help the soldiers and workmen had given the movement, for literally it was they who achieved the overthrow of the old Government. They were treated as confederates, and the process of applying to them the principle of 'Liberté, Egalité, Fraternité' turned their heads completely. At first they submitted to the leadership of the Duma, but subsequently they recognised their own power, based on the only real force that at present exists in the country; they entered into their role of Revolutionists and wished to concentrate the power in their own hands.

Socialistic leaders of the lower classes appeared on the scene, and, being more akin to the populace in spirit, speedily gained a predominating ascendancy in the Soldiers' and Workmen's Council. They took the upper hand, and their first move was to sow dissension between the people and the more educated members of the Duma, inciting them especially against the authority of M. Rodzianko, who as the President of the State Duma took the principal lead. Had M. Rodzianko and his colleagues been wise, they would have foreseen this natural result.

They ought to have been satisfied with the concessions the Emperor was ready to make, and, if they had followed the voice of wisdom, they would, at this critical moment, have given their Sovereign the support of their influence, and above all they ought not to have prevented His Majesty reaching Petrograd, permitting the stoppage of the Imperial train when within a few miles' distance from the capital. That was a grave error which is now deeply deplored. But at that time M. Rodzianko and his colleagues were somewhat inflated at the prospect of the prominent place they were going to take in the pages of Russian history.

Now that they have had time to think, the more thoughtful

blame the Duma for its precipitate action. An ugly story has been spread that the telegrams sent by M. Rodzianko and M. Gutchkoff to apprise the Emperor of what was going on in Petrograd were purposely sent in such a manner as to reach the Sovereign when it would be too late for him to stand forward before the nation and give the required concessions. Many circumstances of those fatal days were unknown to the public, but the leaders of the Revolution knew everything. They were perfectly aware that M. Protopopoff had resigned the post of Minister of the Interior, and that his resignation had been accepted by the Tzar, who likewise wished to grant the country a responsible Ministry. The Emperor did not wish a divorce, but it was decided, with a view to pacifying the people, that the Empress Alexandra, accompanied by her daughters, was to leave Russia on a long visit to England, with the tacit understanding that she would remain abroad as long as the war lasted.

The Empress away, the Tzar would have been independent of her influence and all would have been satisfactory, the Revolution would have been nipped in the bud and all the bloodshed, misery and confusion avoided. The people are up to now ignorant of these facts, which have only lately become known. There was a great deal going on that has yet to be explained. Several members of the Constitutional Democratic faction of the Duma sought the country's safety in the overthrow of the dynasty. M. Gutchkoff was always frankly antagonistic to the Tzar, and he knew that he was antipathetic to the Sovereign; therefore most people blamed him for having put himself forward to claim the Emperor's abdication in Pskov. If the abdication were imperative – and the majority deem it a great mistake – it was the President of the Duma, M. Rodzianko, who ought to have formulated the nation's wish to the Tzar. It turns out now that the nation knew hardly anything of the course events were taking, and it was only the desire of a few scores of men that Nicholas II should give up the reins of government. General Russky, likewise an adversary of the Tzar, is said to have played into the hands of those who wished to dethrone him. All these intrigues and characteristic details are gradually cropping up now, when it is too late.

When the Provisional Government was being formed the first friction arose between the Duma and the Soldiers' and Workmen's Deputies. They objected to M. Rodzianko occupying the post of Prime Minister, and, their forces having become threatening, it was thought wiser to give in to them. Prince Lwoff was elected Prime Minister, and M. Rodzianko remained President of the Duma. Prince Lwoff may be a well-intentioned, clever man, but he is no statesman, and has no experience in administration. In forming the Cabinet he took the portfolio of the Interior, but during more than three months did nothing to prove his activity or ability.

Meanwhile with every succeeding day the soldiers and work-men were gaining power, and their impudence increased in giant strides. The new War Minister, M. Gutchkoff, slackened the discipline, which hitherto had been strictly observed in the army, to a perilous degree. The soldiers were granted all kinds of rights and privileges. They were released from saluting their officers when they met in the street or in public places; they were not to address the officers as 'Your Worship' or the generals as 'Your Excellency', but were to use the nomination of the distinctive ranks, as it is done in France: 'Monsieur le lieutenant, Monsieur le general.' They were allowed to travel in first-class carriages, without paying for their ticket, whereas formerly soldiers could only travel third-class. The result of this stupid permission is that it has become an ordeal to travel in Russia. The best carriages are filled with soldiers, who loll on the velvet seats, whilst the paying travellers, even ladies, have to stand in the corridor glad to be able to enter the train at all.

The same with the tram-cars. Before the Revolution the soldiers stood on the front platform, which serves as an entrance to the inside of the car. Now the tram-cars are crowded with soldiers, who do not pay any fare, and other people have some-times to wait for hours until they can squeeze into the car. Ladies, children and generals have to stand, whilst uncouth soldiers sit sprawling on the benches. It is a painful sight to observe a venerable colonel enter the tram and remain standing, there is no place for him to sit, whilst opposite to him sits a robust young soldier insolently regarding the superior officer without budging from his place. The eyes of the colonel reflect pain and disgust, and he visibly avoids looking at the soldier.

An English officer was going some distance by a tram in which three soldiers were seated, two of them supporting their comrade, who was in the last stage of intoxication. A white-haired general entered. The soldiers continued to sit, and the general remained standing, and had not the right to admonish the inebriated soldier for his misconduct. The English officer was at first a silent witness of this scene, but filled with disgust he went up to the sprawling soldier, took him by the scruff of his neck, and put him outside the door, then approaching the general he said: 'Vasche Prevos-khoditelstvo [Your Excellency] here is a place for you.' No one protested against this act of authority, but, if a Russian officer had acted so, there would have been a fearful row, and all the newspapers would have bayed against the officers oppressing the soldiers.

The discipline was slackened to such an extent that the soldiers ceased to obey orders given by their superiors. The Chief of the Military Circuit of Petrograd, General Korniloff, desired to review the Finland Regiment. At the hour fixed, only three companies appeared, the fourth did not turn up, 'for they only obeyed orders given by the Council of Soldiers' Deputies'. After this insolence, General Korniloff sent in his resignation and returned to the front. The War Minister, M. Gutchkoff, likewise resigned his post, for he could do nothing with the undisciplined army. M. Kerensky replaced him, but, although his popularity among the soldiers and workmen is undoubted, still it is to be feared he will not be able to do much lasting good whilst things remain in the present state.

There have been cases when an attack on the Germans was fixed, the officers appeared, *but not one soldier.* 'They did not consider the attack necessary.' M. Kerensky makes the mistake likewise of wishing to use a moral treatment of persuasion with the soldiers. But no army can exist without strict discipline and implicit obedience. One of the best Russian army leaders, General Romeiko-Gurko, moved by the impossibility under existing conditions of exacting obedience, sent in his resignation. This comprehensible demonstration on the part of an experienced warrior[1] was severely dealt with by the present Minister of War, M. Kerensky. General Gurko received a stern reprimand; his resignation was only partly accepted, for he was deprived of the leadership of an army, but the Commander-in-Chief was requested to give the general another appointment, not higher than the command of a division. General Gurko is too rigorous a disciplinarian to protest against the harshness of the penalty inflicted upon him.

1 General Romeiko-Gurko has gained many laurels in this campaign, as well as in the Russo-Japanese War.

With soldiers, however, the new War Minister is more lenient, and they mostly go scot-free after the most flagrant acts of insubordination. M. Kerensky intends to act on the soldiers' morality by words of reason, and not with harsh reprisals. The Minister evidently does not take into consideration the mental calibre of the simple Russian soldier, nor the customs and habits which for centuries have been inculcated into the army and which had become a second nature to them. The Russian soldier of the past has gained world-wide fame for his wonderful valour and endurance. At a sign from his commander, he would fearlessly rush into the most imminent danger and achieve the bravest feats. An iron discipline and the admiration and respect they felt for their leader brought out their most sterling qualities. Polemical persuasion will never have the same effect on the soldier as a fiery glance, a masterful gesture and a commanding word.

The system of MM. Gutchkoff and Kerensky may theoretically be ever so noble and elevated, but it savours too much of Utopia to be successful in practice. Applied to the Russian soldier it has demoralised the army, and is ruining the soldier who a century ago inspired Napoleon with admiration, and quite recently gave the Kaiser pangs of envy. 'If my army were composed of Russian soldiers I could have conquered the world' has frequently been the German Emperor's remark, but it was the pre-Revolution soldier who caused these tributes from foreign monarchs and army leaders.

The Russian army leaders of the past loved the soldiers under their command, and took a fatherly care of them, and the soldiers would have gone through fire and water for a commander they venerated and trusted. Cases of harshness and undue severity were exceptional, and were never encouraged by the army chiefs. Since the war against Germany, the bond of common danger seemed to draw the officers into a closer union with the soldiers, and never were their relations so cordial. The Revolution, however, has put a complete stop to this. Events have occurred which can never be obliterated, and the covert antagonism that exists now between officers and soldiers, and their mutual distrust of one another, is due entirely to these innovations that have been inaugurated since the democratisation of the army.

The required fraternisation between the military men of all ranks has a fatal influence. The framers of the new Russian army have evidently forgotten the time-old adage that 'Familiarity breeds contempt.' Those responsible for this new order of things are taking a great responsibility in destroying all the old traditions of the army, and, if some miraculous change does not occur, it is to be feared they will be answerable for its complete decay.

To give an undeniable proof of the state of our army, I will quote the report of Lieutenant Yousuff-Khan to the War Minister, M. Kerensky, in which he tenders his resignation:

'I am an officer, and for twelve years have served in the army, devoting my strength and all that is best in me to the service of Russia. Many times have I risked my life in battle, as well as the lives of my dear volunteers from Daghestan. At the present moment I consider it impossible to serve, for there is no army any more. The Russian army is going the way of decomposition and by novel "prikazi",[1] appeals and speeches it continues to be led on the road to destruction. There is no army in the whole world ruled by appeals and orations. An army over which there is no power, where the men criticise the fighting problems and refuse to accomplish them, where no one has obligations but every one has rights; such an army is fatal to the country and harmless to the enemy. I cannot serve in such an army, and I do not wish to be a traitor to Russia; I therefore beg the War Minister to accept my resignation, all the more so as I am a Lesghis, and am not accomplishing compulsory service, but am serving in the army of my own free will out of love for my country, but I have not the strength to serve and be servile.'[2]

Can any declaration be clearer and better formed?

The reply of the War Minister proved that he did not understand the cry of anguish of the officer, assisting at the ruin of the army of which he was so proud. Here is his resolution on the report:

'Until the war is ended there can be no return from the army. Traitors to their country are they who refuse to serve her. The report of Lieutenant Yousuff-Khan tends as strongly to imperil the discipline as the agitation of the anarchists. Shame!'

The news of General Alexeieff's resignation from the post of Commander-in-Chief of the Russian army caused consternation

1 Prikaze = order.
2 This letter and also the whole of this volume was written before the great Russian retreat in Galicia or that from Riga.

and dismay to the public at large. General Alexeieff is a very popular man; the Russian nation trusted him and all hope of success was based on his leadership. His name is connected with two splendid military operations of world-wide fame: (1) the first victorious Galician campaign, when as the Chief of General Ivanoff's staff he planned the movement; (2) the saving of the Russian army during the dismal period of its ammunitionless condition, and the brilliant retreat from Galicia, which in its ingenuity equalled an important victory. Many thought it a mistake that General Alexeieff was not appointed at the beginning of the war as Chief-of-Staff to the Grand Duke Nicholas. This omission was attributed partly to the intrigues of General Soukhomlinoff, partly to the prejudice of His Imperial Highness. The Grand Duke did not get on over well with General Alexeieff, and never gave him full liberty of action.

General Alexeieff was one of the military leaders who gladly welcomed the change when the ex-Tzar took the command into his own hands. At first the new arrangement worked remarkably well, and only during the last months of Nicholas II's reign did occasional friction arise because of the Empress's continual interference.

It is the socialistic party that insisted on General Alexeieff's removal from the leadership of the army. They were displeased with the valiant General's last speech addressed to the soldiers at the front, in which he clearly pointed out that the destructive elements that had insinuated themselves of late amongst the soldiers were the cause of the Russian army falling to pieces. The country was on the brink of a precipice, and could only be saved by the army pulling itself together and deciding to come to the rescue and fight the enemy with the same spirit of valour and endurance which had gained the Russian soldier of former times such a distinguished place in military history. This harangue deeply impressed the soldiers, and increased the disapproval of the socialists.

Military experts, however, are of opinion that General Alexeieff, with all his marvellous erudition and strategical ability, is a remarkable Chief of the Staff, but that he lacks the three principal qualities that make an army leader: boldness, self-assurance, and confidence in the success of his enterprise.

General Brussiloff, the successor of General Alexeieff, though much less learned, possesses these qualities. He has the gift of electrifying himself, as well as the soldiers under his command. He is sixty years of age, but no one would give him his age, for he has retained the active, wiry figure of his youth, his wonderful alertness and energy. His ascendancy over the army is indubitable.

General Brussiloff in turn was forced to relinquish supreme control in favour of General Korniloff, a man of iron determination and uncompromising vigour.

In the first flush of emancipation from the yoke of the old Government, all the former strugglers for liberty were remembered. The dead were honoured with commemorative religious services, the living were set free, or sent for from foreign lands, where they had taken refuge. In the course of a few weeks, the country was flooded with emigrants, most of them socialists and anarchists, arriving from all parts of Europe. Amongst them were many German agents, who slipped in unhindered under the guise of political fugitives. Taking Russian pseudonyms, they became ardent and influential members of the Soldiers' and Workmen's Council, and working for Germany they put all kinds of wild ideas into the simple people's heads.

It is a curious fact that among the leaders of the Labour Party, which at present is the preponderating party in Russia, there are Armenians, Caucasians, Germans and Jews, but not a single real Russian. They began advocating the idea of a separate peace with Germany, without annexations or contributions. They have put ultra-socialistic ideas into their followers' heads, about taking away the land of the proprietors, and arresting capitalists. Under their baleful influence the exigencies of the workmen are taking such dimensions that the closing of all manufactories and foundries will be the probable result. That these increasing demands from the employees threaten a serious danger to the productiveness of industry in Russia leaves them completely indifferent. That it will mean the economic ruin of the country and the renewal of dependence on Germany seems likewise not to trouble them. Such socialistic leaders as Lenine, Trotzky, Grimm, Malinovsky and others, have incited the people against our splendid and trustworthy Allies, instilling the idea that the Germans being our neighbours are our natural friends.

The revolting fraternising at the front between the German and Russian soldiers was likewise the outcome of this socialistic teaching. The most ludicrous and pitiful things are going on all over the country owing to these anarchical socialistic leaders. Great Russia exists no longer. Finland desires to separate herself and demands an autonomy. The Finns argue that conformably to the Treaty of Abo, they were obliged to submit to the rule of the Russian Tzar, who became the Grand Duke of Finland. Now there is no Russian Tzar, the obligations of the treaty exist no longer. The Ukraina likewise wishes to separate from the Russian Republic, so does the Caucasus and Lithuania: the Letts and the Esthonians require an autonomous government. In one word the present state of things threatens the complete dismemberment of the once mighty Empire of Russia.

It is said that only one step removes the sublime from the ridiculous. This can well be proved by the present conditions in Russia, where at least a dozen small towns, following the example of Cronstadt, have declared their ludicrous resolve of not wishing to submit to the Provisional Government, but to have *their own separate republic*. Such was the decision of Schlüsselburg, Tzaritzine, Kirsanoff, etc. Can anything be more utterly senseless?

A formidable mistake which had endangered the safety of towns and their inhabitants was made when the heads of the State Duma, who took the lead in the revolutionary movement, permitted the utter destruction of the well-organised police in Russia. The Prefect of the Police in Petrograd, General Balk, and his assistants were arrested, the police-inspectors, constables and gendarmes were killed by the mob, or put into prison, the police-stations sacked and burnt, and the whole institution for ever destroyed. The very name of policeman was used as an insult. At the same time the doors of the prisons, which had mostly been filled with robbers, burglars and thieves, were forcibly opened and all the miscreants let out. Unchecked they had full scope to break into people's houses and flats and steal all they could lay hands on.

The Militia that was created a few days later to replace the police is quite inadequate to inspire the inhabitants with security. Many of the escaped thieves have joined the Militia, which includes students and college-boys, without any experience or real authority. Their only sign of distinction is a white band with red letters round the left arm endowing them with the necessary power. But the people sneer at them, for some of them are so puny and such cowards that they are the first to run away when a serious broil occurs. They do not even know how to use the fire-arms they are entitled to carry, and some silly as well as several tragic accidents have been caused in consequence.

They are held in profound contempt by the inhabitants, who cannot understand why the Militia receives such high wages, amounting to 200 roubles (£20) a month, whereas the policemen and gendarmes received not more than 50 roubles (£5). Burglaries and thefts have now become common occurrences, disorder and confusion reign everywhere, and bitterly do the people miss the former 'gorodovis' (police-constables) and their protection from the hooligans and other miscreants.

One of the favourite modern robbing systems consists of the men dressing up as soldiers and militiamen (the regulation bandage suffices for the travesty of the latter) and coming to the house they wish to rob on the plea of a search that is to be made. A gentleman the other day being alone in his house answered the bell in person. On being informed of the impending search, he enquired for the warrant. Six revolver-muzzles were instantly levelled at him: 'This is our search-warrant,' was the reply, 'and if you take a movement you are a dead man.'

The gentleman happened to be a rich financier and the booty the robbers carried away was considerable, worth about £16,000. There have been frequent cases of members belonging to the Militia being among the thieves.

Everything now is made uncomfortable for the inhabitants. Bread, butter, milk, etc., cannot be had without standing in a row, sometimes for hours, and waiting your turn. Servants spend nearly all their time in running from one row to the other, neglecting all other household work and manifesting an irritability that is the natural consequence of the fatigue engendered by these waits. Similar rows stand likewise before shoe shops and places where railway tickets are sold. This has even produced a new profession. Local 'camelots' come early and take a place in the row, and when later a lady or a gentleman arrive who do not wish to wait they sell their turn for a guinea or more.

From twelve to two, most shops, especially greengrocers, poulterers, fruiterers and such-like, are closed, to give the shop-assistants leisure in which to have their dinner comfortably. People come from the suburbs to do their shopping and lose a great deal of time because of this innovation, or else they are obliged to go home without the things they want. At six o'clock all shops are definitely shut. Busy people detained at their work until six o'clock can hardly ever find a convenient hour in which to make their purchases. Shopkeepers deplore these new rules, which diminish their receipts, and make them lose good customers. Many of the more experienced assistants likewise disapprove of these new restrictions, but nothing can be done, and no one dare go against the regulations laid down by the Soldiers' and Workmen's Council.

The Revolution in Russia was achieved by the plebeian classes, but during the first days they seemed aristocratic in spirit, actuated by noble impulses and willing to be led by wiser heads than their own. If everything had continued on such lines, the overthrow of the old Government might indeed have proved a blessing to the progress and well-being of the country. But gradually the radiance which had illumined the dawn of the Revolution began to grow dim. The reason for this can only be explained by the fact that at the first sound of the Revolutionary the cad vanishes. Cads are always poltroons, only in flocks do they appear brave.

Noah's second son, who behaved in such a disgusting way to his old father, is considered in Russia the prototype of cads, who in this country have therefore earned the appellation of 'Hams'. Such 'Hams' belong unfortunately to all classes of society, and, as there are nature's ladies and gentlemen, there exist likewise 'nature's Hams'.

During the bright days in February, when the Revolution was inspired with elevated aspirations and ideals, the 'Hams' disappeared as if by magic. They knew their place was not amidst the noble, well-intentioned innovators. They lay low for a time, but they were closely observing the course events were taking, and watching for an opening. Their opportunity came – authority had been completely destroyed by being given into the hands of the liberated people. That was the hour of the 'Hams', and they became the parasites of the Russian Revolution.

At first they acted warily, increasing their impudence as success attended their machinations. Unwittingly perhaps they acted the part of traitors to their country, and the German agents who swarmed everywhere during that period were only too glad to use them as the propagators of their aims and ideas. They sowed the seeds of mistrust towards some of the members of the Provisional Government, they caused dissension and unrest, and brought things to the present lamentable pass.

The Ministers of the new Cabinet are obviously out of their

depth; notwithstanding the wide outlook of their intellect and the nobility of their purpose, they lack the assurance of experience. They spend too much of their time in going to various meetings, and in speechifying at these meetings. And yet time is precious at this moment, and there is so little to lose that it seems a pity to fritter it away on meetings and political committees, which cannot advance matters and do considerably more harm than good.

The Government ought to stop all superfluous revolutionary manifestations and processions, which the people delight in, solemnly carrying about the town dozens of red flags, with high-flown inscriptions printed on them in huge golden letters. The number of such processions that during the past months marched up to the Duma is simply astounding: advanced women, soldiers' wives, factory girls and even schoolboys and little girls in white frocks with huge red bows, taking part in the general political manifestations.

The representatives of the Government have to come out and address them all with gracious encouraging words, whilst the public at large treat these proceedings with derision and laugh at the Ministers. All these manifestations ought to be suspended, the soldiers must join their regiments and do their duty at the front, letting wiser people take care of the country's politics, and the Government must set to work seriously and prove to the sceptical nation that the new order of things means the furthering of Russia's might and happiness.

Chapter XII

THE RULE OF DEMOCRACY

G ERMAN influence was at the root of the Russian Revolution, and German influence is continuing to direct its
development into anarchical channels. People are still
under the impression that the Empress Alexandra had paved the
way towards a separate peace with Germany. It was this threat
that accelerated the overthrow of the dynasty, and caused the
Revolution to be sincerely welcomed by the Right, as well as the
Left parties. Admitting that this surmise were based on facts, the
success of the pacific endeavours was extremely problematical as
there were too many serious impediments in the way. With his
usual astuteness the German Kaiser preferred to call forth disturbances in Russia that would spread all over the country and
reach the army; this would further his cause in any case.

Startled at the unlooked-for result of the disorders, the German potentate was not pleased at the dethronement of the Tzar,
but he soon rallied his forces and resolved to discount the moment
and the present circumstances to his own advantage. The spying-
net was reinforced, and amongst the returning emigrants were
numerous German agents in the pay of the Kaiser. Before leaving
Switzerland they received minute instructions; several of them,
as for instance Lenine, were allowed to pass through Germany.
Arrived in Russia they hastened to act in the interests of their
employers.

The soil it must be owned was a fertile one, for exhausted by
three years of bloodshed and privations, the soldiers were only too
eager to turn a willing ear to the voice of the tempters, who proved
to them the inexpediency of continuing the war. The Russian

people in their simple-mindedness are easily led; they nibbled at the bait and were nothing loth to become pacifists. Still one must remember that such convictions of uncouth minds are only skin-deep, and if a well-meaning patriotic leader would turn up possessing the power to touch their heart and their love for their country, an immediate transformation would ensue, and they would be full of enthusiasm to continue the war.

M. Miliukoff, as Minister of Foreign Affairs, was a thorn in Germany's side, for they knew he would lead the country's politics in a wise and righteous way. No one expected him to be brilliant, but he could be trusted to be true to the Allies and have Russia's interests at heart.

A feeling of mistrust gradually became apparent among the Soldiers' and Workmen's Deputies against the Minister of Foreign Affairs, which culminated suddenly in a fierce onslaught on M. Miliukoff. Hostile demonstrations took place against the Provisional Government; processions of workmen and soldiers carried red banners bearing the words: 'Doloy Miliukoff [away Miliukoff]. No annexations and contributions needed.' It was all the more senseless, for the war had not entered the phase when such questions could be discussed from Russia's and the Allies' standpoint. Consultations and conferences were held, the Government sought a compromise, for they felt this sudden change in the Foreign Office would produce an unfavourable impression on our Allies, but nothing could be done. M. Miliukoff had to retire and was replaced by the Minister of Finance, M. Terestchenko.

One of the first consequences of this change was the revocation of M. Sazonoff's appointment as the Russian Ambassador at the Court of St. James's. The nomination was made by the Tzar, a couple of months before the momentous events that called forth his abdication, and was very favourably received. M. Sazonoff was one of the most popular Ministers in Russia, and his well-known English sympathies, and his zeal to bring about an alliance with Great Britain, made him eminently fitted to fill the part allotted to him. M. Miliukoff shared these general opinions, but in the eyes of the Social Democrats M. Sazonoff was considered too 'Imperialistic', and too much inclined to Anglomania to suit their views. At the eleventh hour, Sazonoff was robbed of the post he was to occupy.

He had completed all his preparations for leaving Russia for several years, and after the sale of all his things, had left his apartment for an hotel, where he was to stay until the day of his departure, which had been fixed for the end of April, o/s.

He was actually *sitting in the train* when a courier from the Prime Minister came up to him with a letter from Prince Lwoff. M. Sazonoff stepped out of the railway carriage, and a few days later it became known that he had definitely quitted the service of the Government. All this produced an extremely painful impression, for it was easy to understand where things were tending, and the Government was severely blamed for thus giving in to the whims of the socialists, who know nothing of politics and diplomatic relations. Up to the present no other Ambassador has been fixed upon.

This was the third concession to the Labour Party. The first was the arrest of the Tzar and his family; the second the putting aside of M. Rodzianko for Prince Lwoff as the head of the new Cabinet. This third concession only served to mark the utter weakness and helplessness of the present Government.

The War Minister, M. Gutchkoff, was the next to give up his portfolio, but he did so of his own free will. Many people blamed him for this, saying that it was principally owing to him things had got into such a tangle, and that he did not see his way to unravel them. The Prime Minister, Prince Lwoff, strove to restrain him from taking this step, but the thoroughly disappointed M. Gutchkoff remained obdurate. The Minister of Justice, M. Kerensky, took upon himself the administration of the War Office.

This 'chassé croisé' in the Cabinet reminded one rather of Kryloff's fable, 'The Quartette', in which a bear, a donkey, a goat and a monkey desire to play a quartette. They buy instruments, music, and solemnly sit down to play, issuing the most heartrending dissonances, instead of the harmonious tunes they wished to evoke. The dismayed musicians endeavour to improve their music by changing places, but do what they can; discordant notes are the result. At this juncture a nightingale flies past, and the amateur musicians hasten to consult the songster as to the means of attaining success. 'We have instruments and music books, tell us only how to sit?' 'To be a musician,' replied the nightingale, 'one must have skill, and you, my friends, no matter where you sit, you are not fit to be musicians.'

The position was getting serious, and authority was in peril, for the Provisional Government possesses no real power and is obliged to connive with the Soldiers' and Workmen's Deputies.

The latter realise the superiority of their position and their pretensions keep increasing. Another change was made in the Cabinet: new Ministries were created, and the additional portfolios entrusted to members of the Socialist Revolutionary party, but this only made matters worse. At present all is in such a tangle of confusion that no one can foresee what turn things will ultimately take.

Meanwhile the workmen's claims on their employers are getting exorbitant, and threaten completely to destroy Russian industry. The workmen have been spoiled by prosperity. Ever since the urgent necessity arose of speedily providing munitions for the army, they have received very high wages, but this unusual affluence instead of inspiring content has only whetted their appetite, and, incited by German provocateurs, their demands know no bounds. The Minister of Commerce and Industry, M. Konovaloff, a manufacturer himself, was well able to gauge the situation; but, finding it absolutely hopeless under present conditions, he sent in his resignation and up to this no successor has been found to occupy his place.

The Social Democratic party pride themselves on not possessing such an absurd feeling as patriotism; they are 'Internationalists', and 'Internationalism' is their watchword. Most of the people do not understand the meaning of the word, but they think it high-sounding and clever, and go on lustily repeating it. When one fathoms the deeper meaning of this 'profession de foi' one is obliged to acknowledge that it is not so abnormal as it appears, for the influential members of the party are *not Russians*, and cannot feel as Russians do.

The conception of liberty in the unenlightened mind of the simple Russian is rather original, and would make people in Western countries open their eyes. They think now that discipline, authority and order are done with. In the name of Liberty all kinds of iniquities can be committed with impunity. They can spit in the streets, in railway carriages and in tram-cars, they can enter a tram-car from the wrong side, roughly push aside a woman or knock down a child who seems to impede their way. They can get intoxicated as often as they please, stagger about the streets in an inebriated condition and behave as objectionably as possible.

The public parks, gardens and squares have become unfit for any decent-minded woman to enter on a holiday, or after seven o'clock in the evening. The benches are occupied with hilarious soldiers or workmen, accompanied by their inamoratas, sitting together in the most indecorous manner, brazenly exchanging kisses and coarse jokes, or singing licentious songs. The pathways are strewn with burnt-out cigarettes, nutshells, orange-peel, and husks of helianthus. The lawns are trodden upon, the flowers ruthlessly gathered; the streets and walks remain unwatered, with perpetual dust-clouds rising, which the misguided pedestrian has to swallow in the name of the newly acquired liberty.

Formerly the police looked after the outward order of the town, but their ineffectual successors, the Militia, do absolutely nothing but pocket their exorbitantly large salary. Everything is left to its own devices, and the external aspect of Petrograd has assumed a tarnished slatternly air most distressing to observe.

People are getting very tired of the Revolution, or rather of the result it has entailed. The position is becoming grave. At the front the soldiers sit with folded hands and do nothing, except fraternise, or mix themselves up with anarchism and marauding. The labour-productiveness has decreased in the same measure as the monstrous wages to the workmen have increased. Most people see clearly, others feel it instinctively, that things cannot go on like this much longer. The Revolution now is more deeply hated than ever was Tzarism. Not a single 'Right', or Monarchical press organ exists and, notwithstanding this fact, the socialists observe with terror the daily extending propaganda of Monarchism, and, what is worse to their prejudiced eyes, this monarchical tendency is taking a serious hold of youthful minds – always the most open to impressions.

While the Social Democrats are daring to insult Russia and deride her glorious past, the 'Martyrs of Ideas' stand forth on the 'Right' side and in the people's opinion have become the 'Martyrs' of Patriotism. In this lies the great danger to the Revolution, because, in the natural disgust evoked by the events that have lately happened in the name of 'Liberty', there is a decisive movement to the 'Right' all over Russia, which is deplored by the moderate Revolutionists. They acknowledge the mortifying facts, but they are of opinion that the reaction that has set in must not tend to idealise the former regime which produced the Revolution.

The newly acquired 'Liberty' is a pure fiction. As a matter of fact there is no such thing in Russia: people have only exchanged an autocratic Sovereign for autocratic Soldiers' and Workmen's Deputies. No one dares give vent to a frank opinion against the existing state of things. The partisans of Monarchism or 'Imperialism' (the new denomination created by the socialists) are persecuted as were the most fanatical nihilists in olden times. The censorship continues to exist, only it has changed hands and is at present directed by the Soldiers' and Workmen's Deputies.

There have been cases where the workmen employed on a newspaper have been forbidden to print the next number because some article had displeased their deputies, or they would inflict the penalty on the publisher of not permitting the paper to be sold by the newspaper boys. There was a moment even when the workmen and soldiers threatened to close the printing offices of those newspapers,[1] which did not meet with their approval. Most of the publishers are naturally obliged to take such possibility into account and 'freedom of speech' has been set at naught, although it had been pompously announced by the Revolutionists.

M. Purischkevitch is another instance of the partiality that guides the Soldiers' and Workmen's Deputies in all their judgements. When in the first days of the Revolution, the worthy member of the Duma made an oration at a meeting in the Mansion House, he gave vent to the following words in allusion to the Empress Alexandra: 'I thank God that Russia has got rid of the woman who was the first German spy in Russia.' His words were frantically applauded, and M. Purischkevitch, who had likewise contributed to rid the country of Rasputine, was magnified into a hero of patriotism.

A few months later this same M. Purischkevitch, profoundly indignant at the events he had witnessed at the front, addressed an open letter to the deputies of the soldiers and workmen, severely blaming them for the way they were imperilling the safety of Russia, and pointing out the dishonourable manner they were conducting the war, obstructing the way to victory by encouraging the soldiers' disobedience, and putting forward all kinds of restrictions, which entirely paralysed all efforts of their chiefs. As to those soldiers who persisted in going over to the German trenches to fraternise with the enemy, he did not hesitate to stigmatise them as traitors to their country. This letter incited the fury of its recipients to such a pitch that they wished to arrest M. Purischkevitch, and it caused M. Kerensky a great deal of trouble to make them understand that such a measure would be

1 For instance, the *Novoe Vremia*.

in direct opposition with the recently established 'freedom of speech'. However, this letter did not appear in any newspaper for the reason that the Soldiers' and Workmen's Deputies prohibited it, and it was only circulated amongst the public in typewritten copies, like the tabooed speeches of MM. Miliukoff, Kerensky, Count Bobrinsky and others, in the time of the old Government.

The Provisional Government, however, was all the time hampered with the fear of transgressing against the rights of Liberty. For this reason it dealt leniently with the anarchist Lenine, although the general opinion was that he ought to have been arrested and taken out of harm's way before he had time to strengthen and spread his forces. The consequence of this most ill-advised tolerance towards such a dangerous agitator is that he has sent his creatures to the principal towns in Russia, and that anarchy and strife are steadily spreading all over the country. The conditions of the Black Sea Fleet were up to this exemplary, but a few days after the visit of Lenine's emissary to Sevastopol there were serious riots amongst the sailors, which induced the Commander, Admiral Kolchak, one of the most able and popular of Russian admirals, to send in his resignation. At this rate the best army leaders and officers are being gradually removed at a time when their services are so urgently wanted.

The soldiers and workmen have been continually put forward since the first days of the Revolution, but there are yet the peasants, who represent the great majority of the Russian populace. A certain anxiety was felt as to how they would take the overthrow of Tzardom. Emissaries from the Duma were sent all over the country to explain to them the position of affairs and attach their sympathies by the promise of an increase of land. Land has always been the most seductive bait for the peasant. One of the greatest insurgents in Russia, who lived about two centuries ago, Stenka Razine, was the first to proclaim the watchword, 'Zemlia y Volia' (Land and Liberty), which has since entwined itself round each peasant's heart. To these alluring words Stenka Razine owed his numerous followers and the success which he and his band of insurgents achieved for many months, before he was finally captured and executed.

The promise of land did not fail to attract the peasants; but they preferred not to wait for the legal distribution and are busily monopolising private estates all over the country. The present state of affairs in the provinces causes general anxiety as to the future; still it is not in the spirit of the Russian peasant to become a socialist, the instinct of possession being too vividly inherent in his nature. The socialists wish all land to belong to the country, though possessed temporarily by the man who works on it; but the socialists make a mistake to found their hopes on the peasants, for they will never be able to fathom the principles of socialism. Their love of their land is elementary, they would do anything to consolidate the possession of land they have a right to.

The origin of the former serfs is unknown to many, and those who once knew have forgotten it. Long before there were serfs by law in Russia, the peasants voluntarily bound themselves to slavery for a certain number of years on condition that the land they lived on should be considered their own. This gave the stimulus about two centuries ago to one of the Russian Empresses to bind the peasants by law to belong to the land they lived on, thus becoming the property and the care of the landowners.

It was in the reign of Boris Godunoff (1598–1605) that the peasants were forbidden to leave the land they lived on and go to another part of the country, thus irrevocably attaching them to one particular estate. Practically they became serfs from that time, but it was in Catherine II's reign that the peasants were legally allotted to the proprietor of the land as his serfs.

The institution of serfs lasted in Russia a little over one hundred years. They were finally emancipated in 1861 by the Emperor Alexander II. The peasants are so deeply attached to their land that they are willing to brave expense and go to law for the smallest particle that is being withheld from them. The affection for their land is more apparent and far deeper than their attachment to the members of their family, for they will not hesitate to become the most implacable foes of their nearest and dearest kinsman if, in sharing their land, the bit one wants is taken by the other. They will make use of the present confusion to annex the land of proprietors or wealthy farmers, without having to buy it, but they will never admit that the land allotted to them by the law of the country should be submitted to the socialistic principle.

Peasant meetings have been convoked and the peasants have sided with the authorities on all questions concerning the war. They have blamed the soldiers for their inactivity, and have pronounced themselves in favour of the prolongation of war until a victory renders it possible to make peace. This hostile attitude of the peasants towards a separate peace with Germany has impressed the soldiers, who in spirit stand nearer to the peasants than to the workmen, for each soldier aspires to return to his native soil and become a peasant.

For some time the relations between the soldiers and workmen have been strained, and they threaten to become more strained still. Most of the workmen incline to the teaching of Lenine and the anarchists; their mind is not subtle enough to see through the treacherous and dangerous precepts, or to comprehend that Lenine is acting solely in the interests of Germany. The workmen and the soldiers, although the latter are in great minority, have put such men as Lenine and Zinovieff on pedestals, and look up to them as to apostles of proletarian felicity.

The misunderstanding that is at present exciting them is provoked by the following incident. Over a month ago, when the Germanophile Lenintzys had attained the zenith of their impudence, they openly annexed several uninhabited private dwellings for the use of their association. The mansion of the Duke of Leuchtenberg was thus occupied for two or three days and robbed of many valuables. The dancer Madame Kschessinsky's solicitor can do nothing to expel the band of anarchists that are living in the artiste's house, where they have completely ruined the costly furniture and the silken and plush draperies. The luxuriously appointed bathroom of the dancer, situated on the second floor is in a disgusting state, and the large white marble basin set into the floor with steps leading down to it is filled for over a yard high with burnt-out cigarette-ends, proving that the anarchists used it exclusively as a huge ashtray.

The day has been repeatedly fixed by the magistrate for the intruders to quit the premises. On the day preceding the last term settled for their exit, the solicitor called at the house to see if they would voluntarily leave the next day without giving trouble as they had promised. He heard sounds of music and laughter and found the garden illuminated, the ballroom brilliantly lighted up and gaudily dressed women merrily whirling round the room in the arms of soldiers and workmen. The Lenintzys-anarchists were giving a ball! The next day was fixed for the judicial hegira, but the authorities were helpless, and the necessary array of men to enforce the verdict was not forthcoming. Since the existence of judicature in Russia this is the *first* case of a judgement that could not be carried out.

The beautiful villa of General Dournovo on the Islands was invaded by the anarchists, who elected to settle their staff in this luxurious dwelling and establish in it their headquarters. The law gave the owner the right to expel the usurpers, according them, however, ample time to find other accommodation. In principle they agreed to leave, but they keep putting off the day of their move. All was done to avoid a scandal, and when they requested another month to find other quarters it was accorded to them and the Procurator Besobrasoff spent a whole day driving about the town in search of suitable house-room for the anarchists.

The last term is approaching and there is a rumour that they will not leave peacably. The workmen will side with them and excesses are dreaded, but should there be trouble the garrison and the majority of the soldiers (except those who are anarchists) will go against the rioters. Besides these armed forces the Government will be supported by 70,000 Cossacks and the 'Wild Division', which is quartered in Petrograd, and is ready at any moment to fight the insubordinate workmen and anarchists. This precaution is considered as an attempt at a counter-Revolution, and the workmen declare they will go to any extreme to safeguard the privileges they have obtained. Strikes, riots and disorders are impending, and only merciful Providence knows how all will end.

Some of the resolutions given out by the Soldiers' and Workmen's Deputies reveal a somewhat distorted point of view. They have decreed that every soldier that is seen in the streets in an inebriated condition must be instantly sent to the front, making a penalty out of what every soldier ought to consider the first duty to his country. The following fact is another instance. Two clerks of the Artillery Warehouse in Cronstadt, Terentieff and Fissoff by name, came to the conclusion that 'except idly prowling from one anarchical meeting to another, they could be of no use to anyone', they therefore addressed a petition to their particular committee begging to be sent to the front. The committee found the request so strange that they could not take the decision upon themselves without submitting it to the General Council of Deputies in Cronstadt. The Council conferred on the subject for a long time giving out the following resolution: 'Shame to the comrades Terentieff and Fissoff for taking an independent departure at such a moment and seeking to be transferred'!

Here is a letter from a soldier, who reveals the real feeling of the army:

Six days ago I returned from the front, where I have spent nearly three years without quitting the trenches, and was all the time in the vanguard. I took part in the battle of Soldau, I fought at Warsaw and Lonsha, was wounded several times, and I am at present in Petrograd on leave. I and my fellow-soldiers are dismayed with all that is happening here. Who cries against the war? Who protests against the enemy? Only those who have not been at the front. Who listen to Lenine and Zinovieff? We are soldiers and acknowledge only the War Minister. As soon as we shall receive his order we shall break the German front. We must vanquish them to liberate our captives from their clutches.

Thirteen of our comrades succeeded in eluding the German vigilance; they reported themselves to the staff of our division. The account of their escape is full of horror; they crawled most of the way for fear of being detected, and the skin was torn off their hands and feet and breasts. They were exhausted with their privations, half-famished with hunger, and it was with the greatest difficulty they reached their country, every minute risking death.

And Lenine, he travelled comfortably and fearlessly through Germany! What does he want? Peace? No, not peace; he only throws bombs from above. If he arrived in Russia with good intentions, why has he not gone to the front, instead of sitting in Kschessinsky's house?

If he wishes for peace, let him set our war-prisoners free. 'Doloy Voinou' (away with the war) is the cry of cowards, of those who have not been in the trenches. We are revolted with the men who won't come to our help, who run away like deserters and hide in the rear.

Help is wanted at the front. Our comrades must come to their senses and follow us. We appeal to each of them. Let them think of us, living in trenches for long months, seeing nothing but the trees of the forest and the sky above. And what are they doing? Forgetting their country and their family, they spend their time with loose women, munching helianthus seeds, selling flowers and cigarettes. Is it the business of a soldier to be doing a jobber's trade?

CORPORAL STEPAN[1] VINOGRADOFF
of the 32nd Infantry Division.

A soldier coming from Mohilev who was a witness of the arrest of the Tzar and of his departure from Headquarters describes the scene quite differently from the account which was given out officially. It was said that a dead silence reigned the whole time, whereas in reality the soldier inmates of the Stavka were terribly upset. When the Tzar took leave of them, thanking them for their services, every one of them wept; the Emperor was visibly moved. When the Sovereign entered the train, which slowly moved off, agonising sobs were heard, and several soldiers had hysterics.

Meanwhile the anarchist members of the Soldiers' and Workmen's Deputies desire to concentrate all power and administration of the country in the hands of the proletariats. They show plainly that they used the Duma and their leaders only as a means to gain their ends. Having done so with great success, they would like to get rid of their former auxiliaries, and in their impudence they have decreed to do away with the State Duma and the Upper Chamber as 'Imperialistic institutions', thus saving the nation the yearly expense of five millions of roubles.

The Duma has never been popular with the nation at large, and the majority consider it has only brought harm to the country; still, this resolution of the Soldiers' and Workmen's Deputies can only be looked upon with contempt. M. Rodzianko takes no notice of this decree, and the sittings continue as usual. At Prince Lwoff's request the Duma is shortly moving into the Palace Marie, where the Upper Chamber dwells. The Tauride Palace is to be adapted for the great convocation of electors, who alone will have the right to decide on the future fate of Russia and establish the form of government.

Weary of the dispiriting state of things that reigns in Russia, people are commencing to realise the personal motives that guided the leaders of the Revolution, and are inclined to blame the members of the Duma for giving the revolutionary movement the sanction of their support at such an important historical moment, when interior disturbances should have been avoided. As long as the Revolution was kept within the bounds of reason

1 Stepan = in Russian Stephen.

and moderation the nation welcomed the change, seeing in it the means to conclude the war victoriously, without the dishonour of a separate peace, and exhilarated with the hope of the future progress of the country.

As things are turning out, the public is becoming displeased, for things are going from bad to worse. The harmony amidst the 'saviours' of Russia, like the hopes of the nation, lasted only about a month. Signs of the Provisional Government's helplessness began to manifest themselves and caused the first qualms of anxiety to be felt. The merit of MM. Rodzianko, Gutchkoff and Kerensky, as well as of the executive committee of the Duma, consisted in the fact of their having so rapidly formed a new Government, thus saving the country from the dangers of anarchy. But anarchy followed nevertheless, as the fatal and unavoidable result of the foregoing events and the seeming deliverance was only a reprieve.

The power of the Provisional Government was only fictitious. As a matter of fact its actions were from the first day openly and officially submitted to the Council of Soldiers' and Workmen's Deputies, thus putting them in authority over the Government. Power under continual surveillance is no power: therefore it is not to be wondered at that the Government was repeatedly obliged to give in to the real masters of the situation and, like M. Gutchkoff, end by leaving the coast clear for their representatives to fill the vacant places.

One of the rooted customs of bygone days among the Russian merchant classes was to secure the presence of one or several generals to assist at the weddings and funerals in their families. The generals attending these solemn occasions in their glittering uniforms, with all their orders and decorations, gave to them a certain brilliancy and importance; the venerable veterans, on their side, were easily prevailed upon to attend such pageants, which were always followed by a sumptuous banquet, at which the warriors were the most honoured guests. This time-honoured custom originated the expressions 'wedding-general' and 'funeral-general'.

The role allotted by the Revolutionists to M. Rodzianko and Prince Lwoff was the historical part of generals assisting at a merchant wedding. Their participation impressed the people with confidence, but they only gave the bride away; they were not the happy bridegrooms.

The renovated Provisional Government, filled with members of the Council of Soldiers' and Workmen's Deputies, is much nearer in spirit to the democratic leaders of the Revolution, but even they are powerless to stem the growth of anarchy in the army and in the country. The utter ruin of everything manifests itself everywhere: in every department, in every jurisdiction, in every single part of the country's administration. The Ministry of the Interior seems to have plunged into Nirvana, from the time Prince Lwoff undertook its direction and continues in the blissful state between existence and non-existence.

The Ministry of Justice seems powerless to stop the most daring violation of the country's criminal and civil laws, which it should be their duty to guard against infraction. The responsible Minister is forced to close his eyes to the revolting acts of the anarchists, who stop at nothing in their brazen insolence. The police, as I have already mentioned, are non-existent, for the Chinese phantoms that prowl about the streets, with the Militia badge round their arm and who are never to be found in an emergency, are not to be depended upon.

The existing tariff for the cabmen was abolished during the first days of the Revolution, and has not been re-established. The cabmen consequently charge fancy prices. For a distance that in former days would have cost from 20 to 80 copeks, they now demand from two to seven roubles, sometimes more than that. The post and telegraph systems are also in a wretched state. The Ministry of Labour is on the eve of becoming the labourless ministry.

A political refugee had been appointed at the head of the Ministry of Food. The Minister is known as a clever theoretist, but he knows hardly anything of Russia and Russian ways, as political circumstances forced him to live and grow old in foreign lands. Nothing has been done to relieve the difficulties of getting food, or to reduce the existing exorbitant prices. The Ministry of Food is more like the Ministry of Famine, as with the increasing shortage of food-stuffs and the high prices which increase ever more quickly than the choice of food decreases, people will soon not be able to find food at all.

As to the unfortunate Minister of Finance, he does not know what to do and, wringing his hands at the desperate outlook, he can only think of the old saying: 'Give me good politics and I will give you good finance.' The Ministry of War is hopelessly struggling with the consequences of its own mistakes and errors. The Ministry of Commerce and Industry is chiefless since the resignation of M. Konovaloff. His resignation will be better understood in England than here, where it created great indignation. To make myself clearer I will give an instance of why he resigned.

One of the most important Russian manufacturers was recently in Petrograd and related that the works which, prior to the Revolution, delivered from eighteen to twenty engines a month now produce only five. Since the Revolution the productiveness of labour has decreased by seventy-five per cent, whilst the wages of the workmen have increased fourfold.

'Perhaps you lack raw material?' the manufacturer was asked.

'Certainly not,' was the reply. 'Last year we had stores of metal and coal to the value of four hundred thousand roubles, whereas at the present moment our stores amount to eight and a half millions of roubles.'

The figures speak for themselves.

The Ministry of Ways and Communications is no exception to the prevailing rule. Greasers and stokers direct many of the most important departments. This has brought the conditions of the Ministry to a state of utter chaos. If the prophecies of clever engineers and private railway companies are to be believed, it threatens the country with a colossal catastrophe.

Out of motives of personal vanity, political leaders in search of popularity play into the hands of the demagogues and the proletariat, without a thought of the unfortunate country which is agonising under the burden of democracy and socialism, or of their countrymen who have been liberated from the autocratic yoke of Tzardom only to become the victims of autocratic demagogues.

Political parties and factions are full of expectation. Political passions are excited by virulent orations. People seem to have nothing to do but frequent political gatherings, make speeches or listen to them. The most busy Ministers are seen at all the most important meetings. Cataracts of high-sounding words are being daily pronounced . . . but where are the deeds which the nation is craving for? Unhappy Russia!

Chapter XIII

THE TZAR'S TROUBLES

THE political troubles that darkened the beginning of the reign of Nicholas I prevented him from achieving several liberal reforms which he had planned, but Alexander II knew he was fulfilling his father's will when, in 1861, he emancipated the serfs.

Up to that moment the gentry, consisting of landowners, were responsible for the material well-being of the peasants who lived on their land, but the Emancipation Act wrought a complete change in these relations, freeing the peasants from their servile dependence, but at the same time relieving the proprietor of their support. A *modus vivendi* had to be thought of to give the peasants the means of gaining a livelihood. The noblemen were compulsorily dispossessed of part of their domains, and the land taken was given over collectively to the community of liberated serfs: the landowners received an indemnification from the Crown, but many wealthy proprietors preferred to pass over the land to the peasants as a gift.

To the rich landlord, owning thousands of acres, the loss of a small portion of his vast property was immaterial, but it impoverished the proprietors of small estates, who hitherto had lived very comfortably. To some of them it spelt ruin. The weakening of the land-owning nobility as a corporation dates back to that period.

The sequestered land, however, was inadequate to satisfy the needs of millions of peasants, and the portion individually allotted to each was very small. They had hardly enough pasture to feed their cattle, and if a peasant's cow wandered on to the squire's meadow the cow was confiscated until the fine of thirty copeks

{173}

was paid. All this created continual friction and heart-burning, causing a feeling of ill-will towards the landlord.

The majority of the emancipated serfs never fathomed the nobility of the Tzar's motives in granting them their long-coveted liberty. They were under the impression that the monarch was hostile to the nobility, and had taken part of their land from them as a punishment. This naïve idea was fostered and encouraged by evil-minded people, who established themselves in the midst of the peasants intent on gaining influence and provoking ill-feeling between the landlords and peasants. An over-honest nihilist who dared to breathe a word against the Sovereign would be pitilessly beaten and hounded out of the village, but the more astute agitators were cautious, pretending to be the Tzar's most loyal and devoted subjects, whilst all the time they devoted their energy to undermining the peasants' loyalty to their former proprietors.

The most incongruous tales were spread, and firmly believed by the villagers, that the Tzar wished to give the whole of the land to the peasants, but that he had been overruled by the nobility. They were convinced that the Emperor hated the gentry, and would not interfere in their favour if their houses were burnt, sacked and pillaged, their forests destroyed, etc. This was the keynote to all the riots and agrarian disturbances that at times devastated the private estates in Russia.

Russia is pre-eminently an agricultural country, and the majority of its population belong to the peasantry. The Tzar Alexander III felt that Russian well-being lay in the rational development of agriculture and forestry all over the country. The Sovereign's desire was that most of the peasants should remain farmers and labourers, live and work on their land or on the land of the proprietors.

All sorts of financial facilities were accorded by Alexander III to the landed gentry, as well as to the peasantry, for acquiring land and obtaining loans for its improvement at a low rate of interest, and with all kinds of privileges as to repayment. This was done to encourage the gentry to keep their estates, and to help the peasants to acquire more land when the opportunity presented itself. To further this aim two agrarian banks were founded, for the nobility and for the peasants' benefit.

The Tzar foresaw the ruin of Russia in the increasing growth of the proletarian element. He disapproved of the wealthy peasant sending his son to the gymnasium and subsequently to the university, instead of having his son taught in a practical agricultural school. All kinds of obstacles were placed in the way of people of the lower ranks giving a good education to their offspring. This has been imputed to the late Tzar as the outcome of retrogression, and is looked upon as a proof of his being a foe of the democracy.

As a matter of fact, the Tzar had the happiness of all his subjects at heart, and he considered the best security of their well-being was for people to remain in their own rank, and to live contentedly in the conditions of life they were born to. In Alexander III's opinion a high education could only have a disastrous influence on the son of a peasant, for the development of his mental faculties would be out of keeping with his unrefined nature, resulting only in discontent with his surroundings, detaching him from his native soil, and inspiring him with contempt for his simple-minded, uncouth parents. Such half-educated young men and women increased the growth of the proletariat. They turned a willing ear to the wild teachings of the socialists, and became an easy prey to the revolutionists in search of political converts.

It was mostly to such inexperienced neophytes that the accomplishment of terroristic acts was confided. It sounds paradoxical, but it is nevertheless the truth, that in Russia the sudden education-craze of raw and totally unprepared minds wrought much harm and caused disaster.

Russian people are inclined to extremes. A sensible middle-class schooling is not appreciated. If a boy be lazy, he will all his life remain a semi-illiterate dunce, hardly able to read and write.

If on the contrary he is gifted with even second-rate abilities, he thinks himself a second Lomonossoff,[1] and aspires to the university, although in most cases he has neither the brains nor the means to finish with honours.

A great drawback of the Russian high schools and colleges was that the boys were more absorbed in politics than in their studies. They neglect their work, but they would attend secret meetings[2] to discuss the defects and misuses of the Government. It is among

---

1 Lomonossoff, one of Russia's greatest men and poets, was the son of a simple fisherman in Kholmogory (province of Archangel). He was born in 1711, and is considered the creator of Russian poetry. He was the first national writer who rhymed his verses.
2 During the old regime such meetings had to be clandestine.

the students that the nihilists and socialists found their most eager auxiliaries.

The young Russians never could understand that they are sent to college to develop their brains and mind, and are not called upon to improve the Government. Because of this political tendency, many parents objected to sending their sons to college, except to the so-called privileged ones (the Lyceum and the School of Jurisprudence), which are expensive, and where everyone is not admitted.

Unfortunately, the democratic Government intends to abolish these privileged colleges, as well as the colleges for girls (institutes) all over Russia which were under the patronage of the Dowager Empress Marie. Henceforth there are only to be gymnasiums and universities accessible to everyone. In their determination to annihilate all vestige of 'Imperialism' the democratic Government is destroying everything, even those perfectly organised institutions that were a blessing to so many.

Some of the villages, especially in the proximity of large towns, are frequently quite deserted by young and able men. The wealthy pursue their studies or their professions; the poor leave their native village to work in manufactories, where the wages and the gay, dissolute town life attracts them. Only old people remain in the villages, and the lack of farming hands is often felt, thus imperilling the security of the harvest. Town life, under the workman's conditions, completely demoralises the rustic youths. They become a rough, riotous lot, and are considered the worst element of the people, held in contempt by the villagers, who scornfully call them 'fabritchnye'.

Alexander III wished to stem this fatal tide, which, in his opinion, was at the bottom of people's dissatisfaction, causing the unhappiness such partially educated people were bound to feel. They are morally detached from everyone and everything originally belonging to them. Their intellect outgrows the mental calibre of their kinsfolk, yet they cannot join the higher classes, owing to their lack of breeding.

During the recent days of revolution, when the Chanceries of Ministries were ransacked, a report of the Minister of Public Instruction was found bearing on this vexed question, with the following pencil mark in Alexander III's hand: 'That is the misfortune, every peasant wants his son to go to the gymnasium.'

The revolutionists got hold of this document, distorted the

Tzar's motive, and long tirades were printed in the daily papers against Alexander III for being the sworn enemy of democracy.

Nicholas II was brought up in his father's ideas, and, having not only a deep affection but a great admiration for his father's wisdom, he endeavoured, especially during the first years of his reign, to emulate him, but the methods of the son were always less arbitrary than were those of his father. One of the most honest and well intentioned of monarchs, Nicholas II was not only hampered by lack of strength of purpose, he was continually pursued by his fatal ill-luck. He never wished to occupy the exalted position of Tzar of all the Russias, and would willingly have escaped his impending fate.

As quite a young man when it was hoped his father's life would last several decades, the Tzessarevitch Nicholas expressed his desire to resign to his brother the rights to the throne. This rumour spread with great persistence, but it was carefully hushed up. The Tzar, fond father though he was, did not see his way to circumvent the laws of heredity. When Alexander III died, the Tzessarevitch knew he was obeying his father's wish, and, without any further demur, he ascended the throne and endeavoured to do his duty; but fate and circumstances combined to render the burden too heavy. His reign was an unfortunate one. The ex-Tzar is perfectly aware of his ill-luck: the following story proves it.

After the disturbances of 1905–1906, one of the Ministers, after sending in his resignation, was received by the Sovereign in private audience.

'And what shall you do now?' queried the Tzar, in the course of conversation.

'I shall spend the greater part of the year in the country,' was the statesman's response. 'I shall be very busy with an historical work.' A short silence ensued, after which the Tzar added:

'How I should like to be in your place, but,' said the Sovereign in a low voice, 'I was born on the day of the long-suffering Job.[1] Strive as I can, no attempt of mine succeeds. Everything I think of, all the plans I wish to carry out, all end in failure.'

The ex-Tzar is quite resigned to his present fate, and shows a brave front to the sentinels who guard him, but his moral anguish must be fathomless. The majority of the sentinel-officers which surround him are rough fellows, who take a certain pride in being

1 6th/19th May.

insolent to the former monarch, but the latter, under the most trying circumstances, remains invariably courteous, calmly ignoring their slights. Since the warm weather has set in, the ex-Tzar spends hours in gardening; his skill excites the admiration of the watching soldiers. The flower-beds which he planned and dug out himself are now a blaze of bright-hued flowers, which he tends with the greatest care. The Grand Duchess Tatiana occasionally shares her father's labours.

When Nicholas II resolved to give in to what he believed the general wish of the people and abdicate, he never thought of leaving the country. His intention was to retire to the Crimea and lead a retired life in Livadia, but the Social Democrats and the Social Revolutionists, in their strenuous endeavour to copy the French Revolution, do not wish any of the reigning branch of the Romanoff family to remain in Russia.[1] To leave the country will be a painful wrench to the quondam Sovereign but he is certain to bear the ordeal with the same dignified patience he manifests in his captivity, and will certainly lead a contented existence, glad to be relieved of the heavy burden of responsibility of ruling over such a vast Empire with so many millions of heterogeneous people.

During one of M. Kerensky's interviews with the ex-Tzar, His Majesty told him that since his boyhood he had always felt a passionate love for his country. 'I was told it was my duty to the country to become its Tzar – I obeyed, although all my inclinations tended to a private life. I was told I must marry for the good of the country – I married. Again I was told that to save the country I must abdicate – I did so without demur. This morning I have been to holy communion, and am quite ready to lay down my life should my country require it.'

The fascinating charm of the ex-Tzar's personality has completely captivated one of his greatest political adversaries. M. Kerensky finds the former monarch a well-informed, interesting conversationalist, with a developed, well-balanced mind and one of the noblest natures he ever met.

Such is M. Kerensky's opinion of the monarch he helped to dethrone. Could any ruler wish a greater tribute?

The state of health of the former Empress Alexandra is very

1 This was written before there was any idea of sending the ex-Tzar to Siberia.

precarious. She is wheeled about the park of Tzarskoe Selo in a bath-chair and is said to have aged greatly. When she is wheeled about the park she mostly keeps her head bent, looking neither to the right nor to the left. The sailor Derevenko, who for years has been attached to the service of the Tzessarevitch, wheels her about, whilst one of her daughters walks beside her, generally preserving a rigid silence. The lawn-tennis court, which used to be the favourite resort of the Imperial Family, stands empty and even the nets have not been set up.

The sailor Derevenko is one of the Tzar's most faithful retainers. His old comrades and other sailors wanted him to leave the Palace, but he scornfully refused all proposals and has remained true to his allegiance.

The Mistress of the Robes, Madame Narischkine, has recently left the Palace. She sent a petition to the Procurator-General, pleading the state of her health, and requesting to be relieved of her duties. The only lady who now attends the ex-Empress at the present instant is the maid of honour, Countess Hendrikoff, assisted by Madame Schneider, who taught the Russian language to the Empress and remained at Court in the capacity of reader. The ex-Empress places great confidence in the lady, and Madame Schneider frequently attends the young Grand Duchesses.

The Dowager Empress Marie is staying in the Crimea in her son-in-law's, the Grand Duke Alexander Mikhailovitch's, palace near Yalta. The rumour of a conspiracy amongst the members of the Imperial Family caused a search being made in all the palaces in the vicinity of Yalta. The Empress Marie was in bed and did not hear the knock at her door. It was suddenly opened by a ruthless hand, and an officer stood before her startled eyes. He offered her the option: to get up in the presence of a woman who accompanied them, or to remain in bed with her hands over the bed-clothes. The Empress chose the latter. All her correspondence and some of her books were taken away to be inspected. Even her pocket Bible, with some inscriptions in her own and in her late husband's hand and her favourite verses underlined, was taken.

The Empress remained perfectly collected, but Countess Mengden[1] – her maid of honour – wept bitterly to see her Imperial

---

1 Her brother, General Count George Mengden, the former Commander of Her Majesty's regiment, the Horse Guards, was killed in the days of the Revolution, though the fact was not mentioned in any of

mistress subjected to such treatment. The Empress's youngest daughter, Olga, and her husband are also with her. A few months prior to the Revolution, the Grand Duchess Olga divorced her first husband, Prince Peter of Oldenburg, and married his aide-de-camp, Captain Kulikovsky, an officer of the Blue Cuirassiers of Gatchino. He was obliged to leave the service in consequence of the Revolution because of his marriage to the Tzar's sister.

The marriage took place privately in Kiev, in the Dowager Empress's presence. The Emperor sent a telegram to wish his sister happiness. A few days prior to the wedding ceremony, a sister of mercy came to the clergyman and expressed her desire to be married by him to an officer. The priest enquired if all the documents were in order.

'The bridegroom's papers are there,' the sister replied, 'but I have no documents.'

The priest then told her he could not marry her.

'But if my brother sends you a telegram?' queried the sister of mercy.

'What has your brother to do in the matter?' laughed the clergyman.

'Even if my brother happens to be the Tzar?' enquired the Grand Duchess.

'That changes everything,' replied the abashed priest, and the wedding ceremony was fixed. Captain Kulikovsky was to have received the title of Count, had not the Revolution intervened.

The movements of the Imperial Family are under continual control. If they want to go to Yalta or prolong their drives in the neighbourhood they must have a special permission. The Grand Duke Alexander Mikhailovitch is a lover of archaeology, but he was requested to desist from his researches. The other day the Empress Marie and her daughters visited Livadia, and went over the new palace of the ex-Tzar, built from the designs of the Empress Alexandra. Marie Feodorovna had never seen this new residence of her son and went all over the palace, showing much curiosity to see her daughter-in-law's apartments which contain numerous sanctuaries, prayer-rooms and secret passages.

When the Grand Duke Nicholas's palace was searched, he

---

the papers. He died a noble death – not wishing to surrender to the insurgent soldiers.

personally took the officers all over the house and showed them everything. The Grand Duke is never seen outside his own palace. He is busy the whole day, writing the history of Nicholas II's reign with all the preliminary details preceding the war. This book, when it is published, will throw a new light on many circumstances and events that to the public now seem dark. His stepdaughter, the Duchess Helen of Luchtenberg, is engaged to be married to Count Tysczkievicz, an officer of the Horse Guards, of Polish descent. The latter was obliged to obtain a special permission to enter the Grand Duke's palace; it was granted to him in view of his approaching marriage.

The financial position of the members of the Imperial Family has very much deteriorated since the Revolution, for they have ceased to receive the yearly income allotted to them by the Imperial appanages. Many of the Grand Dukes and Grand Duchesses are in great difficulties, for they have a great expenditure which cannot be met 'du jour au lendemain'.

The Grand Duchess Victoria Feodorovna is selling her valuables in order to be able to pay the pensions that are due to her old retainers. The Dowager Grand Duchess Elisabeth Mavrikievna is very anxious as to the future. She had a large family to provide for and the cost of numerous palaces and summer residences to defray; most of them will have to be put up for sale. Her eldest daughter, the widowed Princess Tatiana Constantinova Bagration-Moukhransky, was allowed by her late father the sum of 12,000 roubles a year. The Tzar found this income too small for a princess reared in the luxury of a palace, and increased it, paying her 50,000 roubles a year out of his own private fortune. All this will be altered henceforth, and will mean a dire change to the Imperial Princesses.

The Grand Duchess Xenia was the most practical of the family. She made out a list of the pensions that are regularly paid out of the sum that was yearly allowed to her from the appanages, as well as of the charitable institutions she sustains with this money, not a farthing of which is spent on herself or her family. The manager of her affairs went to Prince Lwoff, showed him this list, pointing out to the Prime Minister that all these people and institutions would in the future remain destitute. Prince Lwoff saw the justice of the matter, and gave his word of honour that the necessary money to satisfy these claims would be paid over to the Grand Duchess.

The private fortunes of the ex-Tzar and his family amount to the following sums:

The ex-Emperor Nicholas possesses
a capital of . . . . 908,000 roubles.
The ex-Empress Alexandra . . . . . 1,006,400 „
The Tzessarevitch . . . . 1,425,700 „

The Grand Duchesses	Olga 3,185,500	„
	Tatiana 2,118,500	„
	Marie 1,854,430	„
	Anastasia 1,612,500	„

Apart from this money, the Imperial Family is supposed to have great sums of money deposited in foreign banks, especially in the Bank of England.

The Revolutionists have endeavoured to inspire the people with the belief that the disturbances were instigated by the old Government, but that is untrue. Everyone knew that some agitation was at work in the numerous factories that are situated in Petrograd and in its close vicinity. Strikes were impending; they were expected to commence on January 14th, o/s, on the plea of the reopening of the Duma being put off, for such was the general belief, but the opening took place, and only a day or two later than had been fixed. The delay was caused by the new Prime Minister, who was not ready with his declaration. The disturbances began a month later because of the long queues before bakers' shops, people standing for hours in a biting cold wind, with the thermometer at 15 Réaumur (last winter was an exceptionally cold one), before each person's turn came to get the coveted piece of bread. The workmen complained with reason that, after having worked for so many hours, they could not be expected to spend their time in standing before a shop. If they were family men, they were reduced to return to an unheated, untidy home, where no food awaited them, because their womenfolk were among the queues.

The demonstrations began quite peaceably, the workmen not desiring to give to them a political colouring. The red flag was strictly tabooed. It was the Duma that turned the disturbances into a revolution, for which they were preparing people's minds for some time past, but which was to be carried out after the war was over.

Two reasons made them accelerate their plans. The first was

that the present opportunity was such a favourable one; the second was a fear that, if the war ended victoriously, the Tzar would attain the zenith of his popularity and would become invulnerable to any revolutionary movement.

The ukase dissolving the State Duma until April appeared on February 26th, turning the scales definitely into the deep waters of insubordination to His Majesty's commands.

The ex-Tzar has been accused of having challenged the Duma by this unwise decision, but only a very few people know that the responsibility of this act lies entirely with Prince Golitzine, the last Prime Minister of the old Government. Whenever the Emperor absented himself from the capital, a ukase for the dissolution of the Duma was always delivered to the Premier, duly signed but undated. This was done in case of an urgent emergency, when it would be imperative to act promptly. Prince Golitzine, who never aspired to be an eagle, thought the right hour had struck for him to use his prerogative of dissolving the Duma. But in doing this he only added fuel to the flame. It was M. Kerensky who turned the balance of hesitation still manifest among his colleagues. Once the die was cast they staunchly upheld the side of the people.

Amongst the numerous documents of the Imperial Okhrana, a paper was found dating back to August, 1915, in which the Chief of the Okhrana informs the Minister of the Interior 'that the workmen's strikes and the agitation reigning in their midst were the result of the revolutionary activity of the Social Democrats and the Labour Party of the State Duma, and especially that of lawyer Kerensky, the leader of the latter faction. The revolutionary doings of Kerensky were expressed in the watchword: *Struggle for power and an organising commitee*, and consisted of discrediting the Government in the eyes of the masses.

'To achieve this enterprise, Kerensky recommends to the workmen to have gatherings in the streets and in factories, found workmen's groups for the formation of councils of Workmen's and Soldiers' Deputies, similar to those that existed in the year 1905, which when the moment arrived direct the movement into a determined course with the goal of an Organising Committee in view that would take the defence of the country into its own hands. To ensure the success of this agitation, Kerensky spreads the rumour amongst the workmen that he receives masses of letters from the provinces insisting on the overthrow of the

Romanoff dynasty, and urging him to take the power into his own hands.'

The member of the Duma, M. Bublikoff, took upon himself the mission of preventing the Tzar's return to the capital. Arrived at the junction Dno, where the Imperial train was stationed, he did not dare to stop it outright, but managed to have the train go backwards and forwards, without letting it progress. When the Tzar was informed of these manoeuvres, he gave the order for the train to return to Pskov, and requested M. Rodzianko on the telephone to come over to Pskov and talk things over. Unfortunately M. Rodzianko did not do so, or things might have turned out quite differently.

If the shortage of food was only simulated by the former Government to call forth riots, why is the Provisional Government not able to do anything to ameliorate the conditions in the four months that have elapsed since the old regime was overhauled? Why has the food question become much more complicated since those days? Why have the difficulties to get any food increased tenfold? For instance, before the Revolution it was possible to get flour, whereas at present it is utterly impossible. Even co-operative shops have been forbidden to sell flour, as it is to be kept for the army, and wheaten flour will not be produced until the end of the war. As to the queues before shops, they have likewise increased in length and in number, for at the present moment one must stand in the queue for eggs, milk and butter. As for meat, one can stand for hours and not get anything.

M. Kerensky was the soul of the Revolution, and continues to be the only man who has any influence and can move the masses.

Like the hero of Mozart's opera, he seems to be ubiquitous: 'Figaro ci, Figaro là' could be easily translated into 'Kerensky ci, Kerensky là.' The countless number of meetings that man has harangued is amazing. Somebody calculated the other day that if he got a copek for every word he pronounces on such occasions, he would be a multi-millionaire. His popularity with the soldiers is at its height, and he certainly has the gift of making a striking impression. His outward appearance is somewhat like that of an actor, and, when he prepares for some special occasion and wishes to particularly impress his auditors, he gives little touches to his face and eyes to enhance the eloquence of their expression.

The workmen are not so fascinated by M. Kerensky, and the

anarchists detest him; for although he is a socialist, he is the friend of order, and would like to establish it all over the country. His detractors say that he is extremely ambitious, and has become intoxicated with the power he always coveted, is greatly impressed at the prominent part he is taking and hopes it will soon be even more pronounced. But however sceptical people are in regard to the 'man of the hour', they must own that he has succeeded in conquering the soldiers at the front. Under the magic of his personal fascination, the brilliant attack on the Austrian front was made with such remarkable success.

The Russian victory is entirely attributed to M. Kerensky's power over the soldiers and to his fiery speeches, which were plainly and convincingly expressed and suited to the simple minds of his auditors. M. Kerensky has never served in the army, but he has the soul of a warrior, and his bravery appeals to the heart of the true soldier. The Minister wanted to join in the fight, but the soldiers prevented him; nevertheless he remained all the time in the first line of the trenches.

Without wishing to diminish the merit of M. Kerensky, my love of truth impels me to add the following detail, which has not appeared in any reports about the famous battle. After repeated instances of flagrant disobedience of the soldiers, who refused to advance to the attack, the 'Alliance of Officers' resolved to form regiments consisting exclusively of officers who would take upon themselves the duties of soldiers. The vanguard of the army that went into attack were such 'Officers' Regiments'. The ordinary regiments followed. It is principally owing to the pluck of these brave officers that the attack succeeded so brilliantly, and the battle was gained. Not one newspaper has mentioned this, but it is an uncontroverted fact.

M. Kerensky is very unconventional, and the effect he would produce in a London drawing-room would be somewhat startling. His favourite garment is a leather jacket in which he appears even at solemn functions, as for instance when the senators came to take their oath of fealty to the Provisional Government. At the time M. Kerensky was Minister of Justice. He is not averse to theatrical effects. He once attended a concert at the Opera House. He was carried into a box on the first tier in the arms of soldiers, a sailor hanging on with his arm round M. Kerensky's neck. Deposited in the box, where his wife was seated, he climbed over the rail on to the stage and commenced haranguing the house.

But these lapses into eccentricity can easily be forgiven if he prevails upon the army to do its duty.

It is to be regretted that M. Kerensky's health is not good, and it is to be feared the continual strain upon his nerves may still further weaken it. All kinds of rumours are being spread: one of them is that he is liable to epileptic fits, another that he suffers with his heart. Others again say he is consumptive, but all agree that something very serious is amiss with his state of health.

It would be a mistake to think that everyone in Russia was elated at the news of the first victory after so many months of inaction. The anarchists and the Lenintzys were extremely displeased that the soldiers attempted the attack, and openly showed their disgust. This is a false move on their part, as it shows them up to the people in their true light! Their hostile demonstrations created intense indignation amongst the people, for the general public was overjoyed at the news of the success achieved by our army.

The following instance is a convincing proof of the mistrust with which the regiments at the front regard the soldiers of their reserve battalions, or squadrons at Petrograd who were mixed up in the recent disturbance. Two of the Infantry Guards regiments (the Moscow and the Finland regiments), who had never refused to go into battle, declined to have their ranks completed with soldiers from their reserve battalions. They had heard these men were voting and demonstrating against the war, and formally refused to have any further connection with them.

Soldiers arriving from Petrograd are regarded as a scourge by the army leaders and superior officers at the front, for they bring with them the infection of the moral gangrene that has spread all over the garrison of Petrograd. People have often wondered how it is that the soldiers in the capital are now in possession of such large sums of money! Gambling goes on in their midst at a wild rate. Soldiers win hundreds and thousands of roubles. *Where does this money come from?* That is the important question.

Chapter XIV

THE TRAIL OF REVOLUTION

THIS narrative cannot be terminated without a sympathetic mention of Lord Lansdowne's perfect way of greeting the new Russian Government. Dealing justly, as every true Englishman always does, Lord Lansdowne in the House of Lords referred in words of respect and sympathy to the ex-Tzar, Nicholas II, 'who for nearly three years has been our faithful and noble Ally'. It is characteristic of the present intolerance of anything that is not democratic that this speech was not reproduced in any of the Russian papers, although every cultured and true-hearted Russian read it with gratification, appreciating the tribute given by the eminent English statesman to the former Sovereign.

Nicholas II committed many errors, but the nobility of his character is beyond all doubt. The distinguished English peer's speech was read with great interest in Petrograd, and proved only too truly the power of his subtle foresight.

Russia, in her new guise, regardless of the fervent hopes with which she inspired everyone at the outset, gave a bad quarter of an hour to the Allied Powers, obstructing all efforts to come to a rational understanding. It was as if the Russians had suddenly turned their back on common sense. The first glimpse the Western countries had of Russian people in their gruff uncouthness, without the softening medium of an Imperial Court and of a cultured Government, was not encouraging, but let me convince the English reader that the majority of my countrymen were in despair at the turn things were taking; but they were helpless to stem the current of general disorder.

Everything was, and to a certain extent continues to be, in the power of the Soldiers' and Workmen's Deputies. They brought forward the obstacles and impediments which were prompted from Germany, through the numerous German agents that are swarming in Petrograd at the present moment. These men have gained a solid footing in the Council of Soldiers' and Workmen's Deputies. The Ministers are mere puppets in their hands, as the Council really controls the situation.

Over four months have passed, and people are beginning to sum up the pros and cons of the Revolution, and are inclined to find that, far from being beneficent, the change has up to this only wrought harm. The last months of the ex-Tzar's reign were the most unfortunate. A wave of discontent enveloped the country. The folly of the infatuation with Rasputine's saintliness, and the extraordinary nominations carried through by means of the Empress Alexandra's influence, all the vagaries that went on at Court, had the effect of continual challenges to the nation.

People, even the most favourably inclined, were disgusted at all that was going on, and, although the majority would not have tampered with the revolutionary movement, they willingly accepted the overthrow and sincerely welcomed the new state of things, trusting it would lead to victory, progress and success.

All that has happened since, however, has damped the enthusiasm, and the adherents of Monarchism are daily increasing in number.

The idea of the Revolution had been for a long time hatched by the Social Democrats, and by the Labour Party, with the help of the Constitutional Democratic party, the Cadets, but the latter were unable to realise their plans and became the cat's paw of the socialists. As a matter of fact the Cadet party includes many distinguished theorists and intellectual men of science, but not a single clever one. Their leader, M. Miliukoff, has his limitations, although he is a very learned man. His chief defect is his tactlessness, which frequently leads him astray. He is what the French call a 'gaffeur', and his last 'gaffe', a speech made in the Academy of Music in favour of German music generally and Wagner's compositions in particular, produced an uproarious outburst of indignation against him.

The Cadets had all the trumps in the game, but they played their hand so unskilfully that they failed to win. The Cadets are too theoretical, too much in the clouds, and they had not one gifted man amongst them who could have stepped forth energetically to take up the reins of Government.

A hand of steel in a velvet gauntlet was needed at that critical moment, instead of the many hands that pulled in all directions, without the iron grip that was required.

The first break in the Provisional Government, which resulted in the appointment of several influential members of the Social Democratic Party as Ministers, proved the utter instability of the new state of things in Russia.

One responsible Minister under the Republic has a very stormy record; he was mixed up in the Fonarny Street affair in 1905. A gang of anarchists discovered that on a certain day a large sum of money would be conveyed to the State Bank from the Custom House. The money was to be transported in a closed carriage, with several men on guard. The conspirators had ascertained by what streets the carriage containing the money would be driven, and they lay in wait in a small tavern. When the approach of the carriage was signalled, they came out of the tavern and threw a bomb under the horses' feet. An explosion was heard, which shook the whole street, broke the windows of the nearest houses and completely destroyed a shoemaker's shop at the corner of the street. In the general panic which ensued, the anarchists got away with a great part of the money.

The present state of affairs is impossible to conceive. There is no authority, no courts of justice, no one to appeal to. Everything is submitted to peasant meetings, and dealt with and judged by them amidst a cloud of words. Such is the new state of things. How can the Government expect the nation to have trust in such Ministers? The Russian people are accustomed to look up to the Government, but some of the members of the newly formed Cabinet compel them to look down upon the Provisional Government.

Numerous revolting acts committed in the days of Revolution, though carefully concealed from the public, have become known. The soldiers of some of the reserve battalions, like the sailors in Cronstadt, manifested the utmost savagery and cruelty. Soldiers came to the barracks of the Horse Guards and committed repulsive excesses. It was at that time that General Count Mengden was killed. Colonel Tchertkoff escaped death by the skin of his teeth, because the soldiers of his company stepped forward to defend their Colonel from the murderous attempt of the other soldiers. Count Kleinmichel, a young subaltern, was still in bed when the murderous band broke into his room. He was mercilessly cut to pieces. Another subaltern, Prince P., was walking down the Nevsky Prospect with the girl he was engaged to. A soldier accosted him: 'Give up your sword!' 'Why should I? I am not a prisoner!' was the reply. Hardly were the words out of his mouth when a bullet from the soldier's revolver put an end to his young existence, and he fell at the feet of the girl he loved.

Bands of bloodthirsty soldiers forced their entrance into apartments inhabited by generals and other officers and shot them in the presence of their wives and children. Weeks after the acute period of the Revolution was over, the dead bodies of generals, officers and policemen that had been thrown into the river were washed up. The persecution of the policemen was terrible. Some of them were cruelly mutilated. One 'gorodovoi' (police constable) was sitting with his young wife, who was in the last stage of expectation before childbirth; a throng of soldiers invaded the room they were living in. The unhappy woman threw herself at their feet and implored mercy for her husband. The soldiers happened to be kind-hearted; they felt pity for the young wife and the unborn babe and left the room without even arresting the husband. However, this proved only a respite, for after some time another horde followed, who were less charitably disposed, and they did not scruple to kill the miserable gorodovoi before the eyes of his distracted wife.

There was such a panic amongst the gorodovois that the majority of them bolted. They hid in the most unlikely places, and were dragged out of barrels, chimneys and hay-lofts. The wiser ones gave themselves up and were temporarily arrested. Those at least escaped with their lives. Sixty disabled young soldiers had just arrived from the front having been appointed as policemen, but they had not yet commenced their duties. They were living in the barracks of the Agraxine police-station, and every one of them was butchered.

Such scenes and even worse were numerous, though they were shrouded in the mystery of silence, for no one dare mention these facts. It was with difficulty that the bereaved families obtained the permission to get back the bodies of their murdered relatives and give them decent burials. Whilst these revolting acts of wanton cruelty were going on, the newspapers published yard-long articles of commiseration on the tragic fate of Alexander II's murderers, calling the assassination of one of the noblest and most humane of monarchs, 'the execution of Alexander II'. Such things have had quite the opposite effect from what was intended, and have done much towards reverting and turning people's thoughts back to monarchy.

Many curious scenes happened in those days, which eloquently revealed the people's real feelings. Hoping to interest the English reader, I shall reproduce some of the most characteristic stories which I know to be true.

In Russia Easter is considered one of the greatest festivals. Presents are exchanged on that day, ladies receive abundant flower-offerings from their friends, children get heaps of playthings and servants are invariably tipped by their employers.

On the Easter Sunday following the Revolution one of the new Ministers descended the marble staircase leading from his private apartment, and was deferentially greeted by the elderly 'schweitzer' (porter) of imposing presence, arrayed in his festive livery. The Minister approached him with outstretched hand and warmly returned his respectful Easter wishes. After helping the Minister into his fur coat and into the waiting motor-car, the old 'schweitzer' returned to the hall, looking ruefully at the palm of his hand. For the benefit of the other ministerial retainers assembled in the hall he regretfully remarked: 'Well, I prefer a Minister who does not shake hands, but gives me ten roubles' (a guinea).

A member of the Duma was commissioned to visit one of the girls' colleges (institutes) under the personal supervision of the Dowager Empress Marie. He came intent on explaining the new order of things to the directress and class-dames. Perceiving a life-size portrait in oils representing the Empress Marie, he exclaimed: 'This must be removed.' At these rash words a murmur of indignation was heard from the girls, and, forgetting discipline, they rushed up to the portrait with outstretched hands, forming a bodyguard in defence of the picture: 'Only over our bodies,' cried the irate girls. The directress and the school-dames looked on in sympathetic silence, whilst the dismayed member of the Duma stood helplessly staring at the crowd of pig-tailed adversaries in white pinafores and capes, valiantly arranged in front of their beloved Empress Marie's portrait, glaring at the intruder. Reflecting that after all 'discretion is the better part of valour', he shrugged his shoulders and beat a retreat, muttering: 'What is to be done with such foolish girls?'

Unfortunately, this loyal demonstration will not alter the fate of the institute. The girls have been all dispersed, and will not return next year. Even the scholars of the last two classes are not admitted to pass their final examinations.

A long queue was standing at one of the bread shops, some of the women taking up part of the pavement. A soldier passed the facetious remark: 'Do take up your tails, ladies, there is no room for anyone to pass.' An angry woman turned round: 'Perhaps there is not enough room here,' she said, 'but there is plenty at the front.'

At another shop, where a long tail of purchasers were impatiently waiting for their turn, a woman noticed a soldier, who was one of the waiting customers. 'Why do you come here? You get plenty of everything at the barracks.' 'Better not grumble,' replied the soldier; 'if it had not been for us soldiers, you would perhaps be without bread at all.' 'Nothing to boast of,' was the woman's retort; 'you would have done much better to lie on the oven.'[1]

A small boy sent by his mother to take his turn in the inevitable queue waiting for bread endeavoured to use his diminutive size and slip unperceived to the front of the row. His manoeuvre, however, was noticed by a bearded mujik (peasant). 'Back, youngster, where are you stretching to? Your place is behind.' 'I am not a youngster,' retorted the boy, beating his chest with a small clenched fist; 'I am a free Russian citizen', to the evident delight of the bystanders.

A country yokel was caught by the guard under the bench of a third-class railway carriage, intent on taking his journey without paying for his ticket. The indignant guard dragged him out of his retreat and obliged him to descend at the next stopping place. Full of rancour at this enforced exit, the youth continued his journey on foot along the rails, brooding revenge. He was caught in the act of pulling out the sleepers which support the rails. The express train was expected, and the impending catastrophe was prevented by a hair's breadth. On being questioned as to his motives, the country bumpkin answered sullenly that he wished

---

1 The warmest and most comfortable place in a Russian 'isba' (cottage) is considered the large oven, built with tiles. It is the favourite refuge of the tired members of the family in want of rest.

to be revenged on the guard who had turned him out of the train. 'But the accident would not have concerned him; this is another train with different guards.' 'Leave me in peace! What are you badgering me for? Liberty reigns now, and everyone can do as he likes,' was the unexpected answer of the fellow who had nearly caused the death and suffering of many travellers. His way of appreciating 'liberty' is, alas! not an uncommon one. Many uncouth minds share his opinion.

A gentleman is in the habit of taking his dinner daily at one of the best and oldest restaurants in Petrograd, where the same waiter always attends him. The habitué entered the restaurant a day or two after the great change. On seeing the waiter, the gentleman gave him a cheerful nod.

'How do you do, Simon?' he remarked.

To his astonishment the up-to-then obsequious waiter drew himself up to his full height and with nose well in the air, replied: 'I am no more Simon, I am Simon Ivanovitch now.'

'Oh, very well,' said the gentleman, as he seated himself at the table and prepared to eat his meal.

On leaving the restaurant he politely went up to the waiter and, shaking hands with him (without giving the usual tip), said, 'Good evening, Simon Ivanovitch.' The next day and the day following the scene repeated itself; the gentleman on entering and on leaving the restaurant shook hands with the waiter, adding invariably: 'How do you do, Simon Ivanovitch', or 'Good-bye, Simon Ivanovitch.' On the fourth day the gentleman was met by a deprecating waiter with the appeal: 'I am tired of being Simon Ivanovitch, I want to be Simon again.'

A lady's maid came to her mistress who happened to be the wife of a Senator and a Princess by birth.

'We are equals now, Madam,' quoth the maid with an impertinent toss of the head.

'I congratulate you,' was the quiet reply of the lady, taking up her book and continuing to read.

When Easter arrived a few weeks subsequently, the lady, who had a large establishment, prepared the Easter gifts for the servants. She divided the allotted money in equal parts and putting each into an envelope wrote on it the name of the recipient. A few hours after the distribution the deeply offended lady's maid entered and, in a tearful voice, reproached her mistress for putting her on the same level as the laundress and kitchenmaid.

'I could not act differently,' responded the lady, 'for you are all equals now.'

'There will always be a difference – the kitchen-maid is not my equal.'

'Nor are you mine,' was her mistress's reply, 'and yet not so very long ago you pointed out to me yourself that henceforth we were all equals.'

'I see, Madam, that you evidently don't understand anything about the differences of position', and the irate damsel flounced out of the room.

During the first days of the Revolution, when most of the houses and flats were searched, and at the same time pillaged, many strange scenes occurred. The wife of a member of the Upper Chamber, Princess Kourakine, was alone in her luxurious flat when the soldiers came to search for hidden firearms. The entrance door to the apartment leads out of a lofty hall, the top part of the door having glass panels. The soldiers rang, but, impatient at the footman's delay in answering the bell, they broke the glass panes, and from the vestibule entered the spacious and beautifully furnished drawing-room, where the Princess, being an invalid, was reclining on a lounge amidst a heap of soft, downy, lace-bordered cushions.

Princess Kourakine is an old lady of seventy-three, with a sweet face and snow-white hair, which give her the air of an eighteenth-century marquise. Her attitude towards the intruders was superb. She did not flinch when the soldiers entered, nor did she alter her pose. Telling them in her quiet ladylike voice that she was not well enough to show them over the house, she took the keys from a small basket and gave them to the soldiers with her grandest air, adding that they could switch on the electric light and inspect the whole place. Visibly impressed by the old lady's dignified behaviour, one of the soldiers looked at the Princess in a reassuring way: 'Don't be alarmed, Granny, we shall do thee no harm.' In a very short while they left the house, without having caused the slightest damage.

Captain M., a young man of about thirty, was on service in one of the naval barracks in Helsingfors, when a search party arrived. On their question: 'Have you got any concealed firearms?' the Captain emphatically replied 'No.' He then had to conduct the soldiers all over the place to verify the truth of his assertions. Boldly leading the way, Captain M. felt great misgivings, for he was not at all sure whether firearms had been stored away or not, and he knew that if rifles or machine-guns were found he would be ruthlessly put to death. Fortunately the Captain had been right – there were no firearms. But the moral tension during the two hours which the search lasted was so intense that, when the Captain returned home, his family was astonished to see that his thick auburn hair had grown snow-white.

Many cases of nervous breakdowns and mental alienation have been the result of the terrors during the acute period of the Revolution.

Rich people are trying to sell their possessions, for fear of sharing the fate of General Dournovo's collections of beautiful things, which had been amassed by generations and contained some rare art gems. American antiquarians have hastened to Petrograd and are lavishly laying out their money in acquiring pictures and art treasures belonging to the Russian aristocracy. Prince Youssoupoff has sold all his collections for eight millions of dollars. Countess Kleinmichel has sold her beautiful mansion on the Serguievskaia, the scene of so many brilliant festivities, with all it contained, as well as her famous 'Cottage' on the Islands. The Countess is taking her remaining goods and chattels to an hotel where she will settle for the winter.

Prince Saltykoff sold his marvellous collection of old china for £25,000. Jewels are being sold in quantities. People are trying to dispossess themselves of all they can, and turn their valuables into money. Only estates cannot be sold, not even the smallest portion of land. The Senior Notary has received orders not to ratify any sales of land. This is done for two reasons: in anticipation of the impending agrarian reform, and to prevent the prevailing scare from impelling the landowners to sell their estates, as was the case in 1905–6.

Some people have had the courage to go for the summer to their country seats, but the moral atmosphere there is not an edifying one. A lady went with her family to a small place she owns between Petrograd and Moscow. She has not been molested, but when she arrived from the station in a carriage drawn by four horses, the peasants greeted her with the words: 'Today you are driving – it will be our turn tomorrow.'

The family of Count Scheremeteff are spending the summer in Finland. Their beautiful country-place, Oulianka, close to Petrograd, is uninhabitable, for it has been invaded by soldiers belonging to the anarchists, and has been robbed of half its beautiful things.

All the old revolutionists, who for years have lived in banishment in the wilds of Siberia, or as emigrants in foreign lands, have returned to Petrograd. Amongst them was an old septuagenarian lady, Madame Breschko-Breschkoffsky. Being one of the oldest revolutionists, dating back to the time they were called nihilists, Madame Breschko-Breschkoffsky has earned the name of the 'Grandmother of the Russian Revolution'. A great fuss was made over her return. The station was decorated with flags, the Imperial rooms thrown open and all the revolutionists, with M. Kerensky at their head, carrying a huge bouquet of flowers, were assembled on the platform to greet the old lady.

The train arrived. M. Kerensky stepped forward, flourishing the nosegay in his hand, prepared to utter one of his most telling speeches, but no revolutionary grandmother stepped from the train, and under the disappointing circumstances he had to leave the words of greeting unsaid and followed by the crowd of advanced thinkers, looking rather foolish, he entered his motor-car and was swiftly driven away.

This happened several times, for the old lady kept changing the itinerary of her journey home, and arrived a month later than was at first expected. It became quite ridiculous; the newspapers one day flourishing trumpets at her supposed arrival, and announcing the next that the rumour had been a false alarm. When at last the much-heralded 'Grandmother' did arrive, she was woefully disappointed with her younger colleagues. She was shocked at what was going on in Petrograd and when she witnessed some of the demonstrations against the Provisional Government and heard the repeated cries of 'Doloy Voynou' (away with the war) she wept bitterly. At that moment, seeing the unruly sprouts that she had helped to sow, strange feelings must have filled her heart. Perhaps she felt regret for some of her past actions.

At the present moment the energetic lady is travelling about the country, going to all the garrison towns, haranguing at soldiers' meetings, endeavouring to instil in her auditors a sense of duty, and incite them to go to the front and fight for their country. In Simferopol the soldiers promised her not to have the red banner hoisted in their regiment! Who would have believed that a day would come when one of the principal leaders of the revolutionary movement would speak against the red badge!

What happened in the Russian army closely following upon the bright dawn of the Revolution can only be compared to the 'revolt of mercenaries' in Carthage in the pre-Christian era; but the Carthaginian soldiers had the excuse that their wages had not been paid them for a considerable time, whereas the Russian soldiers were always well provided for during the old regime. After the Revolution, they were made heroes of and were subjected to a system of pampering that entirely spoiled them. It was the fatal *first 'Prikaze'*[1] that did all the harm; the privileges and rights that were all of a sudden showered on the soldiers put an end to discipline and nullified the very qualities for which the Russian army was famed.

This 'Prikaze', sanctioned by the War Minister, M. Gutchkoff, was drawn up by three of the most influential members of the Labour Party: the member of the Duma, Tcheidze, M. Tchernoff, the present Minister of Agriculture, and M. Stekloff. This Prikaze was the first drop of deadly poison that filtered into the army, threatening its complete decay. It must be added for the honour of the soldiers that they would not have gone against their oath of fealty to the Tzar had they not been led by the chiefs of the revolutionary movement into believing that the Tzar had voluntarily renounced all rights to the crown a few days prior to the abdication. They therefore considered themselves free agents.

The soldiers were in the position of men suddenly deprived of their religion. Life had run on in such an even, monotonous groove for so many years that they felt utterly out of their depth at the sudden alteration in the current of their existence. Not having a high moral standard of their own, all the meaner qualities of their natures rose to the surface.

One of the principal psychological reasons why the Russian soldiers suddenly became laggards in battle has not been taken enough into consideration, either at home or abroad. The average Russian soldier does not care a brass button for politics, which he does not understand. He was not interested in the reasons which called forth the European conflagration. It was enough that the battle-call was given; the Tzar desired them to fight, they obeyed in the name of God and *for the Tzar*. From the moment this motive

1 Order.

ceased to exist, the war lost all 'raison d'être' in their eyes. They clamoured for peace at all hazards. Why, indeed, should they go on fighting? A sense of duty to our Allies is unknown to them, and they do not acknowledge the right of the Provisional Government, composed 'of mujiki[1] like ourselves' to make them risk their lives for political benefits which they neither appreciate nor comprehend.

It is for the first time that the world comes into direct contact with the Russian people, without the smoothing mediation of a cultured Government, and the dazzling impression of a brilliant Court. That the effect has not been a pleasing one has been gradually acknowledged by all the Western countries.

Another result of the Revolution is that it has entirely vulgarised the country. Russia with her sparkling façade – somewhat oriental in its splendour – is no more to be recognised. All that was beautiful, imposing and brilliant has disappeared – and what has remained is vulgar, paltry and mean.

The American democratic delegates have just left Petrograd, sorely disappointed with the Russian democracy. Their verdict is that Russia is a long way off from a Republican Government. The majority of people are not fit for self-government; they have no idea of the value of time, no consciousness of duty, no standard of moral integrity. As a country Russia represents great riches, but these riches are only in the latent state of possibilities, requiring development, and the land's finances at the present moment are far from being in a brilliant condition.

The roots of our industry are being systematically sapped through the imprudence of the workmen. How can a Republic flourish under such conditions? But the Social Democrats in Russia have not the political insight to admit this.

The incongruity of things in Russia is largely due to the vast difference that lies between the cultured and educated higher classes and the rest of the population, the majority of which is represented by peasants, or people coming from their ranks. There is likewise a sort of go-between class of educated but totally uncultured people, who not only do not possess breeding themselves, but profess a thorough contempt for those who do. This latter class of people is the most dangerous of all.

At the present moment everything is getting topsy-turvy. A

1 Peasants.

well-educated lady can obtain work at a bank or in an office at a salary from 75 to 150 roubles a month, and may consider herself lucky to be engaged on such terms. A simple factory girl, on the other hand, can without difficulty earn 200 roubles a month, and the wages of women tram-guards have been raised to 160 roubles a month. A man with a university education thinks himself fortunate to be employed with a salary from 250 to 500 roubles a month, whilst a skilled workman, at the present rate, earns 30 roubles a day. Manual labour is valued much higher than intellectual work.

The favourite modern appellation of the well-dressed, well-bred man is 'bourjouy' (derived from the French 'bourgeois'). Everybody who is not a workman or an anarchist is contemptuously referred to as a 'bourjouy'. Now, as a matter of fact, there are no 'bourgeois' in Russia.

We have numerous families who belong to the small gentry, but they have their titles of nobility. Some people are of opinion that it is a mistake in the general state of things in Russia that such a burgher-class does not exist to fit in between the real gentry, bordering on the aristocracy, and the peasants. In former times all the landowners, even those possessing only a limited number of acres, belonged to the class of untitled nobility, and the labourers and workmen were peasants. There is a class of people called 'mestchane', but they do not correspond to the French bourgeois, or the German burghess. The 'mestchane' are peasants that dwell in towns.

Now that the Romanoffs have been set aside, and Russia exists no longer as an Empire, there has been a tendency, especially in the first days of the Revolution, to destroy the Imperial eagles, wherever they were placed. This proves the utter ignorance of the people, as well as of their leaders, for the eagles had nothing to do with the Romanoffs.

For over five centuries the eagles have represented the national Russian coat-of-arms. They were introduced into the Russian nation's crest in the reign of Ivan III (1462–1505, surnamed 'the Good' – he emancipated Russia from the yoke of the Tartars). The eagles were brought to Russia from Byzantium by Sophia Paliologue, the wife of Ivan III, and the latter had the eagles belonging to his wife's race adopted in Russia. The Griffin belongs to the Romanoffs' private coat-of-arms.

Since the war special officer-classes have been instituted in the

Page School. These are attended by even, some of them, married men, in order to pass their military examinations and go to the front as qualified officers. One of these temporary pupils of the Page School entered a tram-car, and his smart uniform attracted the notice of two gruff-looking soldiers, calling forth sneering remarks, made in a loud voice, on the 'military bourjouy' that has just come in. Hearing the comments concerning himself, which were meant to reach the ears of an appreciative tram public, the young man calmly turns to the two soldiers and in a distinct voice says: 'I do not conceal that I am *not* a "Leninet" [follower of Lenine], and do not live on money received from Germany.' The laugh that ensued was at the expense of the soldiers, who looked extremely foolish.

It is noticeable that, when such conflicts occur now, the public sides against the soldiers. One day a white-haired general of venerable aspect entered a first-class railway carriage going to Tzarskoe Selo. On the seat opposite to him sprawled a soldier puffing a cigarette, and from the tail of his eye observing the attitude of the general. The latter took no more notice of him than if he had been empty space. Taking out another cigarette, the soldier familiarly leaned across towards the general, holding out his cigarette case.

'Well, comrade, let's have a smoke together,' he said insolently.

White to the lips, the general draws his revolver from his pocket, and handing it to the soldier says:

'Please shoot me outright, but do not dare to accost me in such an impertinent manner. I never was and never shall be your comrade.'

The other occupants of the carriage were disgusted with the soldier's impudent outbreak, and openly sided with the general. The abashed soldier hastily beat a retreat to a third-class carriage.

Another consequence of the Revolution is that women have been accorded all kinds of rights. In that respect we have outstripped the Western countries. In Russia women will henceforth take a prominent part in all administrations and governmental institutions. Countess Panine has been nominated the Assistant Minister of the Charitable Board, a new Ministry, destined to take the place of the former institutions of the Empress Marie. We have women senators, women members of the town councils, without mentioning a new regiment which has been formed of young women. This regiment has been duly drilled, presented with a special standard, went to the front, and fought magnificently. Advanced thinkers among Russian women are delighted at this transformation, though the public at large looks on with a smile of derision. The illustrated papers are full of caricatures representing the distracted husbands pacifying squalling infants, rocking cradles, or looking after the pots and pans in the kitchen, whilst the wife struts off to her business duties with a preoccupied air and a heap of papers under the arm.

What else can be said to complete this account of the March Revolution in Russia, its motives, causes and results, except to add the fervent hope that the laboriously painful crisis which the country is traversing may soon come to a climax, which will enable the rejuvenated nation to come forth in its old might and grandeur, like the Phoenix of the Arabian desert, rising from the ashes with new strength to proceed towards progress, success and prosperity.

A new dynasty is spoken of and several more or less likely representatives of old races are named as the most probable candidates to the throne of Russia. The old custom of the former Tzars is to be revived, for the Sovereign to choose a Consort, worthy of her future position, from among the highest ladies of the land. The new Tzar – Russia cannot exist without a Tzar, although many months may elapse before Tzardom, which is now in abeyance, will be again restored to its old glory – the new Tzar will do well to take the sad experiences of his predecessor to heart, and not let a German Princess lead the country to destruction.

I have finished. Let me express the hope that this candid account of the great historical days of February and March, 1917, will help to enlighten the English readers as to the circumstances that led up to the Revolution, and will convince every unbiassed mind as to the urgency of the impending change, as well as from what danger the country was saved by the Left factions of the Duma's bold resolution to lift the red flag of Revolution. The facility and rapidity of throwing off the yoke of the dynasty, the instantaneous transfer of the numerous regiments' allegiance to the side of the people, and many other events of the following days, seemed to crown and rivet the success of this extraordinary parliamentary enterprise, unforeseen in the Statutes. It gave the Provisional Government the possibility of launching the country, agitated with the unsuccess of the war, privations and the fear of the future, on the road of honour, energetic activity and success. Such a problem threatened not only the ruin of the external enemy, but scored over the Russian anarchical preacher's impotence. The period of revolutionary festivity and manifestation seemed all too short and too simple in the eyes of many of my countrymen. All the springs of the apparatus were pressed, theoretically called upon to act in beautiful concord with the Provisional Government, and the latter was forcibly convinced that it was only a frontispiece, a symbol of something that was not rooted in the nation and possessed no power.

It is said that 'les extrémités se touchent' and the days of April, 1917, when the Russian army seemed to fall to pieces, when a separate peace with Germany was removed from the Cabinet, once more placed our Allies before the tempest of ruin and treason, the clouds of which were gathering in Russia during the last months of the monarchy and which, so it was fervently hoped, had been chased away by the harmony that reigned amongst the people, the army and the Duma.

What the future holds no one can forecast. Possibly a strong man will arise – a Washington, a Cromwell, or a Napoleon – a man who will appreciate that no country that has just emerged from a Revolution, and is in the midst of the greatest war she has ever fought, can be ruled by eloquence, no matter how forceful or inspired.

Available as a companion volume

RUSSIAN COURT MEMOIRS 1914–16

With an introduction by Alan Wood

This book, first published in 1917, provides an insight into life among the upper classes in Russia at a time that was to prove pivotal in world history. The anonymous author was writing from within the intimate circle of the court of Tsar Nicholas II in a period when the country was only months away from a revolution that was to destroy everything for which he stood.

The purpose of the book was to paint a portrait of Russia's royal family, court entourage and metropolitan society during the early years of the First World War and also to lay the responsibility for that war squarely at the feet of Germany. Written throughout in a strongly individualistic style, the text expresses the author's often extraordinary views on contemporary political and social events.

The author's firm declaration that 'Russia is not a revolutionary country' and his utterly condescending opinions about the mass of his compatriots show the fatal limitations of the privileged élite of which he was a member. *Russian Court Memoirs* unwittingly describes the final period of influence of a clique which, through its exclusivity, had become blinded to the realities of life in its own country.

RUSSIAN PORTRAITS

CLARE SHERIDAN

Edited by Mark Almond

In late 1920 the sculptress Clare Sheridan, cousin of Winston Churchill, clandestinely left England bound for Soviet Russia. She departed, without telling family or friends and without the knowledge of the British Government, in the company of the Bolshevik Kamenev, who had offered her the opportunity of modelling busts of the revolutionary leaders.

This book, a diary of that remarkable journey, recounts how Sheridan abandoned her aristocratic English background and arrived in a country which was entirely alien to her and whose leaders had been portrayed in the West as monsters. It then describes her meetings with some of the most important figures in the Revolution, such as Lenin, Trotsky and Dzerzhinsky. Although Stalin is missing from her gallery of portraits, many of those who would later fall victim to his purges are presented here, for once, without his awful shadow.

Based in Moscow, Sheridan did not glimpse much of life beyond the city, but she did enjoy a unique access to the Bolshevik leaders which makes *Russian Portraits* a fascinating picture of events at the very heart of an embattled revolution.

THE ARGONAUTICA EXPEDITION

THEODOR TROEV

Foreword by Tim Severin

The legend of Jason and the Argonauts, and their quest for the Golden Fleece, has long fascinated classical scholars. Intrigued by the discovery of a curiously shaped golden ingot in the Black Sea, which led to a new theory concerning the origins of the myth, Bulgarian writer and explorer Theodor Troev suggested a voyage following the route of the Argonauts to the land of the Golden Fleece, Colchis – present-day Georgia. The aim of this expedition was to investigate the possibility that maritime and cultural links had existed between what is now the Bulgarian coast and other points in the ancient world and also to establish what it really was that Jason and his crew had sought on their journey.

In this book Theodor Troev describes his research into the story of the Argonauts, the preparations for the expedition, the voyage itself, and the discoveries that he and his crew made in Georgia and along the northern coast of Turkey on their homeward journey. He also tells of his team's encounter with the expedition led by the renowned British explorer Tim Severin which at the same time was tracing Jason's voyage in the replica galley Argo. The book will delight all those interested in Greek mythology, archaeology, travel and adventure, and the new hypotheses that emerge from it will make a valuable contribution to the study of the ancient world.

CHARLES KNIGHT – A FORGOTTEN GENIUS

DEREK STOW AND JUDITH HUNTER

Charles Knight – writer, publisher, editor, historian, reformer, critic and commentator – made a major contribution to the history, literature and art of the England of the nineteenth century. Yet to most people his name is unknown.

Working within the 'Society for the Diffusion of Useful Knowledge', Knight aimed to bring the world of learning and education to the Victorian masses. In the process he produced and largely wrote the publication for which he is best remembered, the *Penny Magazine*. Appearing between 1832 and 1845, and achieving a huge circulation, this was a magazine of quality and integrity, illustrated by the work of some of the country's finest engravers, on sale at a price that made it available to all. Among Knight's numerous other publications were a pictorial Shakespeare in eight volumes, *London* in six volumes and his magnificent two volumes of *Old England* which contained over 2,500 engravings, some of which are reproduced in this book.

Charles Knight's story is also a chronicle of a period of great social change which witnessed the revolution in industry and travel caused by the dawning of the steam age. Knight actively worked with many leading politicians and reformers of the time and journeyed throughout the country in a constant effort to encourage the regard for fairness and people's rights which formed the basis of his beliefs. He also developed a friendship with Charles Dickens and appeared on stage with him.

Forming a unique record of Knight's life and achievements, the book has been written by Derek Stow, author of *Charles Knight's London*, and Judith Hunter, Curator of the Royal Borough Collection at Windsor. Their text is complemented by extensive material from Knight's memoirs and those of his grand-daughter Alice Clowes.